DEVELOPING
ACHIEVEMENT
MOTIVATION
IN ADOLESCENTS

EDUCATION FOR HUMAN GROWTH

DEVELOPING
ACHIEVEMENT
MOTIVATION
IN ADOLESCENTS

EDUCATION FOR HUMAN GROWTH

ALFRED S. ALSCHULER

EDUCATIONAL TECHNOLOGY PUBLICATIONS
ENGLEWOOD CLIFFS, NEW JERSEY 07632

To Irene

PREFACE

After working with patients in psychotherapy, one finds normal high school teaching surprising. Individual needs are largely ignored in favor of group progress towards pre-set standardized goals. Careful diagnostic assessment of each person's strengths and deficits rarely is done, thus precluding an individualized program for growth. Students' feelings are of secondary importance compared to their ability to intellectualize. In contrast, in work with patients, what is not *personally* relevant is irrelevant. Commitment to the patients' welfare is more important than adherence to any academic viewpoint, whereas most teachers' primary allegiance is to the curriculum. I realize, of course, that most high school students, even in their moments of rebellion, are not "sick" and are not in need of psychotherapy. However, it is equally obvious that normal schooling systematically neglects the psychological needs of individual students, ultimately to the detriment of a more healthy society. The contention of this book is that schooling can and should consciously promote the psychological growth of students.

When David McClelland and I began to create and assess educational methods for promoting psychological growth, it seemed natural to try out our procedures on the development of achievement motivation in adolescents. Not only did we know a great deal about the origins and consequences of this socially important motive, but we also heard and heeded the ubiquitous cry of teachers for effective methods of motivating their students. Further, from a practical point of view, achievement motivation training is particularly well timed for students about to choose between academic and vocational tracks at the beginning of high school and about to make career choices at the end of high school. From a developmental point of view, during this period adolescents begin to form clear ideas about their unique being in the world, in large part from recognition by others of what they like to do well. Training courses that encourage their special concerns for excellence, and help them achieve what they want, contribute to the formation of their identity.

Although our primary goal was to identify the combination of educational tactics and strategies that most effectively increase *any* motive, we decided to study the education of one human motive in depth and generalize our conclusions to the deliberate education of other aspects of mental health. In the years since the beginning of our work, there has been a phenomenal increase in "growth centers" for promoting mental health. These non-formal training centers for adults and the many new methods that have been incubated there now are finding their way into schools. Many methods and strategies that work for adults in psychological health resorts are inappropriate, incomplete, and premature for adolescents in schools. The conclusions from our research about the development of students' mental health in formal educational settings should be particularly helpful to administrators and supervisors who are entrusted with protecting as well as promoting the psychological growth of students.

In devising workable solutions for teachers, we learned about two separate aspects of schooling as a system: (1) schooling as a meta-individual system of rules, roles, procedures, and policies, and (2) schooling as practiced by individual classroom teachers. Workable solutions in psychological education had to meet the needs of both aspects of schooling. Not only did the motivation training have to be effective in the classroom, but ways of introducing this innovation in schools had to be devised so that conflicts over norms, procedures, policies, and values were kept at a minimum, and competition for limited resources of time, money, and manpower was reduced as much as possible. If we did not attend to both aspects of schooling, our motivation training did not survive in schools after we left. Our solutions to the problems of training in classrooms are presented in Part Two of the book. (Teachers who are not familiar with statistical analysis of psychological data can skip the "results" sections and still benefit from the introductions, descriptions of procedures, and discussions.) Our methods of working with schools as systems are discussed in Part Three. This section of the book should be particularly useful to curriculum planners, professors of education, teacher trainers, and other creators of educational technology who are responsible for introducing improved content and practice in schools. The single most important conclusion from the years of work, summarized at the end of Part Three, is that schooling can promote the psychological growth of children and adolescents in a variety of ways. The challenge now is to develop this new field of education for the benefit of all.

Numerous people have assisted this work from its inception. I have acknowledged most of them in the specific chapters where their efforts were most manifest. Several individuals and institutions have provided such overall support that acknowledgment here is appropriate. I am indebted to David C. McClelland, who began this work, whose advice was consistently productive, and whose colleagueship has profoundly influenced my professional career. The United States Office of Education provided the major portion of funds for the project during the first five years. It is a fine record of longevity despite competing pressures for funds. The Program in Humanistic Education at the State University of New York at Albany supported the final year by granting time for writing. This book has had more antecedent manuscripts than I can remember or count. Nancy Raeburn and Rita Lee provided consistently excellent secretarial help from beginning to end. My wife Irene has provided all manner of support, from encouragement when the data seemed impossibly confusing to useful ideas when the results were clear but the causes were obscure. During the lengthy vicissitudes of this book she has maintained saintly patience.

Alfred S. Alschuler
Amherst, Massachusetts

LIST OF FIGURES AND TABLES

xi

CONTENTS

xv

DEVELOPING
ACHIEVEMENT
MOTIVATION
IN ADOLESCENTS

EDUCATION FOR HUMAN GROWTH

PART ONE
Introduction

1.
The Origins and Nature
of Psychological Education*

At the joint frontier of psychology and education a new movement is emerging that attempts to promote psychological growth directly through educational courses. Psychologists are shifting their attention away from remedial help for the mentally ill to the goal of enhancing human potential in normal individuals. Educators, on the other hand, are beginning to accept these courses along with the unique content and pedagogy as appropriate for schools. At present there are psychological education courses designed to increase achievement motivation, awareness and excitement, creative thinking, interpersonal sensitivity, joy, self-reliance, self-esteem, self-understanding, self-actualization, moral development, identity, nonverbal communication, body awareness, value clarity, meditative processes, and other aspects of ideal adult functioning. Some of these courses have been taught experimentally in schools, although most of them have been developed and offered in other settings, such as industrial training programs, Peace Corps training, and private educational institutes.

Psychological educators who have worked in isolated independence are beginning to meet together to foster mutual collaboration, and new centers of psychological education are emerging that offer these courses to the general public.** A

*Portions of this chapter appeared in the Spring, 1969 issue of the *Journal of Humanistic Psychology.*

**The first conference on "Affective Education" was held in August, 1968, in Sausalito, California, under the sponsorship of the American Association of Humanistic Psychology and Esalen Institute. In April, 1969, 1970, and 1971, number of large research and development projects have been funded to introduce this type of education into schools, and continuing national publicity increases the demand from students and parents. The psychological education movement clearly is gaining momentum.

Paradoxically, psychological education as a discipline is unorganized and inchoate. For the most part, psychological educators remain highly individualistic innovators within the field. Despite its many strong historical roots, this movement is viewed by many as a new fad of unknown origins. In spite of the many goals, procedures, and trainer skills common to all psychological education, there are only three graduate programs in the country to train psychological educators.* In short, this burgeoning educational movement is not yet recognized as a legitimate discipline.

Ideology and Origins

Like past ideologies of personality change, psychological education grows out of a vision of human potential. This vision, and the methods of change associated with it, can be understood clearly only in the perspective of past ideologies.

In pre-Christian Greece, those individuals who could not get along in the world, whom we would call "mentally ill" today, were viewed as possessing divine inspiration. Visions were not insane, but prophetic. These divinely inspired souls were feared

conferences for national and international leaders were sponsored by the Menninger Foundation and the American Association of Humanistic Psychology. The best-known organizations are Esalen Institute, situated in Big Sur, California; National Training Laboratories, situated in Bethel, Maine; and Western Behavioral Sciences Institute, La Jolla, California. At the latest count there were about 100 other "growth centers" actively in operation in the United States.

*The Center for Humanistic Education, School of Education, University of Massachusetts, Amherst, Massachusetts; the Center for Confluent Education, University of California in Santa Barbara, California; and the Program in Humanistic Education, State University of New York at Albany, Retreat House Road, Glenmont, New York.

and respected—not pitied, punished, or burned as they were centuries later. Certainly the medicine man who spent his time collecting herbs and smelling urine was not fit to touch the divinely possessed. Dictated by these beliefs, a sanctuary at Epidaurus was created in the sixth century B.C. that compared favorably with most health resorts of the twentieth century A.D. The treatment was lavish for those individuals who were inhabited by the deities and could not function well in society (Henry, in Zilboorg, 1941).

With the rise of Christian institutions and the belief in a chain of communication between God, priests, and man, those people seen previously as divinely inspired came to be seen as representatives of the devil, on a plane with the priests but direct challenges to the priests' God-given power on earth. Thus, it was incumbent upon men to demonstrate the superior strength of God by casting out the demons from the unfortunate bodies of the bedevilled. The resultant treatment consisted of beatings, collar harnesses in dark, damp cells, starvation diets, and—failing all else—burning at the stake. These treatment procedures were dictated by a vision of goodness and evil as surely as Plato's 50-year educational program was dictated by his vision of the wise civil-servant ruler and what was necessary to produce such a philosopher-king.

Despite several crusading attempts, demonology and its associated restorative methods were prevalent through the latter part of the nineteenth century. It remained to physicians to claim for medicine what had previously been religious concerns. In the process of asserting that "madness" was an organic "disease" and thus "curable," physicians brought with them a new ideology and method. The assumption was made that a science of mental illness must begin with a classification of diseases, similar to the classification of elements in chemistry and other physical diseases. When these new disease entities had been identified, research into the organic causes could begin. As a result, physicians studied alcoholism, aphasias, and paralyses, and attributed them to such things as the lever actions of the limbs, disturbances of the muscle sense of the limbs, and organic brain disease.

In particular, Emil Kraepelin's classification system brought to fruition the establishment of mental illness as an ideology and as a legitimate branch of medicine. We are heirs to this revolution. The care of the mentally ill is entrusted to doctors. The mentally ill are placed in hospitals, and there is widespread use of healing chemicals. Obtaining case histories, an art perfected by Kraepelin, remains a standard procedure. Legally required diagnostic labels given to the hospitalized mentally ill bear the stamp of Kraepelin's formative thinking. So pervasive is this thinking that it requires of us almost a Copernican revolution of thought even to consider the possibility that mental states and visions may not be "disease symptoms" needing a cure. Our belief is firmly rooted in Kraepelin's scientific ideology, just as incarceration and punishment were methods emanating from deep-seated beliefs in demonology.

Psychoanalysis, the second psychiatric revolution, was a child of this scientific ideology. One of Freud's chief contributions was to persuade others that "mental illness" could have psychological as well as physical origins—that forgotten psychological traumas could leave permanent psychological scars and debilitation as surely as physical traumas (e.g., broken limbs), if not treated, would leave physical debilitation and scars. Further, Freud showed that a psychological "talking cure" was possible if the "patient" re-experienced the original trauma and worked it through, much as an operation opens the body to correct the source of a disease so that it can heal properly. Because Freud believed that psychoanalysis was a method of learning about one's self as well as a method of medical treatment through emotional re-education, he recommended that experts from a number of disciplines be trained to do psychoanalysis (Freud, 1927). However, the medical doctors who brought psychoanalysis to this country have kept it tightly locked within *their* profession, to be used solely as a healing technique.

The psychoanalytic ideology has stimulated many developments in the last 50 years, two of which specifically paved the way for psychological education. First, numerous additional methods of affective re-education have been created, ranging from variants on the "talking cure" (client-centered therapy, direct analysis, sector therapy, play therapy), to varieties of group therapy (marital, family, ward, psychodrama), to complete environmental control (Kibbutzim, "brainwashing"), to the many short exercises designed to promote a specific, limited affective experience (game simulations, role plays, programmed units). In addition, learning theory has developed to the point where numerous techniques are available to help people systematically unlearn certain behaviors, and learn other, healthier behaviors (Wolpe and Lazarus, 1967). In short, a large repertoire of methods exists besides psychoanalysis to foster affective education and behavior modification.

A second development was stimulated in reaction to Kraepelin's and Freud's exclusive attention to mental illness. Most psychiatrists and psychologists were seldom at a loss for words to describe even the subtlest nuances of mental illness or to hypothesize about the origin and vicissitudes of psychoses. However, psychiatrists and psychoanalysts were considerably less eloquent when asked to describe "mental health," maturity, or ideal psychological functioning. Bound to the ideology of "mental illness," "disease," and "cure," mental health was either the absence of psychological symptoms or "the ability to love and work," a definition which made mental health inaccessible to the very young and the very old. Beginning with Carl Jung's descriptions of "individuation" (Jung, 1959a, b), attempts were made to characterize the ideal states of human development (Allport, 1961; Erikson, 1959; Jahoda, 1958; Maslow, 1968a, b; and Piaget, 1962). Whether the description was a list of traits, states, healthy crisis resolutions, or capacity for cognitive operations, the rationale for the descriptions was the same. The impetus was to fill a gap by describing in detail the ideal states of human development.

After the articulation of what lay at the positive end of the spectrum of human functioning, it was a natural step to use the existing repertoire of change techniques to promote those ideal states. However, psychological education courses were not created and implemented so logically, so systematically, or so simply. Although psychological education was an immediate, reasonable, and enticing possibility, until recently the need for this new approach to promoting growth had not crystallized within the communities of psychotherapists and educators.

Psychotherapists have begun to realize that their traditional methods and settings are inadequate to deal with the magnitude of psychological problems in society. The extent of violence in the streets stands in bold defiance of the inefficient, long-term, one-to-one therapeutic relationships that take place in small offices and safe hospital rooms. The number of existing and potential psychotherapists is hopelessly inadequate because the problems are not just among the mentally ill and because any type of remediation, ipso facto, is too late. From this perspective, psychotherapy is not so much wrong as basically inappropriate to alleviate widespread racism, aggression, interpersonal insensitivity, moral irresponsibility, and non-self-actualization. More efficient methods are needed to promote psychological growth, thus preventing these human problems from occurring, and making remediation unnecessary. New settings are needed that reach the larger population. In the current climate of urgency it is not surprising that psychologists are looking seriously to the educational system, because of its universal coverage, its large source of potential psychological educators, and the appropriate emphasis on learning and personal growth.

Conversely, educators are turning to psychologists, not for additional help in increasing the rate of knowledge acquisition, but to find out what the schools can do about prejudice, violence, lack of motivation, and uncurious, uncreative students. Schools are doing almost nothing to prepare students *vocationally and psychologically* for life after high school. Thirty percent, or 15 million of the 50 million students in school, will not graduate from high school. This staggering number of dropouts will enter the labor market unprepared. A total of 40 million students will not complete college, and only 6 million of these students will have had any significant amount of vocational education. For the vast majority of students, what they are learning in school is not so much wrong as basically inappropriate.

It is increasingly clear, however, that more vocational training in particular, or better curricula, teacher training, and physical facilities in general, will not be sufficient. The "Coleman Report" on *Equality of Educational Opportunity* (1966a) has shown that student attitudes towards themselves and about the responsiveness of the world to their efforts are more strongly related to academic gains than are differences in curricula, facilities, or teacher training. In addition to vocational training, schools will have to take greater responsibility for promoting the growth of attitudes conducive to learning and to continued psychological growth. In a recent study of 440,000 high school students across the country, the American Institutes for Research concluded that schools fail to help students develop a sense of personal responsibility for their own educational, personal, and social development, and that schools must prepare students more fully for citizenship and mature adulthood (Flanagan, 1967). Thus, from a teacher's point of view, there is double reason for and double gain from courses designed explicitly to promote aspects of psychological growth: increased learning in school and more effective, socialized, self-actualizing adults after school.

Psychological Education Procedures

In the last ten years, individual psychotherapists and teachers working independently have created a number of prototype psychological education courses. The course procedures are the first clues to the course goals, since it is through these procedures that the desired psychological states are fostered in the course. For example, Outward Bound courses attempt to promote "self-reliance" (Katz and Kolb, 1968). Most of the course exercises ask students to engage in physically difficult tasks like scaling a cliff or swimming 50 yards underwater in one breath. Outward Bound courses usually end with a solo survival experience in the wilderness, where the trainee lives off the land. Procedurally, "self-reliance" is defined as mastering these challenging physical tasks. Similarly, it is possible to infer some of the goals of other psychological education courses by focusing on their procedures. When this is done, four common goals emerge.

First, most courses contain procedures to develop a constructive dialogue with one's own fantasy life. In synectics training, a creativity course, students are asked to "make the strange familiar" by fantasizing themselves inside a strange object, or to "make the familiar strange" by fantasizing about a common object (Gordon, 1961). In other creativity courses, remote associations are encouraged in order to attain a new, useful, and creative perspective on some problem (Allen, 1962; Brown, 1964; Parnes and Harding, 1962; Olton, 1966; Osborn, 1963; Uraneck, 1963; Whiting, 1958). In other psychological education courses students are taken on guided tours of day dreams and night dreams and on fantasy trips into their own bodies (Perls, Hefferline and Goodman, 1965; Schutz, 1967). In achievement motivation courses, students are encouraged to fantasize about doing things exceptionally well and are taught how to differentiate between achievement imagery and plain old task imagery. Later in the course these achievement images are tied to reality through careful planning and projects (Alschuler, 1970; Kolb, 1965; McClelland, 1965b; McClelland and Winter, 1969). These procedures often bring previously ignored aspects of one's personality into awareness. Usually this is a joyful, enhancing experience in contrast to psychoanalytic dream analysis and free association, which are oriented to uncovering unconscious conflicts. The implication of these procedures is that most adults don't make constructive use of their fantasy life and have forgotten how to enjoy fantasy in a childlike, but healthy, way.

A second set of extremely common procedures involves nonverbal action, such as silent improvisations, free expression dance movements, meditation, the exaggeration of spontaneous body movements, and a wide variety of games. Often it is easier to understand psychological concepts when they are learned motorically rather than simply comprehended intellectually. For example, in achievement motivation courses, the concept of "moderate risk taking" is taught through a dart game in which the student must bid on his performance and only "wins" when he makes his bid. A very low bid earns few points while a very high bid is nearly impossible to make. The game experience subsequently is generalized to other life situations. In sensitivity training and encounter groups, nonverbal exercises are used to increase channels of communication. Some personal feelings can be expressed more effectively in motions than in words. Other times nonverbal activities are used because they increase one's expressive vocabulary and are simply joyful experiences. As with constructive fantasizing, proponents of these methods believe that this type of expression, communication, and learning is underdeveloped in most people (McClelland, 1965b; Moore, 1960; Murphy, 1967;

Howard, 1968; Newberg, 1969; Perls, Hefferline and Goodman, 1965; Ruesch and Kees, 1956; Schutz, 1967; Spolin, 1963).

A third set of typical procedures focuses on developing and exploring individuals' emotional responses to the world. In most courses, how people feel is considered more important than what they think. Without these emotional peak experiences, ranging from laughter and exhilaration to tears and fear, the teacher is likely to consider the course a failure. For example, if an adolescent is scaling a cliff in an Outward Bound course and does not feel any fear, he will not increase his self-confidence through his accomplishment. Similarly, techniques in sensitivity training foster intense emotional confrontation with other group members. Trainees are encouraged to express their feelings openly and honestly. They learn to recognize their anger, for example, and to resolve it maturely, rather than allow it to create continued inner turmoil. In achievement motivation courses, strong group feelings are developed to help support the individual in whatever he chooses to do well. In all of these courses there is a shared belief that *affect* increases meaningful learning and that the capacity for the full range of feelings is a crucial human potentiality often underdeveloped in adults. As a result, a wide range of techniques to enhance affect have been created (Borton, 1970; Bradford *et al.,* 1964; Litwin and Aronoff, 1966; Schutz, 1967; Yablonsky, 1965).

A fourth characteristic set of procedures emphasizes the importance of living fully and intensely "here-and-now." The emphasis takes many forms. In Gestalt awareness training, the goal is philosophically explicit (Perls, Hefferline and Goodman, 1965). In most courses it is subtle and implicit. Usually psychological education courses are held in retreat settings which cut people off from past obligations and future commitments for brief periods of time. The isolated resort settings dramatize the "here-and-now" opportunities to experiment with new behavior. In general there is less emphasis on future "homework" or past personal history as an explanation for behavior. A vivid example is Synanon, a total environment program for addicts, which promotes "self-actualization" and in the process cures addiction. Synanon requires the addict to stop taking drugs immediately upon entering the program. Other "bad" behavior which stands in the way of self-actualization is pointed out as it occurs. Historical explanations for bad behavior are considered excuses and are not tolerated (Yablonsky, 1965). In other psychological education programs, the games, exercises, group process, etc., are model opportunities to explore, discover, and try out new behavior here-and-now. Most of these courses consider references to the past and future as escapes from the present opportunity. The assumption is that if a person can't change here-and-now, where the conditions for growth are optimal, he is not likely to continue growing outside and after the course.

These four types of procedures are within the Freudian tradition. The critical moment of growth in psychoanalysis occurs during the cure of the transference neurosis when the patient has an intense *emotional* realization of how he has *acted out* his irrational childhood *fantasies* in the *here-and-now* therapeutic context. The catharsis stemming from this new awareness allows the patient to change in meaningful ways, first in the therapeutic relationship and then outside. These same elements exist in most psychological education courses, but they are transformed. Students discover the creative power of their fantasy life, not the neurotic aspects of unconsciously motivated fantasy. Highly sensitive, understanding communication is experienced by attending to nonverbal cues, whereas in psychoanalysis, behavioral tics and "acting out" are probed for their neurotic messages. Intense feelings are more often ecstatic than angry and unhappy, as in therapeutic catharsis. In both types of change procedures, the assumption is made that long-term change results from the changes which occur in the here-and-now relationship.

These four typical procedures carry an implicit cultural diagnosis. It is as if the creators of psychological education courses said that most people are highly verbal, future-oriented doers who place extreme value on analytic rationality. The result is that other aspects of human potential are left undeveloped or are destructively expressed. What is needed is the growth of healthier, more sensitive multi-level communication, the integration of irrational fantasies into constructive responses, and greater capacity of ecstatic emotional experiences. The relation between psychological education goals and the current social problems is a key reason why it is important to introduce these courses in schools on a widespread basis. A person who has developed sensitive nonverbal communication is less likely to express himself hatefully or violently.

The learning that results from these courses differs from existing academic and vocational courses in several important ways. Psychological knowledge is experiential, in contrast to academic knowledge (mathematics, science, history), which is appropriately abstract. Psychological knowledge is firmly rooted in the person's feelings, fantasies, and actions, and is not merely deposited in the student's internal data bank. This is the difference between knowing about the revolutions of 1848 and experiencing the anxiety and uncertainty of changing a life style quickly, as when a parent dies or when one has an accident. It is the difference between knowing probability statistics and taking action when the odds are 50:50 for success. Obviously, psychological knowledge is as important for a student's repertoire as his academic knowledge or vocational skills.

There also are some similarities in psychological, academic, and vocational courses. Like foreign languages, science, history, and mathematics, psychological education teaches a new vocabulary and pattern of thought. Like vocational courses and athletics, psychological education courses teach new action skills through "exercises," "games," "role plays," etc. And, like psychotherapy, psychological education is concerned with feelings. These statements are straightforward and unremarkable. But, consider for a moment how many courses attempt to promote a synthesis of *all three.* Typical high school curricula are divided into academic "thought" courses and vocational "action" courses (typing, shorthand, auto mechanics, etc.). It is not possible to divide psychological knowledge into separate compartments. For example, Interpersonal Sensitivity is a way of thinking, feeling, and acting in ongoing relationships with other people. Therefore, psychological education courses attempt to create and enhance this synthesis within the course itself in order to foster its occurrence outside and after the course.

In contrast to typical school goals, psychological education courses aim for long-term life changes, not short-term gains in mastery. More precisely, psychological education attempts to increase long-term "operant" behavior. Operant behavior is voluntary, seemingly spontaneous, and not necessarily required by the situation. What a person does with his leisure time is an indication of his operant behavior, since it stems from stable internal cues and needs few external cues to come forth. Respondent behavior, whether it is affective, cognitive, or motoric, requires external cues and incentives before it will occur, just as an examination question brings forth respondent knowledge that otherwise probably would not have been demonstrated. In practice, most school teaching calls for respondent student behavior: multiple-choice and true-false questions, reading assigned chapters, solving a given set of mathematics problems correctly, or writing an essay to a prescribed theme. Interestingly, respondent measures of learning do not predict long-term operant behavior very well; perhaps because when school is over no one follows a person around defining the problems, presenting test questions, and evaluating the response (McClelland, 1968). Success and fulfillment in work, marriage, interpersonal relations, and leisure time result more from operant than respondent behavior. Educational theorists have begun to draw attention to the importance of teaching that leads to operant, voluntary, internalized behavior (Bloom, 1956; Krathwohl *et al.*, 1964). However, the key academic and vocational success criteria very likely will continue to be end-of-semester tests, standardized achievement tests, and other short-term respondent measures that fail to predict what the student will remember later and whether he will choose spontaneously to *use* what he learned. In contrast, psychological education courses aim for long-term, voluntary changes.

Psychological education courses will change in the future as a result of many influences. As in the past, some new courses will be developed for specific institutional needs. For example, industry was one of the chief financial backers for courses in creativity training, because they wanted to increase the patent output of their research scientists. Recently the Peace Corps commissioned the development of self-assessment workshops to replace the psychiatric, illness-oriented diagnosis that had existed in Peace

Corps training programs (Katz, 1970). It is easy to envision other new courses: identity formation courses for Upward Bound adolescents; individuation courses for elderly men and women; training in the "helping relationship" for parents, supervisors, teachers, and coaches. Although these courses will have different problem foci, most likely they will include the enhancement of fantasy, feelings, and nonverbal communication in intense course experiences.

It is also possible that the dramatically increased interest in these courses will breed psychological hucksterism. At present there is little long-term research to prove, disprove, or improve the efficacy of the courses. There are few formal training institutions for psychological educators, no certification boards, and no national professional organization specifically to promote and monitor the quality of training. In the face of growing demands for courses, these lacks are serious, and the future of psychological education must include some attention to them if the movement is to become a viable and effective discipline available to the general population. There is hope that these courses may be introduced in public education on a national scale, soundly constructed, effectively taught, and properly sequenced. However, this will require long-term institutional support. Thus, the future of psychological education will be strongly influenced by how soon and how extensively university programs in education and psychology discipline the movement by bringing to it their inclinations to theory, their competence in research, and their facilities for training legitimized psychological educators.

Plan of This Book

To be solvable, problems in this inchoate field must be sequenced. Not every need can or should be met at the same time. The creation of a professional organization, the establishment of certification criteria, and the development of training institutions all assume the existence of a discipline whose boundaries, structure, and unique forms of excellence are reasonably well defined. However, a discipline (which implies the careful trialogue between empirical research, theory, and practice) does not yet exist in the field, and needs to be introduced first, if these other formal organizational contributions are to build on substance rather than on hope. The thrust of this book is to build substance through the careful, empirical study of educational methods for promoting psychological growth. The problems chosen for study are both immediately practical (e.g., how do you get and keep students' attention), and specific instances of basic problems in human change (e.g., what principles govern the locus, length, and selectivity of attention). Each chapter attempts to generate widely generalizable, and undeniably useable, knowledge.

2.
Achievement Motivation: Its History and Impact

Certain ideas in man's fantasy life are causally related to the rate of a nation's economic development. Although this statement may sound like a line from a book of black magic, the relationship between "achievement fantasies" and economic progress has been demonstrated through a series of research studies conducted by David C. McClelland and co-workers around the world over the last quarter-century. In brief, men who have many achievement fantasies and think about making things concretely better tend to act in certain special ways. The related expressive style is best described as "entrepreneurial" behavior. When there is a relatively high percentage of achievement thinking and entrepreneurial behavior in a country, or, in other words, *high achievement motivation,* it eventually is reflected in a quickened rate of economic development (McClelland, 1961). One obvious implication is that increasing the amount of achievement thinking in a nation should result in faster economic progress, a prime goal of many underdeveloped countries and many disadvantaged peoples here and abroad. Psychological education courses designed to strengthen adults' achievement motivation have been successful in stimulating more energetic, innovative, and entrepreneurial behavior among adults (McClelland and Winter, 1969). The success of these courses led to the questions that are explored and reported in this book: Can adolescents' achievement motivation be increased? What types of educational inputs maximize the gains in motivation?

The Definition and Measurement of Achievement Motivation

In retrospect, it is not difficult to understand how an interest

19

in measuring human motivation moved from the laboratory into the field. McClelland's first goal was "to develop a method of measuring individual differences in human motivation [which would be] firmly based on the methodology of experimental psychology and on the psychological insights of Freud and his followers" (McClelland, 1961). According to Freud, motivation is reflected in the fantasy lives of individuals, much as the nature of a person's health or illness is reflected in blood samples. Interpretation of dream fantasy is one principal method psychoanalysts use to assess a person's motivations, hidden conflicts, and wishes. A second widely used method of eliciting fantasies of individuals is Professor Henry Murray's Thematic Apperception Test (TAT). The TAT is a set of ambiguous pictures depicting a variety of common situations. Persons taking the TAT are asked to tell imaginative stories about what is happening, what led up to the situation, what the characters are thinking and feeling, and how it will turn out. Both the TAT and dream analysis lacked a rigorous quantitative method of determining the strength and extent to which motives were operating in a person's life. It was here that McClelland integrated a scientific method with the Freudian approach by devising a rigorous method of quantifying human motivation reflected in TAT stories.

The first task in devising this method was to prove that motives are reflected in TAT stories. Just as Hull had experimentally manipulated drive states in animals (e.g., Hull increased the hunger drive by depriving animals of food for varying lengths of time), McClelland began by experimentally manipulating strength of food motivation in humans. McClelland obtained TAT stories from groups of Navy men who differed in the number of hours for which they had gone without food. The results showed that different degrees of hunger were reflected in different amounts of food imagery in the TAT stories. In other words, fantasy TAT stories could be used to measure the strength of motivation (Atkinson and McClelland, 1948).

The next steps were to choose a uniquely human motive, experimentally vary its intensity, and identify the resultant changes in TAT fantasies. McClelland chose to study the need for achievement (n-Ach), one of the most interesting motives previously defined by Henry Murray (Murray, 1938). The intensity of achievement motivation was varied by giving different instructions to groups ___ individuals just before they wrote their TAT stories. ___ s told that people who did well on the fantasy test ___ businessmen and administrators. It was assumed ___ involving instructions would arouse achievement ___ AT responses of this group were compared to TAT ___ up given "neutral" instructions and to a third ___ ven "relaxed" instructions. The specific kinds ___ vere present in the achievement group's TATs ___ eutral" and "relaxed" set of TATs became the ___ on of achievement motivation (McClelland *et* ___ since this definition, or measure, is so critical to an understanding of the subsequent work, it will be presented in some detail here.*

The achievement motive is a pattern of planning, actions, and feelings associated with striving for some kind of excellence, as opposed, for example, to the search for power or friendship. An Achievement Image (AIm) is defined as competition with some standard of excellence, e.g., competition with others, competition against one's own past performance, striving for some unique accomplishment, long-term involvement in the mastery of a difficult discipline. The TAT story below contains an example of a "unique accomplishment" achievement goal.

> The boss is talking to an employee. The boss wants the employee, an engineer, to start working on a *specially designed* carburetor for a *revolutionary* engine. The job will come off okay and the engine will *revolutionize* the automobile industry.

If, and only if, a story contains an Achievement Image, the story is

---

*For a more detailed way of learning this coding system, the reader is referred to the following sources: *Teaching Achievement Motivation*, A. Alschuler, D. Tabor and J. McIntyre, Middletown, Connecticut: Education Ventures, Inc., 1970; *Achievement Thinking*, A. Alschuler and D. Tabor, Middletown, Connecticut: Education Ventures, Inc., 1970; *Motives in Fantasy, Action and Society*, J. Atkinson (Ed.), Princeton, New Jersey: D. Van Nostrand, 1958.

searched for other aspects of achievement planning as an indication of the extent and intensity of achievement motivation. The following elements of achievement planning are counted:

Need: expression of a desire to reach an achievement goal. "He wants very much to solve the problem."

Hope of Success (HOS): stated anticipation of success in attaining a goal. "He hopes to become a great surgeon."

Fear of Failure (FOF): stated anticipation of failure or frustration. "He thinks he will make a mess of the job."

Success Feelings (SuF): stated experience of a positive emotional state associated with a definite accomplishment. "He is proud of his acceptance to graduate school."

Failure Feelings (FaF): stated negative emotion associated with failure to attain an achievement goal. "He is disgusted with himself for his failure."

Act: statement that something is being done to attain an achievement goal. "The man worked hard to sell more books."

World Obstacle (WO): statement that goal-directed activity is obstructed by something in the external world. "His family couldn't afford to send him to college."

Personal Obstacle (PO): statement that progress of goal-directed activity is obstructed by personal deficiencies. "He lacked the confidence to overcome his shyness."

Help: statement of someone's aiding or encouraging the person striving for achievement. "His boss encouraged him in his ambitions."

Achievement Theme: the major plot or theme of the story is achievement, rather than affiliation or power.

The following is an example of a typical story produced in response to a TAT picture:

A student is trying to answer questions on an exam and is finding the test too difficult to do as well as he had wanted. The student is not stupid, but he has a girlfriend and didn't study as hard as he should have. He is unhappy that he didn't study harder, and hopes he has acceptable answers. He would cheat, but it is an honor exam, and he has too much character. He will get a D on the exam and will turn over a new leaf and devote the proper time to study.

This story contains examples of AIm, Act, PO, FaF, HOS, Ach Thema.*

It is clear that achievement motivation as defined above is not identical with our traditional notion of achievement as observable accomplishments, e.g., high test scores, attaining prestigious elected office, or earning a high salary. Achievement motivation is a process of planning and striving for excellence, progress, doing things better, faster, more efficiently, doing something unique, or, in general, competing. It is not the accomplishments per se. Achievement motivation may be involved in a variety of activities. Thus, for example, a long-distance runner, gourmet chef, organ-pipe cleaner, and architect all may have equally high achievement motivation. Increasing the strength of a student's achievement motivation will not necessarily lead to better grades in school, nor always to becoming a businessman. Increased n-Ach may result in a variety of specific increased concerns for excellence.

The Spirit of Hermes:
Personal Characteristics of
People with High n-Ach

Having objectively defined n-Ach, and established its reliability as a measure, McClelland opened the door to the hitherto neglected area of empirical research on motivation. In the years following McClelland's original research, hundreds of studies were

*For more exhaustive accounts of the development of the coding scheme, and of the vigorous methodological examinations which it has undergone, the reader is referred to Chapters 7, 8, 9, 10, and 11 in Atkinson, 1958; Brown, 1965; Heckhausen, 1967; Klinger, 1966; Birney, 1959; Kagan and Moss, 1959; and de Charms, 1968.

conducted to explore further the nature, relevance, and effects of achievement motivation. Several of these studies, concerning the personality characteristics of people with high n-Ach, had a particularly significant impact on subsequent theorizing and research. Investigators discovered that individuals with high achievement motivation tend to act in certain characteristic ways:

1.   Such individuals are interested in excellence for its own sake rather than for the rewards it brings.

        Men high in n-Achievement will not work harder at a task when money is offered as a reward (Atkinson and Reitman, 1956). They evaluate roles on the basis of the opportunities for excellence rather than those for prestige (Burnstein, Moulton and Liberty, 1963). Their achievement concern is not affected by having to work for the group rather than for themselves (French, 1958). They pick experts rather than friends as work partners (French, 1956; McClelland and Winter, 1969).

2.   Individuals with high achievement motivation prefer situations in which they can take personal responsibility for the outcomes of their efforts.

        They like to control their own destinies rather than leave things up to fate, chance or luck (French, 1958; McClelland *et al.*, 1955, pp. 286-287; Heckhausen, 1967, pp. 91-103). They like to make independent judgments based on their own evaluations and experience rather than rely on the opinions of other people (Heckhausen, 1967, pp. 134-136).

3.   They set their goals carefully after considering the probabilities of success of a variety of alternatives.

        Their goals tend to be moderate risks in which their efforts are neither doomed to failure nor guaranteed of success (Heckhausen, 1967, pp. 91-103). The goals are challenging ones in which the outcomes are most uncertain (McClelland, 1958; Atkinson and Litwin, 1960; McClelland,

1955; Atkinson *et al.*, 1960).

4. They are more concerned with the medium- to long-range future than men with low achievement motivation.

They have a longer future time perspective (Ricks and Epley, 1960; Heckhausen, 1967, pp. 42-45), show greater anticipation of the future (McClelland *et al.*, 1955, p. 250), and prefer larger rewards in the future over smaller rewards in the present (Mischel, 1960). Perhaps because of this acute awareness of the passage of time, men with high n-Ach see time as passing rapidly (Green and Knapp, 1959; Knapp and Green, 1960), and don't feel they have enough time to get everything done (Knapp, 1962). In order to keep track of progress towards their goals, they like to get immediate, regular, concrete feedback on how well they are doing (French, 1958; Moss and Kagan, 1961).

McClelland hypothesized that the pattern that emerges from these traits is very often characteristic of the energetic, entrepreneurial character type. He found a close fit between these empirically identified traits and the characteristics of entrepreneurs as described by economic and social theoreticians: namely, skill at making long-range plans, energetic activity directed towards specific goals, preference for situations in which personal responsibility is more important than impersonal forces, moderate risk taking, and the desire for immediate feedback on the results of one's actions (McClelland, 1961, Chapter 6). Persuasive as this descriptive fit may be, it required further empirical documentation. Such evidence came from two sources. Using the alumni records of college students who took the TAT some fifteen years earlier, McClelland (1965c) found that almost all (83 percent) of the alumni in entrepreneurial roles had had high n-Ach scores fifteen years earlier. Conversely, few (21 percent) of the men in nonentrepreneurial roles had had high n-Ach scores. These are rather remarkable findings, considering the comparative lack of longitudinal research in psychology and the typically low predictive power of most psychological tests. Consider the fact that a half-hour sampling of thoughts of college students predicted career activity fifteen years later!

Another set of studies documents the association of n-Ach with entrepreneurship. The archetype entrepreneur in Greek mythology is Hermes, as described in the "Homeric Hymn to Hermes," written around 520 B.C., when Athenian n-Ach was high, compared with later periods. In this hymn Hermes is described as innovator, inventor, businessman, concerned with getting ahead in the world as fast as possible. He made a fortune by constructing a lyre from a tortoise shell. Hermes was not above trickery. "Born in the morning, in the noonday he performed on the lyre, in the evening he stole the cattle of the archer god Apollo" (Brown, 1942). Then Hermes swore to Apollo and Zeus that he, the newborn babe, was innocent. "The real point of the story is its realistic reflection of the conflict which was going on between the traditional propertied classes, represented by Apollo, and the nouveau riche merchant class, who adopted Hermes as their patron. In such a conflict the merchants were clearly the aggressors, just as Hermes is, in their demands for a greater share of the wealth and higher social status" (McClelland, 1961, p. 303). Hermes makes technological innovations, embodies restless energy, motion, little waste of time, and strives for higher status and greater wealth.

The empirical question is whether these and other aspects of Hermes' life style also are characteristic expressive styles of people with high n-Ach. Based on research by Aronson (1958), McClelland concluded that restless (nonrepetitive, discrete) doodles are characteristic of high n-Ach individuals. Like Hermes, the winged-foot messenger of the gods and patron of travelers, high n-Ach people, and peoples, travel more, more widely, explore further, and have higher rates of emigration (McClelland, 1961, pp. 313-317). A variety of data suggest that high n-Ach is related to upward social mobility (McClelland, 1961, pp. 317-322; Crockett, 1962). Just as Hermes was a superb athlete, cultures with high levels of n-Ach tend to have more competitive games and sports (McClelland, 1961). In short, many of the life style traits of people with high n-Ach bear a striking resemblance to the character of Hermes, the entrepreneur. Although interesting as an empirical study of a mythological character type, this research has greatest value in filling out our picture of what a person is like who has high n-Ach. It helps suggest why a country with a comparatively large number of high n-Ach individuals will tend to develop economically more rapidly.

The Origins and Consequences of Achievement Motivation

An equally important question to answer concerns the factors which encourage the development of n-Ach in individuals. There are many approaches to this question. Undoubtedly, cultural values, status structure systems, educational processes, peer group interactions and child-rearing practices all influence the development of n-Ach. Most is known, however, about the impact of child-rearing practices and cultural values.

Winterbottom studied the parents of thirty middle-class boys aged 8-10 (as reported in McClelland *et al.*, 1955, pp. 297-304). After determining the strength of n-Ach in these boys, Winterbottom examined the child-rearing practices of the parents. She found that the mothers of boys with high achievement motivation (1) tended to set higher standards for their children, (2) expected independence and mastery behavior to occur at an earlier age than did the mothers of boys with low achievement motivation, and (3) more often were affectively rewarding; i.e., kissing and hugging were common rewards. Additional corroboration for this relationship between child-rearing patterns and levels of children's achievement motivation were obtained in several other studies. Rosen and D'Andrade (1959) studied parents and children in six different American ethnic groups and varying social classes: French-Canadian, Italian, Greek, Negro, Jewish, and "old American Yankee." Despite complex class differences, Rosen and D'Andrade found that self-reliance training promotes high n-achievement, provided the training does not reflect generalized authoritarianism or rejection by the parents.

These results were extended in cross-cultural research done by Child, Storm, and Vernoff (McClelland *et al.*, 1955). They reasoned that child-rearing patterns reflected pervasive cultural values. To establish this relationship, Child *et al.* collected ethnographic data on child-rearing practices from thirty-three cultures. The measure of cultural values was obtained from an analysis of the folk tales told to children of the thirty-three cultures, since folk tales often are used to convey values to children. Child *et al.* found that cultures in which there was direct training for achievement also had folk tales with high levels of achievement motivation. On the other hand, cultures which are characterized by rigid or restrictive child-rearing practices (punishing children for failure to be obedient and responsible) have folk tales with relatively low levels of achievement motivation. The research of Child *et al.* confirms in large part an earlier study by McClelland and Friedman (1952).

These studies describe an important social-psychological pattern. Certain cultural values are reflected in child-rearing practices which foster high achievement motivation in children. Further, high achievement motivation in a child often crystallizes into an entrepreneurial personality and subsequent career as a manager or administrator. It was at this point in the research that McClelland placed these findings into a larger theoretical context. Weber (1930 edition) had discussed the relationship between the pervasiveness of the Protestant ethic and the rise of capitalism. McClelland suggested a social-psychological interpretation for Weber's hypothesis. The Protestant ethic represented a stress upon independence, self-reliance, and hard work—the achievement values which McClelland had shown to result eventually in entrepreneurial activity. McClelland reasoned further that increases in these cultural values should herald subsequent increases in economic activity. Potentially this hypothesis provided a partial psychological explanation for the economic flourishing and decay of nations throughout history.

The research documenting this interpretation of economic history is presented in great detail in McClelland's book titled *The Achieving Society*. Only two key studies will be described here. In the first, McClelland compared the economic productivity in 1950 of all the Catholic and Protestant countries in the temperate zone. The average economic productivity of the twelve Protestant countries was compared to the average economic productivity of the thirteen Catholic countries. The measure used to compare economic productivity was the kilowatt hours of electricity consumed per capita. There was a striking difference in favor of the Protestant countries. In the second key study, McClelland obtained measures of the level of achievement motivation in 22 countries both in 1925 and in 1959 by counting the frequency of achievement themes in samples of third and fourth grade readers. Three measures of the gain in economic productivity were obtained for the period 1925 to 1950: (1) change in national income as measured in international units per capita (Clark, 1957), (2) change in kilowatt hours per capita of electricity produced, and (3) a combination of the above two measures of change. The level of achievement motivation in 1925 predicted the rate of economic development from 1925 to 1950, while the level of achievement motivation in 1950 does not correlate with the rate of economic productivity for the same period. This striking confirmation of McClelland's theory was extended in several subsequent research studies. Levels of achievement motivation were measured in the literature of Spain and England from the 1500's through the 1800's. In both cases, the rise and fall of achievement motivation preceded the rise and fall of economic productivity by about 25 to 50 years. Similar relationships were obtained for achievement motivation levels and economic productivity in Greece from 900 to 100 B.C. and pre-Incan Peru from about 800 B.C. to 700 A.D., further supporting McClelland's hypothesis (McClelland, 1961, chapter 4).

Some Perspectives on Achievement Motivation

Although the research on n-Ach is impressive in quantity, quantitativeness, and ingenuity, it is not the only human motive to be studied and not necessarily the most important one. N-Ach was chosen from among over twenty theoretically discrete motives described by Henry Murray (1938). A number of these motives have received systematic attention, especially the need for affiliation (n-Aff) and the need for power (n-Pow). N-Aff, for example, shows rather complex relationships between birth rate, infant mortality rate, and economic development (McClelland, 1961, p. 164). N-Pow is not related to the rate of economic growth. However, if n-Pow is relatively high in a country, while n-Aff is relatively low, that country tends to be predisposed to an authoritarian regime. McClelland obtained comparative figures on n-Aff and n-Pow in 1925 and 1950 for a total of 63 cases. (Since most countries were measured both in 1950 and 1925, the actual number of countries is about half the total number of cases.) Of the 12 examples of ruthless police states in the sample, all but one were above the mean in n-Pow and below the mean in n-Aff (McClelland, 1961, p. 168). In 1950, the United States was relatively high in n-Pow. It is somewhat comforting to know that n-Aff was also quite high in 1950, thus perhaps mitigating against the ruthless use of power. From the point of view of this chapter, the important thing to realize is that high n-Ach, n-Aff, or n-Pow does not make a man, or country, better or worse than others. And more important than any one motive alone is the configuration of motive strengths.

A second important fact to understand is that we have been discussing "operant" n-Ach, not "respondent" n-Ach. Operant behavior tends to occur even when the situational cues or demands for it are relatively weak. Respondent behavior requires stronger situational cues and demands before it is elicited. Most people whose operant n-Ach behavior is relatively weak, nevertheless can respond appropriately and effectively when the situation calls for achievement-oriented behavior. The crucial difference for people with strong operant n-Ach is that they more actively seek out or initiate entrepreneurial activities, and where the situation allows for a variety of appropriate responses, they are more likely to act in an achievement-oriented way. McClelland argues that the level of *operant* n-Ach in a country makes a significant impact on the rate of economic growth or decline.

Third, the explanation of economic growth presented by McClelland is plausible and substantiated empirically in large measure; but, in itself, it is not the complete answer to the riddles of why some countries develop their economies more rapidly. For example, the description of child-rearing practices conducive to the development of n-Ach is a bare-bones delineation. The exact nature and impact of schooling on n-Ach has never received detailed, extensive treatment empirically. Similarly, the function of peer group interaction in the early school years, the influence of industrial recruitment and management practices, and the impact of the social structure status systems are important in developing achievement motivation. Yet less attention has been given to these influences.* In short, probably there is as much not known about n-Ach, its origins and impact, as there is known. Nevertheless, in this era, where practical social problems demand solutions before the final theoretical answers are known, it seemed worthwhile to search for methods of increasing n-Ach.

Increasing Adults' Achievement Motivation

In the final chapter of *The Achieving Society*, McClelland summarized the voluminous n-Ach research in terms of several recommendations for accelerating a country's rate of economic development. Although true to the supporting empirical research, these suggestions were utopian, requiring nothing less than breaking the culture's orientation to tradition, increasing other-directedness and market morality, decreasing father dominance, fostering feminist movements, encouraging new religious movements similar to the Protestant Reformation, increasing achievement themes in popular cultural literature, and providing for a more efficient allocation and use of existing n-Ach resources. These suggestions could be considered hypotheses subject to empirical test in a social experiment. At the very least, this would require two countries, only one of which would benefit from the implementation of these national policy goals. At the end of the experiment the psychologist-social reformer would compare national economic statistics of the two countries to see if the policies worked. McClelland realized this was impractical. Also, there is the fact that prediction and control are the two ultimate criteria for a theory's validity. By the second criterion, his theory had not been tested. Thus, McClelland reformulated the problem as follows:

---

*For a more elaborate critique of this point the reader is referred to the last section of Roger Brown's chapter on n-Ach in his book, *Social Psychology*. In general, the two best summaries of the research on n-Ach are Roger Brown's chapter and Heckhausen's book, *Anatomy of Achievement Motivation*. See the bibliography in this work for complete references to these books.

national economic statistics reflect the combined efforts of, among many factors, individual entrepreneurs. If the n-Ach of individual men can be increased, there should be a resultant increase in their success and accomplishments as entrepreneurs. This is a more manageable problem, to which McClelland and co-workers have addressed themselves in the last several years.

Increasing adults' achievement motivation means, first, instilling the spirit of Hermes, teaching men to be more often concerned with excellence and to adopt achievement-related action strategies in pursuing their goals. All of these elements of achievement motivation are well specified, thus making the task a straightforward teaching problem. Manageable as this may sound, there is very little evidence in the professional literature indicating that motivation can be increased, especially in adults. The prevailing pessimism is strong. Most psychologists believe that to be even minimally successful requires tremendous effort over a long period of time. In fact this pessimism extends to practically all traditional methods of changing personality. Many psychoanalysts believe that character is formed by the age of five and remains substantially unchanged thereafter. Empirical research on motivation, including n-Ach, shows that ordinarily it is relatively stable over a number of years (Skolnik, 1966; Birney, 1959; Moss and Kagan, 1961); almost all forms of psychotheraphy are equally ineffective for adults (Eysenck, 1961) and for children (Levitt, 1957). These studies show that 60 to 70 percent get better even if they are *not* treated. This is equally true for counseling and tutorial programs (e.g., Cambridge-Somerville Youth Project; see McCord and McCord, 1964). Bergin (1966), in his review of studies, even showed that psychotherapy makes a significant number of people *worse.* When pooled with those who improve, the average is about the same as untreated groups.

The possibility of changing personality, or of increasing motivation, is not a dead issue. Within the field of psychotherapy there is evidence that "behavior modification therapy" is comparatively more effective (Wolpe, 1958). This approach to change argues that all behavior is learned, that symptoms can be unlearned and other, healthier behaviors learned, or taught (Bandura and Walters, 1963; Wolpe, 1952). Contrary to most other forms of psychotherapy, behavior modification uses highly systematic procedures to change very specifically defined symptoms, not the total personality pattern. Psychoanalysts have argued that this approach is superficial and that the removal of symptoms without curing the "causes" will lead to new symptoms that take the place of the old ones. However, Baker (1969) demonstrated in a study of behavior modification therapy for bed wetters that the technique was relatively effective, that there was not a substitution of symptoms and, on the contrary, that other traits not related to bed wetting also seemed to improve. Perhaps the most interesting aspect of Behavior Modification Therapy is its new strategy for change. In each individual case the goals are objective, limited, and measurable aspects of behavior. For any given goal, several re-learning procedures are used systematically (Wolpe and Lazarus, 1967). In a review of compensatory programs, Jensen (1969) shows that the most effective programs have limited and specific objectives and use systematic plans for reaching these objectives.

McClelland's strategy for change is similar. Many methods are systematically used to increase the salience and frequency of specific n-Ach thoughts, feeling, and actions. It is assumed that every individual has within his repertoire a number of different thought patterns and goals. Men differ in the salience or hierarchy of these motives within them. The motives highest in the hierarchy occur most often and are associated with the greatest number of situational cues. In this sense they are the strongest operant motives. The aim of n-Ach courses is to raise achievement motivation within the existing hierarchy by increasing the number of situational cues to which it is tied.

> If one thinks of a motive as an associative network, it is easier to imagine how one might go about changing it. The problem becomes one of moving its position up on the hierarchy by increasing its salience compared to other clusters. It should be possible to accomplish this end by such tactics as (a) setting up the network— discovering what associations, for example, exist in the achievement area, and then extending, strengthening, or

otherwise "improving" the network they form; (b) conceptualizing the network—forming a clear and conscious construct that labels the network; (c) tying the network to as many cues as possible in everyday life, especially those preceding and following action, to insure that the network will be regularly rearoused once formed; and (d) working out the relation of the network to superordinate associative clusters, like the self-concept, so that these dominant schemata do not block the train of achievement thoughts—for example, through a chain of interfering associations (e.g., "I am not really the achieving type") (McClelland and Winter, 1969, p. 43).

Stated in this way, increasing achievement motivation is more like strengthening a weak muscle than redoing a person's childhood.

In order to maximize the chances of increasing n-Ach, McClelland decided to be *eclectic*, using any and all procedures for change that had some support in the literature on personality change, and *systematic* in the use of these procedures to increase achievement motivation. Four areas of research and theory were surveyed to identify useful techniques: animal learning research, human learning experiments, experience with different types of psychotherapy, and the attitude change research literature. From these areas McClelland identified four basic types of inputs that should increase the probability of yielding higher levels of operant achievement motivation.

A. The Achievement Syndrome

Increasing achievement motivation in the most literal sense means: (1) clarifying and labeling the cluster of achievement thoughts by teaching the elements of achievement planning; (2) relating these thoughts to the appropriate expressive style (moderate risk taking, initiative, using concrete feedback, planning ahead carefully, etc.); and (3) tying these thoughts and actions to appropriate life contexts (e.g., entrepreneurial-type situations). To the degree that this syndrome is clarified, made salient, sensible, and relevant, the motive will be strengthened.*

There are numerous specific procedures for accomplishing these course goals.** Participants can be taught to score their own TAT stories, and subsequently to code their own spontaneous thoughts as well as television programs, newspaper editorials, folk tales, religious books, and conversations. The critical task is to clearly conceptualize and label n-Ach thoughts so that they will be difficult to forget. The expressive style is taught through game simulations in which the actions are adaptive and valuable. Participants learn, practice, and see the results of acting this way in situations where the real-life consequences are not severe enough to prohibit experimentation-learning. Group discussions help clarify how and why these actions are natural outgrowths of the achievement thought pattern. Through the analysis of case

*McClelland and Winter, 1969, chapter 2, cite extensive supporting evidences and spell out these propositions in somewhat greater detail as follows:

A1. The more thoroughly an individual develops and clearly conceptualizes the associative network defining a motive, the more likely he is to develop the motive.

A2. The more an individual can link the newly developed associative network to related actions, the more the change in both thought and action is likely to occur and endure.

A3. The more an individual can link a newly conceptualized association-action complex (or motive) to events in his everyday life, the more likely the motive complex is to influence his thoughts and actions outside the training experience.

**The description of course inputs is relatively brief here because they are described extensively elsewhere, i.e., McClelland and Winter, 1969, chapters 2 and 5. Also, a full-length book-manual has been written to describe achievement motivation training and how to teach yourself to become a course trainer: *Teaching Achievement Motivation: Theory and Practice in Psychological Education*, A. Alschuler, D. Tabor, J. McIntyre, Middletown, Connecticut: Education Ventures, Inc., 1970. This book is accompanied by sets of curriculum materials that operationalize the theoretical course inputs, i.e., *Ten Thoughts, The Origami Game, The Ring Toss Game, Who Am I*, and *Aiming*, by Alschuler and Tabor.

studies, lectures by successful men, and discussions of the student's own life situation, the ideas and actions are tied to real-life contexts. Other methods of teaching are used as well: video tapes, programmed text units, tape-slide units, movies, etc.

S. Self-Study

No change in life style or pattern of thought is accomplished without problems and conflicts. Inevitably the adoption of increased achievement thinking and actions raises other issues regarding ideals, values, and ethics. These too are considered in achievement motivation courses, to make the change satisfying and integrated. More specifically, course participants are encouraged to consider: (1) to what degree achievement motivation meets the demands of reality in an increasingly specialized and professional world; (2) how the spirit of Hermes fits with their image of who they are and what kind of person they would like to be; and (3) in what ways the values of achievement fit with their dominant cultural values.* These issues can be raised in a variety of ways, but typically have included periods of meditation, group discussions of self-images and ideals, discussions of cultural values as expressed in religious books and folklore, and discussion of research showing the relationship of achievement motivation to economic development. The role of the trainer during these discussions is that of an informed but impartial resource who is committed more to careful consideration than to convincing and

*From McClelland and Winter, 1969:

S1. The more an individual perceives that developing a motive is required by the demands of his career and life situation, the more educational attempts designed to develop that motive are likely to succeed.

S2. The more an individual can perceive and experience the newly conceptualized motive as consistent with the ideal self-image, the more the motive is likely to influence his future thoughts and actions.

S3. The more an individual can perceive and experience the newly conceptualized motive as consistent with prevailing cultural values and norms, the more the motive is likely to influence his future thoughts and actions.

persuading. Often this results in some individual counseling. At other times the trainer simply is a good listener. Implicit in this examination is an open choice. Participants are free to choose not to strengthen their achievement motivation. The aim is to promote a highly informed, well-considered choice.

G. Goal Setting

What differentiates achievement motivation from power motivation and affiliation motivation or any other motive is first and foremost the nature of the goal: striving for excellence as opposed to influence or friendship. A man may be in business, may be taking initiative, using feedback, etc., and still be more concerned with having friends than improving his business. A politician may see influence as the means to attaining needed reforms which promote various kinds of excellence. In every case the goals define the motive. The training courses encourage achievement goal setting in three major ways. Before the course proper begins, participants are told about achievement motivation, the impressive research findings, the results of previous courses, the experiences of successful entrepreneurs, and the convictions of prestigious academicians associated with well-known universities. (1) Every attempt is made before the course begins to develop the belief in participants that they can and will increase their concern with excellence. To the degree that a man believes something is possible and desirable, he will make it happen. The culmination of the course also focuses on goal setting in two additional ways. (2) Each participant is encouraged to examine his life and to formulate an achievement goal to which he publicly commits himself within the group. In this way participants make concrete their goals and obligate themselves to obtaining regular, careful, specific measures of their progress. (3) This record keeping provides concrete feedback, reinforcement, a way of locating blocks and solutions, and, in general, an opportunity to engage in continued planning. The precise goals always are chosen by the participants, in order to keep the goals individually relevant.*

*From McClelland and Winter, 1969 (continued on Page 38):

I. Interpersonal Supports

As described thus far, the training course may seem highly rational. Emphasis has been placed on clear cognitive labeling, articulation of action strategies, understanding the research, analysis of related larger issues, goal setting, and record keeping. Obviously, humans are not simply thinking machines into which a new "computer program" can be inserted. Achievement motivation also is the excitement of challenge, the joy of working hard for a goal, often the frenzy of trying to meet a deadline, the pride in innovating, the fear of failure and disappointment at not succeeding. Through the game simulations, course participants have an opportunity to experience and consider their emotional responses to achievement situations. Yet, in another way, achievement motivation courses provide an emotional climate which allows for change. (1) Usually, the courses are held in retreat settings which take the participants away from the daily pressures and demands of work, family, and friends. Besides fostering a feeling of unusual privilege, it allows time for serious emotional self-confrontation. (2) The other group members, all of whom share this unique experience, begin to form a new group identity with new ties of friendship and feeling which last beyond the brief course. The new reference group can act as a continued stimulus to and reinforcement of what was learned during the course. (3) One of the key functions of the trainer is to encourage this group formation, not as its leader, but as a catalyst. The trainer's style is "non-directive," open, warm and accepting, consistent with the

G1. The more reasons an individual has to believe that he can, will, or should develop a motive, the more educational attempts designed to develop that motive are likely to succeed.

G2. The more an individual commits himself to achieving concrete goals in life related to the newly formed motive, the more the motive is likely to influence his future thoughts and actions.

G3. The more an individual keeps a record of his progress, towards achieving goals to which he is committed, the more the newly formed motive is likely to influence his future thoughts and actions.

posture of client-centered therapist. This, too, allows participants to face increasingly deeper emotional issues raised by the course.*

Conducting an achievement motivation course requires more than simply exposing participants to sets of educational inputs. The inputs need to be systematically organized, and the training group, as a small social system, needs to be managed.

To provide this perspective, McClelland and Winter draw upon Parsons' analysis of the functional imperatives of a social system (see Table 2.1 and page 40).

Table 2.1

The Functional Imperatives of a
Social System, after Parsons•†
(cf. Black, 1961, p. 331)

	Instrumental Activities	Consummatory States
Task performance (external orientation)	Adaptation (technology) [Achievement Syndrome—A]	Goal Attainment [Goals of business expansion—G]
System maintenance (internal orientation)	Pattern Maintenance (norms, tension management) [Self-Study—S]	Integration (System Survival) [Interpersonal Supports—I]

• McClelland and Winter, 1969, p. 359.
† Course inputs are in brackets.

*From McClelland and Winter, 1969, chapter 2:

I1. Changes in motives are more likely to occur in an interpersonal atmosphere in which the individual feels warmly but honestly supported by others as a person capable of guiding and directing his own future behavior.

I2. Changes in motives are more likely to occur the more the setting dramatizes the importance of self-study and lifts it out of the routine of everyday life, thereby creating an in-group feeling among the participants.

I3. Changes in motives are more likely to occur and persist if the new motive is a sign of membership in a new and continuing reference group.

He [Parsons] argues that it is possible to distinguish two main functions of any social system—one oriented outwards toward the environment, which he labels task performance; and the other oriented inwards, which he labels system maintenance. The goals and means of attaining each differ. Thus, a psychological experiment such as the achievement motivation training course has two distinct aspects. The task performance aspect is to expose businessmen to certain psychological inputs with the goal of changing their business behavior. However, for this task to be performed, a system maintenance goal must also be achieved, that is, the course as a social system must survive . . . The achievement syndrome (A) is the technique by which the goals of business expansion set by the participants' classes of educational inputs relate to the task to be performed as a result of the creation of this miniature social system. On the other hand, the Self-Study (S) educational inputs seem designed to help the person manage the tensions and value changes within himself and his relations to others, which are likely to result from pursuing the task performance goal. Similarly, the interpersonal supports (I) educational inputs seem designed to fulfill the requirement for integration either within the personality as a system or within the society to which the individual returns (McClelland and Winter, 1969, pp. 359-360).

Of the four sets of training inputs, only the Achievement Syndrome (A) is unique to the training program. In other words, although the research was designed originally to test the causal relationship between achievement motivation and entrepreneurial behavior, the questions answered should generalize to other types of psychological education as well: Can the motivation of adults be increased? What are the relationships between the four training inputs and specific course yields? What type of people benefit most from motivation training?

The Results of Achievement Motivation
Training for Adults

Seventy-six men in Kakinoda and Vellore, India, comprised

the basic sample of businessmen who were given achievement motivation training and were studied by McClelland and Winter. These men were compared to matched controls in Vellore and Rajahmundig, India, towns similar to Kakinoda. The basic data on change were obtained through a series of intensive interviews given over a two-year period following the training. A four point "Business Activity Code" was developed to assess the degree of change: -1 for demotion, firing, fewer responsibilities, less pay, etc.; 0 for an impasse, business improvement not due to the person's efforts, routine job advancement, improvement in family life; +1 for specific plans to improve his business and some action taken; +2 for unusual increase in the firm's business due to the person's activity, salary increases more than 25 percent, etc. By this measure, the training programs were reasonably effective (see Table 2.2).

Table 2.2*

Percentages of n-Ach Trained and Untrained
Entrepreneurs Classified as Active
(+2) During Two-Year Periods

	Before the course 1962-64	After the course 1964-66
All trained in n-Ach (n = 76)	18%	51%
All controls (n = 73)	22%	25%

$\chi^2 = 18.91$; p $<.001$

*Adapted from McClelland and Winter, 1969, p. 213.

Beyond this increased entrepreneurial activity there are more specific indices of their new energy.

They work longer hours. They make more definite attempts to start new business ventures, and they actually start more such ventures. They make more specific investments in new, fixed productive capital. They employ more workers. Finally, they tend to have relatively larger percentage increases in the gross income of their firms. The aggregate effects of the courses include, to date, the mobilization of approximately R_s, 376,000 of specific new capital investments and about 135 new jobs. Measured by these figures, the courses certainly seem to have had an economic effect (McClelland and Winter, 1969, pp. 230-231).

However, not all businessmen benefit from the course. Almost half of the men (49 percent) were not unusually active in the two years following the training. A careful comparison of the "changer" and "inactive" men showed that they were systematically different before the course; 92 percent of the changers (n = 27) were "in charge" of their businesses or were the decision-makers in their extended family life, while among the inactives (n = 34), only 50 percent were in charge in either situation (χ^2 = 12.00, p <.001). Besides being "in charge," the changers tend to have a different view of themselves:

Achievement motivation training is especially likely to change men who are in charge of their businesses, probably because they have the scope and independence to carry out new ideas and plans. Furthermore, if a man already is somewhat dissatisfied with himself, but sees himself as someone who can initiate specific action to solve specific problems, he is likely to respond to the training with specific visible activity (McClelland and Winter, 1969, p. 272).

Perhaps the most striking psychological difference in the "changes" produced by the training is revealed in their TAT stories in the two years following the course. These stories contain increased references to activity rather than essence goals, to taking initiative rather than relying on external resources, to solving problems rather than avoiding them, or more generally, a syndrome that can be described as more efficacious thinking.

Not every course was equally effective in influencing the participants to change. By comparing the effects of courses with differing numbers and types of inputs on men "in charge," it was possible to roughly gauge the value of various inputs. The comparison suggests that no one input is either necessary or sufficient to produce change. However, when training is viewed as the establishing of an effective social system, the results are clearer.

> At least some minimal level of course inputs relevant to each of the four functional imperatives is necessary to achieve effectiveness . . . Intensive attention given to two or three of the four prerequisites is not likely to be as effective as some attention to all of them. At a minimum, we are convinced by our experience that exclusive attention to task performance without any attention to system maintenance is likely to result in complete failure of the enterprise (*Ibid.*, p. 360).

In fact, the "system maintenance" issues were less well resolved by the course than the "task performance" issues. For the men *not* "in charge," the course message—to think and act more efficaciously—did not fit. They were not as dissatisfied with the way they were to begin with, and they had fewer opportunities to exercise the problem-solving, achievement-orientation taught in the course.

In perspective, nevertheless, McClelland and Winter did show that adults' motivation can be increased when the training is an effectively managed social system. This entails the integration of the task with the personality of the participants and with the demands and opportunities in participants' lives. Only under these conditions will motivation aroused in the training program be maintained.

Consider for a moment one implication of these results. The United States is engaged in enormous foreign aid programs, including the shipment abroad of dollars, equipment, food stuffs, and Peace Corps volunteers. A major assumption behind this aid is that increased opportunities will foster more rapid economic progress. Achievement motivation training represents a radical alternative. The investment is made in *men* instead of materials, in motivation rather than in opportunities. This type of aid would be focused on key individuals, and thus be relatively inexpensive compared to programs which attempt to feed an entire nation.

Motivating Adolescents' Achievement

Aid to education has been invested primarily in the external, material side of teaching and learning—newer school buildings, newer curricula, better equipment. One central aim is to create equal educational opportunity for all citizens. Yet Coleman (1966a), in his nationwide study of educational opportunity, concluded that certain student attitudes accounted for more variance in the amount of learning than teacher training, physical facilities, or curricula combined. The key attitudes were students' self-concept and the degree to which they believed they could control their own destiny through their efforts. Students who believed that fate, chance, and luck were more important than hard work did less well. Lefcourt (1966) reviewed the research on this attitudinal variable and concluded that we know very little about its social origins or how to increase it through training. The aims and outcomes of achievement motivation training are temptingly close to this crucial desire to master one's destiny. The restless striving for excellence, self-confidence, calculated risk taking, and desire to have personal responsibility for what happens are central to achievement motivation and also, perhaps, to a sense of "fate control."

Beyond this similarity, there is also empirical data showing that n-Ach is moderately related to how well a person does in school. McClelland *et al.* (1955) found a low significant relationship between n-Ach and school grades of college students. Other researchers have found small but statistically significant relationships between n-Ach and academic performance of superior high school students (Uhlinger and Stephens, 1960). "Underachievers," on the other hand, appear to have very low achievement motivation (Burgess, 1957; Garrett, 1949; Gebhart and Hoyt, 1958). Morgan (in Atkinson and Feather, 1966) showed that in equal-ability grouped classrooms, n-Ach was strongly related to grades attained. For these practical and socially meaningful reasons, it seemed appropriate to see if adolescents' achievement motivation could be increased.

The first achievement motivation training course for high school students was given to bright, underachieving boys enrolled in an intensive remedial summer school program at Brown University (Kolb, 1965). Twenty of the 57 boys in the summer program were chosen randomly to receive the additional motivational training. The remaining 37 boys served as the control group.

Kolb demonstrated that adolescents' striving for excellence could be increased for relatively long periods of time. However, his research raised a number of practical questions. The effects of the training were most pronounced for high socioeconomic status (SES) boys who, Kolb hypothesized, returned to environments that supported and encouraged the achievement values they had learned. Although this is plausible, it is also possible that low SES boys simply did not find *school* the best arena for them to exercise their increased motivation. They may have become more entrepreneurial outside and after school where they are more "in charge." It is possible that different types of students use the training in different ways. Older students may apply their achievement motivation in different ways from younger students. Girls may use n-Ach in different areas from those used by boys. These questions simply are extensions of those asked by McClelland and Winter: What are the yields of achievement motivation training? For whom is the training most effective?

At a theoretical level there is an important question raised but left unanswered by McClelland and Winter. Their data indicate that the courses were more effective in reaching the "task performance" goals than in resolving the "system maintenance" issues. At an individual level, this means finding additional ways of managing tension, reducing intra- and inter-personal conflicts, setting new norms, and facilitating the integration of the new motive into the person's life. At an institutional level (or large group), increasing system maintenance means finding more methods of reducing the conflict between an individual's achievement motivation and the situational press for other motives, e.g., compliance, obedience, etc. It means devising ways of introducing achievement motivation training into schools so that this type of psychological education will be integrated into the system—and both will survive. Much of the current efforts to increase innovation in education have succeeded initially in reaching their goal, only to find that the resultant conflicts set up in the school subvert the progress made.

As with much of social science research, the core problem in the current efforts became clear only after a series of specific investigations, with each success or failure progressively delineating the boundaries of the central unanswered question. When we began this research in 1965, we were asking two questions: Can adolescents' motivation be increased? What combination of course inputs maximizes the motivational yield? Partial answers to these questions allowed us to put the question more broadly and yet more precisely: What conditions increase the likelihood that initial changes produced by the training program will be maintained? In learning how to increase adolescents' motivation we were not interested solely in the temporary creation of an aroused motive. It is comparatively easy for the psychological educator to arrange the learning environment so that the desired information is grasped and repeated, the behavior produced, and the feelings experienced. It is considerably more difficult to make motivation resilient, information synergistic, behavior skillful, and feelings more matured. We wanted to identify the conditions that allowed aroused motivation to be sustained long after the special learning environment of the course was absent.

Nevertheless, we were never interested in forcing permanent increases in motivation, but instead, in being more complete in our pedagogy. We considered it our end goal to make it possible for those students who chose to increase their n-Ach to do so in as many ways and for as long as they so desired. Thus, when we reached what appeared to be the maximum degree and variety of yields from n-Ach training itself, we turned to one of the most significant social environments in which achievement strivings occur—the school. Our hope was to devise ways of restructuring classroom learning procedures to be more conducive to achievement motivation. In this way we hoped to provide additional support for students who wanted to exercise their achievement concerns, and increase the overall yields of n-Ach training. As we observed normal classes in regular subject matter areas, we began to see specific conflicts our students faced. The structure of learning, the rules, scoring system, and student roles did not always allow individual goal setting and moderate risk taking, or encourage the restless spirit of creative independence. Devising ways of altering these structures, we predicted, would increase the likelihood that aroused n-Ach could be sustained and enhanced in more areas for longer periods of time.

Although we collaborated with teachers in restructuring motivational learning opportunities in the classroom, after the research team left the school, the "decay" curve set in. Most traces of the seemingly productive collaboration slowly vanished. We had to become concerned with the conditions which increase the likelihood that aroused institutional changes will be sustained. In practical terms, solving this institutional problem was instrumental to maintaining conditions receptive to the flourishing of increased student motivation. At both levels we had to solve the problem of facilitating "maintenance."

The problem is familiar and as prevalent as attempts to innovate in ongoing social systems. It seems almost as if such conflicts were in the service of an innate institutional conservatism that transcends individuals, and maintains the status quo.

According to the theoretical formulations of Parsons (Black, 1961), "system maintenance" is one of the two functional imperatives of any social system. The other is "task performance." If a system is to attain its goals and survive, it must maintain norms and values and reduce the inevitable conflicts and tensions created by changes adopted to accomplish its mission more effectively. Innovations in education have concentrated more on advanced technology for more efficient goal attainment than on system maintenance, i.e., ways this technology can be assimilated into the system with minimum *disruption*, or procedures for helping the system accommodate to the changes.

As we have indicated already, the survival of an individual's aroused motivation appears to depend in large part on solving system maintenance problems at several levels—within the course as a system, in the individual's relations to classroom norms, values, and procedures, and in helping the school adjust to and maintain institutional changes.

A system's ability to attain its goals and to survive are highly interdependent: goal attainment is not possible if the system doesn't survive, and survival is not possible if goals are not reached. Since system maintenance patterns support the task orientation, the successful management must proceed from an understanding of the system's goals and values. Parsons (1959) argues that formal schooling is one of the primary agents of socialization and that, as such, its goals are (1) to *generate commitments* (a) to basic social values and (b) to the performance of a specific type of role within the structure of society, and (2) to *develop capacities* such as (a) role competence, skill, and expertise, and (b) "role responsibility." Parsons argues further that from the point of view of society, another basic goal of schooling is (3) to *allocate manpower.* In essence this means determining who shall have access to higher education. Since completion of high school has come to represent a minimum satisfactory level of educational attainment, the responsibility of allocating manpower means determining who shall go to college and who shall not. This allocation function seems to be accomplished in large part by the end of the ninth grade, when students are enrolled either in the college or vocational program. There is relatively little shifting after this time into or out of these educational tracks. Given finite educational resources, personnel, funds, and materials are devoted mostly to (2a) developing competence or skills to perform the individual's role as a college student or in a non-college vocation. Far fewer resources are devoted directly to (1a) developing broad social values (i.e., citizenship) and (2b) "role responsibility" (i.e., the configuration of motives appropriate to the specific role).

Achievement motivation training encourages commitments to (1a) basic social values, such as independence, acceptance of personal responsibility for the consequences of one's actions, and actively attempting to master the environment according to standards of excellence (Dreeben, 1967). Even more directly this training attempts to develop (2b) entrepreneurial "role responsibility." In theory this is consistent with the functions of schooling as an agent of socialization. In practice, the implementation of these generally acknowledged goals requires some of the finite resources of schooling—time, funds, personnel—and thus is a challenge to the current allocation of resources to (2a) the development of role competence. For example: As long as our research project provided the teaching personnel and funds to conduct achievement motivation training, administrators arranged students' time for the training. Here, our participation added to the total resources and allowed the schools to accomplish all of their socialization goals more completely. When we left, however, schools typically did not redistribute their limited resources to maintain the training because this would have meant devoting less energy to what they considered their primary socialization task—developing role competence. There appear to be three basic alternatives helpful in avoiding this conflict: (1) change the school's value hierarchy of socialization goals, (2) find other social systems in which entrepreneurial role responsibility is more highly valued, and (3) show that this training is instrumental in developing greater role competence. Any of these alternatives would reduce conflict, increase the likelihood that motivation training will be maintained, and help the system accomplish its mission more effectively.

This social system analysis also provides a framework for understanding Kolb's basic maintenance problem (1965): of the underachievers he trained, only high SES boys sustained increased grade point averages for 1½ years after the n-Ach course. Schools allocate manpower and socialize role expectations for college and vocational areas primarily on the basis of "ascribed factors" (principally socioeconomic status) and "achieved factors" (i.e., being a "good" student in terms of grades and deportment; Parsons, 1959). Kolb trained only "poor" students, i.e., underachievers. It is reasonable to expect that Kolb's lower SES students would apply their entrepreneurial, n-Ach training in areas related to vocational roles in and outside of school and not in academic courses oriented to success in college. In fact, Kolb did not find lasting improvement in grade point averages for the low SES boys and he did not assess possible gains in the vocational areas. The high SES, poor students in Kolb's study entered the course with conflicting role expectations. It can be argued that increased n-Ach was seen by them as instrumental to becoming a "good" student and was applied in academic areas. This reduced their conflict and enhanced their ability to attain their goal of role competence.

McClelland and Winters encountered a maintenance problem which also is more understandable when viewed from a similar social system perspective. The n-Ach training was least effective for those men "not in charge," i.e., men for whom neither ascribed role responsibility (head of household) or achieved role expectations (decision-maker in business) were consistent with the entrepreneurial orientation taught in the course. Whether and how this system conflict was resolved by the men is left unanswered by McClelland and Winter for lack of relevant data. It is unlikely that the family decision-making patterns or the prerogatives of subordinates in a business would accommodate sufficiently to their increased desire for personal responsibility. It is equally hard to imagine just what non-business contexts would be more receptive to an increased entrepreneurial drive. Given these major conflicts, increased n-Ach probably was experienced as tension producing, a challenge to the norms and values expected of their social roles and as non-adaptive in their salient social systems.

These examples illustrate the importance of a social system perspective in maintaining changes produced by motivation training, and psychological education in general. The investigations described in this book in one way or another all deal primarily with the question of maintaining change. For us this has meant finding resolutions for system maintenance conflicts and tensions engendered by the training. These problems occurred in the training program itself as a system, in the conflict between an achievement orientation and role responsibilities within normal classrooms, and in the larger social systems of schools. Our ultimate goal has been to increase the long-term role competence and role responsibility of students by developing prototype solutions from achievement motivation training for the field of psychological education.

PART TWO
Research Studies on
Achievement Motivation Training

3.
Maximizing Attending Behavior*

In planning our first two courses for adolescents, an obvious target population was the group of boys popularly called "seat warmers"—those who dislike school and basically are waiting for their 16th birthday and a job opportunity so they can drop out of school. We hoped that an n-Ach course would increase their commitments to such basic social values as independence, acceptance of personal responsibility for the consequences of one's actions, and active attempts to master the environment according to standards of excellence. We also hoped that the course would teach entrepreneurial role responsibility and improve their performance and attitudes in school. Of the 21 boys who came to the five-day courses, eleven dropped out by the end of the third day. Thus, in addition to a preliminary assessment of the ultimate yields of training, we were forced to come to grips with a fundamental system maintenance problem in managing the course—how do you maximize attending (attendance and attention) behavior?

Procedure
Recruitment. In January, 1966, a letter was sent by the principal of a Boston suburban school system to 32 "seat warmers" in the 10th grade, inviting them to come to a one-hour

*This chapter was co-authored by David McClelland. The research reported here resulted from the hard work and creative efforts of Manohar S. Nadkarni, Richard deCharms, Knowles Dougherty, John Lennon, Ron McMullen, Steven Solomon, Gordon Alpert, Jeffrey Griffith, David Kolb, and Jim Reed.

presentation about the project. Twenty-two boys attended and heard the courses described as something that would help them understand themselves better and improve their school work. They were told that the course was for people with unused "potential," "late bloomers" who could benefit from courses like those given to businessmen around the world. The course was scheduled for the week of their winter vacation in a rural residential setting on the edge of the metropolitan Boston area. In individual interviews, 14 said they wanted to go, 2 said "no," and 6 said "maybe." The program was also explained to the parents of the boys in an evening session at the school arranged for the benefit of those who were curious enough to attend. Parental permission to attend the course was required by the school. Eight boys showed up for the five-day session in the country, two of whom dropped out on the third day.

A second group was recruited in a similar manner for the April vacation. Alumni of the first course were paid to help in recruiting individuals. A general presentation was attended by 26 out of the 41 invited. From this group and others contacted, 18 said they wanted to attend, 7 said "no," and 9 were in the "maybe" category. Twelve actually showed up for the course (including 3 who had said "maybe"), of whom 8 went home on the second day, and one on the third. An additional boy was brought along by an assistant trainer, who was the parole officer to whom the boy had just been assigned after having been released from a detention house. Only 4 boys from the school actually completed the course; 2 alumni of the first course joined them for the last 2 days.

Matched controls. This left a total of 10 boys who had completed the course and 11 who had been exposed to some of it and dropped out. Each boy was carefully matched for age, IQ, and grade point average in the five quarters before the training with a boy from the large group who had heard about the course, expressed an interest, but for one reason or another had not attended. No boy who had said "no" at the outset was included among the controls. Thus the trained and control groups were roughly equated for initial expressed interest in self-improvement. One might, of course, suppose that those who actually showed up had more motivation, but the supposition is probably incorrect on two counts: (1) many of the boys in the control group wanted to come but were genuinely prevented by the necessity of work, illness, etc., and (2) subsequent events showed that many who went were not so much interested in self-improvement as they were in having a "good time."

Training. The courses were patterned almost exactly after those given for adult businessmen, and fully described elsewhere (see McClelland and Winter, 1969). In fact, the key trainer was the same man, M.S. Nadkarni, who had conducted courses for businessmen in India. He worked in collaboration with teachers and guidance personnel from the Harvard Graduate School of Education and from the staff of the high school involved. The course inputs included (1) learning about the "achievement syndrome," the planning pattern, action strategies, and feelings of people with high achievement motivation; (2) some exercises in self-study; (3) setting personal goals for after the course; and (4) learning individual responsibility from group living. The full course totaled about 50 hours. The partially trained group (i.e., those who dropped out after 2 or 3 days) were exposed to about 10 to 15 hours of the course, consisting largely of learning the achievement syndrome and engaging in a self-analytic group session.

The first course seemed, on the whole, reasonably successful. The 6 who stayed for the whole time became quite enthusiastic about achievement motivation, its effects on their own lives, and their role in spreading the concept to others in the school. In interviews about 10 months later, they made the following comments:

"Pretty good course. Smartens you up a little. Realize now school is important. Need it to go places. Try to better self and stay in."

"Liked all of it. Before I didn't care about things, my family, nothing. When I left the course, I really wanted to do something. Had a great talk with my father, before never exchanged two words with him. Now when

I get bad marks, the n-Ach course makes me feel guilty. I am keeping my marks up."

"Excellent, very good course. Learned how to run a business. Helped me decide what I want to do. When I was little I wanted to be a priest. Then decided hairdressing was the job for me. Came back from course and got addresses of schools. Before I was nervous, now I am relaxed and can talk to people."

The second course was a near-disaster. A good many of the boys came prepared to cut loose, and they did. What happened can best be described in their own recollections eight months later:

"Stunk! Every time you asked the Indian guy a question, he asked a question back. It was up in a wilderness."

"Mass destruction. We did $1,000.00 worth of damage and still had plenty of alcohol left. There were no restrictions. Kids are not used to that kind of freedom. It went to our heads. The course brought out insanity. But, I think I got something out of listening to others anyway."

"I couldn't see the point of it. I saw no purpose to the games. It was a waste. Everybody started with the idea of causing trouble. They went wild. I didn't get anything out of it."

"There was no respect for the group leaders. If they were stern, the kids would have stayed in line."

The leaders were pretty much the same as those in the first course, and so were the procedures, but, for a variety of reasons, the right atmosphere was not created. The students had been told by the boys who recruited them that they would have a great time. They came to the resort-like course setting during their spring vacation ready for a "wild time." Once there, they looked around and immediately identified the group and themselves as a "bunch of kooks" rounded up by Harvard psychologists to have their "brains shrunk." The course trainers, for their part, made a conscious decision not to be jailers or disciplinarians, since this would deny the boys the opportunity to take personal responsibility for their own actions. The boys brought liquor with them and responded to the challenge by going wild, not sleeping, being rude, not participating in sessions, and inventing war games of their own. The instructor-led self-analytic sessions were threatening and the instructional "games" seemed "stupid." Not surprisingly, most of them left the second day, and they made up 8 out of the 11 of the "partly trained" group. Of the 4 who stuck it out, most of them had a more positive attitude towards the course later, but a negative attitude towards the "crazy kids" who had gone wild.

Results

Nearly all participants and controls were interviewed some 8 to 10 months after training. Some were interviewed again 2 years later. Grades were obtained from the school and averaged for 5 quarters after the training. One full participant dropped out of school and joined the Army soon after the course. Four out of 28 in the total pool of control subjects studied dropped out. The numbers are too small to draw any conclusions about the effect of training on dropping out of school, though it should be noted that the course was not specifically aimed to keeping the boys in school, if it seemed better to them in terms of their carefully chosen goals to do something else.

The main results are summarized in Table 3.1, where the effects on individual boys from the fully trained group are set side by side with the changes occurring in their matched controls. The matching was done blindly on the basis of the first three columns after a boy's name only, without any knowledge of posttraining grade point average. Seven out of nine of the fully trained boys gained at least a letter grade step in their average (e.g., from D to D+, or .33 points), as contrasted with only three boys among the controls. As far as could be determined from the school records,

Table 3.1

Effects of n-Ach Training
on Grade Point Average (GPA)
of 10th Grade Male Underachievers

Full Training (n = 9)

Name	Age	IQ	5 Quarter GPA[1]		
			Before	After	Change
Steve	18/8	86	.60	1.42	+ .82
Bill	17/7	90	1.44	1.60	+ .16
Paul	16/9	102	.94	1.36	+ .42
Owen	16/9	122	1.18	(2.3)[2]	+1.12
Joe	16/4	113	1.40	1.96	+ .56
Jimmy	16/3	105	.96	1.98	+1.02
Stephen	16/1	100	.86	1.20	+ .34
William	16/0	105	1.20	.80	- .40
Bob	16/0	111	.58[3]	1.78[3]	+1.20
Averages: (number gaining +.33 or better: 7)		104	1.02	1.60	+ .58
Partly trained[4] (n = 11)		108	1.42	1.59	+ .17

No Training (control) (n = 9)

Name	Age	IQ	5 Quarter GPA		
			Before	After	Change
George	17/9	86	.90	1.04	+ .14
Chris	18/5	82	1.28	1.46	+ .18
Ed	17/3	97	.92	1.00	+ .08
Tom	17/0	120	1.12	2.24	+1.12
Mike	16/9	118	1.34	.94	- .40
Brian	16/8	107	1.16	1.34	+ .18
Norman	16/6	89	.50	.30	- .20
Ken	15/8	104	1.18	2.20	+1.02
Kim	15/9	103	.80	1.40	+ .60
Averages: (number gaining +.33 or better: 2)		101	1.02	1.32	+ .30
Controls[5] (n = 11)		107	1.38	1.65	+ .27

1. F = 0; D = 1; C = 2; B = 3; A = 4.
2. Family moved to another state; grades are reported by the boy, not exactly comparable but clearly a large improvement.
3. From another school.
4. Dropped out after 1 to 2 days of training.
5. Five from the above control group used again here to produce close individual matching.

the three control boys who showed such marked "spontaneous" improvement had not received any special "treatment." Fisher's exact test shows that the p-value of obtaining such a difference by chance is less than .04 in the predicted direction. The trained boys' overall averages rose from a solid D to a low C-, while the untrained controls went from a D to a D+.

As for the partly trained boys who dropped out, their performance is compared with that of a new control group drawn from the same pool of subjects appearing in the first matching basis. Five of the subjects appearing in the first control group were also used here to produce close matching. Obviously the slight increase in the average for the course dropouts is more than equalled by a larger increase in their matched controls. As the dropouts themselves said, they got nothing out of the course. It is of some interest to know why they dropped out. Since a number of tests were given them at the outset, it is possible to check for initial differences in various characteristics. They did not differ from those who stayed on fantasy measures of n-Ach, n-Aff, or n-Power, on IQ, on occupational level of the father (predominantly skilled blue-collar workers), on Debilitating Anxiety Test, or on the extent to which they valued achievement or described themselves as internally controlled on Rotter's I-E scale. They only differed significantly on deCharms and Rosenbaum's (1962) self-esteem scale. Seven out of 11 of the dropouts scored above the group's median score, as contrasted with only 2 of the 10 who stayed, $p < .05$. In other words, it looks as if it took greater self-confidence to go to the staff and ask to go home. The dropouts were also doing somewhat better in school, so that they may have felt under less pressure to stay.

The better academic performance of the fully trained boys after the course is also reflected in other measures, such as days absent from school, which indicates their attitude as well as actual illness. In fact, the boys refer to absences often as "skipping school." On the average, the 2 control groups and the partly trained were absent an additional day per quarter in the 5 quarters after the training, as contrasted to the 5 quarters before. The fully trained boys were absent one day less a quarter on the average. Or, to put it another way, 6 out of 9 of them went to school more often afterwards, as contrasted with 3 out of 9 of their matched controls. The differences are not significant, but certainly suggest a better attitude toward school on the part of the fully trained boys.

When the boys were interviewed at some length 8 to 10 months after training, there was still a marked difference in the attitude of those who had been fully trained, as evidenced by their answers to the interviewer's first non-directive question: "What are the most important things in your life? What are the most important things you do or think about now?" Among the 9 boys interviewed from the partly trained group and the 10 from the 2 matched control groups, most of the answers concerned sports, having a car, playing in a band, or just getting out of school. Only 4 out of the 19 boys in these groups mentioned doing well in school or thoughts about work or a career. In contrast, every one of the 9 fully trained boys mentioned serious education or work-related goals, most of them specific. Only one mentioned a sport as of prime importance to him, but that was because his whole family was in baseball, he was on the town championship team, and furthermore he felt he had to have a college education, which meant studying harder now. The difference between the fully trained students and the others is highly significant, though it is hard to know, of course, how much they were talking to please someone who represented what was for nearly all of them still a very valuable and respected part of their lives. But the fact that they were able to give details of the plans they had made, or talks they had had about future jobs or schools, indicated that it wasn't all just giving what they knew to be a desired response. They were doing the things that they had said at the end of the course they were going to do. One example, which is fairly typical, will help give the tone of their reports to the interviewer.

Jimmy had decided at the course that he wanted to be a hairdresser. By the middle of his senior year in high school he reported he would start in the June or September following. He picked the career because it pays well and he has really put his mind to achieving his goal. He had a part-time job and saved about $500 to use for tuition at the hairdressers' school. He applied to the school and had an invitation to come for an interview. He planned to try to get a job at the telephone company while going to school, because it would be better than the part-time job he had at a dry cleaner's. He was trying for the "honor roll for the first time since 3rd grade" and his grades were up (see Table 3.1). Obviously he had done a lot of concrete thinking about and planning for his future.

Typical of the control boy reports is Ken's. He said sports are most important to him, football and particularly skiing—in winter, snow skiing, and in summer, water skiing. He also spent a lot of time with his girlfriend and is a "bug on mechanics." He used to race go-karts, wants to race his car at the Connecticut dragway, but has lost his license for speeding. He never liked school and never does the work. He said he just hasn't done much serious thinking about his future.

Discussion

What exactly do the results show? Is it reasonable to believe that five days of intensive training can significantly change school attitudes and performance, and perhaps even affect career planning beneficially? Certainly any such belief needs to be subjected to a healthy dose of skepticism. The numbers are small, and the probably least-adjusted fully trained boy is not included in the statistics because he dropped out and joined the Army. To be sure, there were dropouts among the controls too, and we can't be sure that the Army wasn't the right course for this boy, for there is certainly room for doubt that the course affected him much. Furthermore, it must be remembered that the training didn't "take" at all for half the boys—particularly during the second training session, when the majority left after a day or two. Thus, if the overall evaluation included every boy who had at least started the training, one would have to conclude that the project as a whole had failed to produce any effects. Isn't it unfair to draw inferences only from the improvement of those who stuck out the training? Doesn't that prove they were "better stuff" to start with? The facts suggest otherwise. So far as school performance is concerned, they weren't better off, but worse off. Also, they had lower self-esteem. They appeared to have stayed partly out of weakness rather than ego strength. And it hardly seems fair to include the effects of training on boys who were not exposed to much of it. Certainly, it would be unwarranted to draw extensive conclusions of any kind from such a small pilot study. It gains significance largely because it is one of the very few studies which show that intervention can produce a significant improvement in performance of such "hard core" problem boys (Jensen, 1969). Futhermore, the educational input is cheap compared to some of the expensive failures reported in the literature (e.g., the Cambridge-Somerville Youth Project, see McCord and McCord, 1964).

The most salient problem raised by this research is how to get high potential dropouts to stay in a course designed to reduce their dropout potential. The problem is a dramatic, special instance of a ubiquitous educational issue: how to maintain attending behavior (attendance and attention) so that learning can take place. It is the first maintenance problem that must be solved if the course as a system is to succeed. While such a conclusion may seem so obvious as to be almost trivial, it does not figure largely in the literature on personality change. On the one hand, if positive results are obtained, as they were here for about half the group, then observers conclude it was "mere suggestion" or the "Hawthorne effect"—forgetting that such a statement means little because it is clear that sometimes a suggestion "takes" and sometimes it doesn't. The problem is to find out how to create an atmosphere in which suggestion will take—which is another way of saying that far more than "mere" suggestion is involved. On the other hand, previous research has tended to try to isolate the "educational inputs" (games, fantasy, training, etc.) which are "really" responsible for what changes occur afterwards. Our experience here suggests that this isn't quite the right way to define the problem. It is not a question of this or that input which, when "applied" to pupils, produces this or that effect, but rather *a question of what organizational or motivational inputs can create an atmosphere in which the boys are interested enough in the educational inputs and under sufficient control to get something from them.* The stress has to be more on the interest value of the inputs, and the structure of the learning situation, than on the exact nature of the study units themselves, at least for boys of this type, who have already mentally "dropped out" of school learning situations. Viewed this way, one might conclude that putting on a motivational training course is something like putting on a play. If you succeed in capturing the audience's attention long enough, the message gets across. Otherwise, you have failed and the audience is not influenced.

Getting and maintaining attention seems to be largely a matter of creating moderate discrepancies from what is known, experienced, expected, or valued. As most teachers know, when a student is given a problem far beyond his capabilities, he becomes confused and does not engage in problem-solving behavior. Problems that are too simple are boring, and also fail to elicit students' attention for very long. Moderately difficult or discrepant problems are best for learning. Kagan (1967) has gone so far as to argue that the necessary and sufficient conditions for learning are (1) contiguity of the material to be learned and (2) attentional involvement through the creation of moderate novelty. "Reinforcement," from this point of view, is only one method of making a situation moderately novel, whether it is the delightfully surprising appearance of a food pellet for a rat in a Skinner box or a teacher's warm pat on the back for a correct answer. Too much of either fails to be reinforcing, since the organism is satiated with food or praise. This helps explain the findings in studies of learning that a sequence of "continual reinforcement → periodic reinforcement → aperiodic reinforcement" is best for fixing a desired stimulus-response bond in organisms. In each phase of this reinforcement sequence, moderate novelty is maintained *relative* to the changing norms of experience or expectations.

From this point of view, many major (not moderate) discrepancies were created for the boys in the training programs, especially those in the second course. They were told it would be fun, but the trainers wanted them to write and think as in school. Yet it certainly wasn't like school in other respects: it was held in a resort setting over vacation and there were "games." Unlike school, there were no "rules" or punishment for bad behavior in this specially selected group of pure "troublemakers." They couldn't see how "going wild" would help them get better marks or a better job. This highly unfamiliar situation with so many discrepancies from patterns of schooling and vacation fun was experienced as confusing, threatening, and—for half of them—as something to be discontinued. Maintaining attention in motivation courses would be maximized, one would predict, if the context, rules, reference group, and espoused values were less radically different from familiar learning situations. Thus, the technology of maintaining attending behavior seems to rest first on a clear understanding of the existing norms, values, roles, and expectations in participants' familiar learning situations. This provides the basis for creating a *moderately novel* learning experience. In contrast, the transfer of specific inputs or techniques used successfully in one group to another, different group may violate the principle of relativism underlying the creation of "moderate" discrepancies. Setting up a small, intimate group with few rules and little protocol in a retreat setting may be engaging for adult businessmen but intolerably discrepant for potential high school dropouts.

The effects of the training on those boys who stayed through the course, while not dramatic, are suggestive. Their grade point average went up over a period of a little more than a year. It is difficult to tell whether the increase is as socially significant as well: What does it mean for a boy's average to go from D to C-? On the other hand, while the interviews were not rigorously coded and tabulated statistically, the differences in the extent of career planning are striking, and if confirmed on a larger sample, would seem to be very important in the lives of these boys. However, assessing the long-term impact of a course is a complex problem. The results reported here included what happened for about a year after the training ended. So much else was happening as the course faded into the past, one might well wonder whether it could continue to influence them.

The most that can be said for the course is that it seemed to get those who stayed thinking more seriously about their futures and in many cases trying harder to achieve goals they had set for themselves tentatively during the training program. This needs to be investigated more thoroughly in order to understand the contexts, systems, and conditions that facilitate the application of the course. Perhaps the primary question raised by the course is how to increase attending behavior. These two questions, plus several additional ones, are explored in the next experiments in maximizing n-Ach course yields.

4.
Planning Patterns and Action Strategies*

The first necessary, but not sufficient, condition for the maintenance of achievement motivation training as a system is adequate attending behavior by participants, i.e., their physical presence and psychological attention. Having identified numerous possible sources of our failure to sustain attending behavior in the first experiment, we tried to find solutions to all of these problems in this second experiment. The methods we developed illustrate how the principle of creating moderate novelty can be used to generate appropriate procedures for sustaining attention.

A second purpose of this experiment was to collect a wider range of data on the yields of achievement motivation training. Even though increases in grade point averages are most persuasive to educational administrators, there are a variety of other important possible consequences of the training. There is no *a priori* reason for expecting that all yields will be found in school settings. In fact, past research on n-Ach indicates that the yields will be in entrepreneurial contexts where people are "in charge." The first experiment suggests, for example, that long-range career planning is developed by n-Ach training. It may also be that other non-school attitudes, preferences, and behaviors characteristic of the entrepreneurial character type are influenced by the training. From a systems point of view, it is important to assess the nature and extent of the impact. Only then is it possible to know how the new n-Ach skills are adaptive, what system goals it helps to attain,

*I wish to thank the following people for their efforts in conducting this research: James McIntyre, Bob Hindmarsch, Michael Dole, Gordon Alpert, Judy Walker, and D.C. McClelland's Social Relations class.

and what goal conflicts are likely to arise. This knowledge would help also in solving some system maintenance problems, e.g., developing more appropriate expectations and goals in participants, resolving the conflicts that occur and becoming more helpful in overcoming conditions that restrict these high probability yields.

A third purpose of this experiment was to identify, if possible, what teaching the achievement motivation syndrome contributes to the net effects of the course—i.e., if Goal Setting (G), Interpersonal Supports (I), and Self-Study (S) are taught, but Achievement Syndrome (A) is not, how severely will the yields of the course be reduced? In order to hold constant the effects of quantity (i.e., all four types of inputs versus only three types of inputs), it was necessary to substitute another syndrome for achievement motivation in the comparison training program. Since it is the syndrome inputs, not G, I, or S inputs, that differentiate n-Ach from other types of training, it should be possible through this comparison to identify yields uniquely related to teaching the achievement syndrome.

It makes sense to carry the analysis of the Achievement Syndrome one step further. Teaching "Achievement Planning" and "Achievement Action Strategies" is not likely to be equally meaningful or effective for adolescents. Piaget states that it is a fundamental development in intellectual growth when adolescents can perform certain logical operations on their own thoughts. Until this period of "Formal Operations," beginning around ages 12 to 14, children can only perform these operations on physical reality—i.e., during the period of "Concrete Operations." This developmental sequence suggests that learning the Achievement Action Strategies through the games, exercises, and role plays will be more effective than learning to conceptualize and alter one's pattern of thought, at least until the child develops "Formal Operational" thinking. Boocock and Schild (1968) argue that game simulations are extremely effective in teaching complex subject matter content. Cherryholmes (1966), in her review of educational research on simulation, concludes, to the contrary, that there is no empirical evidence for the superiority of this method in teaching cognitive content. Cherryholmes states, however, that in all studies she reviewed, the authors report dramatic increases in interest, involvement, and motivation. Thus it may be that games are particularly well suited to teaching experiential content like motivation. From the perspective of Piaget's theory and evidence on simulations, the effects of the achievement motivation course probably will not be reduced by omitting the teaching of achievement planning for children in the period of concrete operations. In contrast, the yields should be decreased significantly if teaching the action strategies is omitted. Once the yields unique to achievement motivation training have been identified in the first set of comparison courses, it should be possible in a second set of comparison courses to assess which Achievement Syndrome inputs are essential to teaching and maintaining achievement motivation in young adolescents.

Procedures

The Sample. The course participants consisted of 52 boys from 33 elementary and junior high schools in the metropolitan Boston area. The majority (32) were recruited from a morning summer school where they had classes in mathematics, English, and science. The boys were attending summer school for a variety of reasons—advanced work, remedial work, and just for fun. The remainder of the boys were recruited from another summer school and from the neighborhood surrounding the school where the achievement motivation courses were taught. The boys were divided into four groups: *Achievement Full* (course inputs from the areas of Goal Setting [G], Interpersonal Supports [I], Self-Study [S], and the full Achievement Syndrome), *Affiliation Full* (inputs from G, I, S, and the Affiliation Syndrome, rather than the Achievement Syndrome), *Achievement Action* (inputs from G, I, S, and the Achievement Syndrome, but omitting the planning pattern), and *Achievement Planning* (inputs from G, I, S, and the Achievement Syndrome, but omitting the action strategies). The boys were assigned to groups on the basis of grades in school, and race—the only two items of background information known for all 52 boys at the beginning of the summer. Subsequently, additional information was obtained and is included in Table 4.1. This table compares the groups in the two sets of

Table 4.1

Background Characteristics of Groups Receiving Motivation Training

Variable	Achievement Full (n = 14)	Affiliation Full (n = 13)	Achievement Action (n = 11)	Achievement Planning (n = 14)
Age	12.1[1]	11.6	12.3	11.7
Grade in School Completed	6.8 (n = 12)[2]	6.7	7.2 (n = 10)	6.5
Race				
Black	6	6	5	6
White	8	7	6	8
Socio-economic status[3]	4.5 (n = 12)	4.4 (n = 11)	4.4 (n = 8)	3.6 (n = 12)
Stanford Achievement Test[4]				
Math	5.8	6.0	5.5	6.2
Verbal	6.9 (n = 13)	5.9 (n = 10)	7.1 (n = 10)	6.8 (n = 13)
Motivation[5]				
n-Ach	0.9	0.7	1.3	0.9
n-Aff	1.1	0.7	1.1	0.6
n-Power	0.1 (n = 12)	0.0	0.2 (n = 10)	0.1 (n = 12)

1. The numbers given are means.
2. When comparison statistics are based on incomplete data, the actual sample size is in parentheses.
3. Based on Hall, J., and Jones, D.C., Social Grading of Occupations, *British Journal of Sociology*, 1950 (1); 1 (high administrative or executive) to 7 (unskilled manual labor).
4. Numbers represent the Grade Equivalent Achievement at the beginning of the summer.
5. N-Ach, n-Aff and n-Power imagery only were scored for three stories. This gives a possible range from 0 to 3.

experimental courses.

In general, the pairs of groups are well matched. None of the differences are statistically significant. An attempt was made to obtain IQ scores on all the boys from their school files. Unfortunately, scores were available for only about 50 percent from nine different tests given at various times. Therefore, meaningful comparisons on this variable were not possible. The average age of the boys is well below that expected for the full acquisition of formal operations. Thus, the Action course should be more effective than the Planning course. Since the Planning group is approximately at grade level in mathematics achievement, whereas the Action group averages a little over 1½ years behind grade level, if anything, this biases against obtaining results in the predicted direction. The difference in "verbal achievement" between the achievement and affiliation groups, while not statistically significant, favors the achievement group.

Recruitment. The boys were recruited through a speech given by one of the course instructors. In this first step in creating a temporary social system, the major thrust of our recruitment was to define the group as a highly desirable one in which to have membership. He emphasized that this was a special course originally designed for adult businessmen to help them reach their goals. Through reference to prestigious groups like "researchers at Harvard University who have discovered important differences between people who achieve and those who don't," he attempted to give volunteers a positive image, in contrast with the "seat warmers," who were publicly identified as "high potential dropouts." The recruits were told the course was "only for boys" in an appeal to the fashionable clannishness of the age group. To intensify this sense of belonging to a special and valued group, they were promised T-shirts with group emblems, soft drinks and dessert to eat with their lunches, transportation home, and "fun and games" as they learned. They also were informed of another group in St. Louis being studied by the researchers, with whom they would be competing. We encouraged them, in this way, to unite against a common competitor and to begin from the outset to be concerned with achievement goals.

Of the 55 boys who heard this presentation, 52 signed up for the course and attended. This 95 percent initial attendance rate compares favorably with that of the high school dropouts; of an original 48 who received a presentation and individual interviews describing the course, only 20 boys (48 percent) attended the course. It is not possible to ascertain whether this difference in acceptance rates is due to a difference in age, public identification of their reference group ("potential dropouts" vs. "the fortunate few who can have a very special adult course"), the style of presentation, or a combination of these factors. In both cases we were asking boys to spend more time in school during their vacation, a handicap for us that required particularly effective recruitment procedures. Even when evaluated by itself, a 95 percent initial attendance rate seems to be quite good.

Treatment. Each group met twice a week for 2 hours over a period of 5 weeks for a total of 20 hours of training. The "Achievement Full" and "Affiliation Full" groups were taught by a professional teacher and a college student from the Harvard research project. Another teacher and a second student from Harvard taught the "Planning" and "Action" groups. All four groups received identical inputs in three areas: Self-Study (e.g., "Who Am I"),* Interpersonal Supports, and Goal Setting (e.g., "Aiming").* Only the Achievement Full group learned achievement planning *and* action strategies as well as relevant case examples—i.e., the entire Achievement Syndrome. The Affiliation Full group, instead, played games that depended on luck and chance rather than on skill or knowledge of the Achievement Action strategies. Intra-group reactions and relations to these games were used as the experience base for meaningful group discussions about "getting along with others," "making friends," "good sportsmanship," resolving conflicts, and other affiliation-related topics. The "action" group did not learn achievement planning, but concentrated on such action-skill games as "The Origami Game," "The Ring Toss Game," and "The Darts-Dice Game."** In contrast, the

---

*These curriculum modules and the associated manual, *Teaching Achievement Motivation*, A. Alschuler, D. Tabor, and J. McIntyre, are published by Education Ventures, Inc., Middletown, Connecticut, 1970.

**Ibid.

Achievement Planning group concentrated on activities described in "Ten Thoughts,"* and omitted all action games that taught achievement strategies.

In attempting to translate McClelland's 12 original propositions (McClelland and Winter, 1969) for acquiring a motive into a more relevant teaching strategy for these students, a natural, logical, and psychological sequence of goals emerged. Most of the original propositions are incorporated into this heuristic paradigm:

1. Get and sustain students' attention by creating moderately novel learning situations.
2. Allow the student to experience intensely the thoughts, actions, and feelings that comprise the motive.
3. Help the student clearly conceptualize the motive he has experienced.
4. Help the student intellectually relate the motive to his dominant values, ideal self-image, and the demands of his salient life situations.
5. Guide the student in practicing the application of this goal-oriented pattern of thoughts, actions, and feelings.
6. Internalize the motive by progressively withdrawing the support of the learning situation while the student takes increasing responsibility for maintenance.

The omission of several of McClelland's 12 propositions (warm and supporting relationships with the instructors, valued continuing reference group, retreat setting) helps clarify the nature of this sequence. According to Parsons' conception of the functional prerequisites of a social system, this is a strategy for the successful "goal attainment" in a psychological education course. The propositions omitted from this task orientation sequence all have to do with methods of course-system maintenance—i.e., methods of establishing norms and values and reducing conflicts.

The six sub-goals form a logical sequence in the sense that each is required before the next can be accomplished. Before the motive can be experienced, students must be in attendance and

Ibid.

attending. Before the student can clearly and meaningfully conceptualize the motive, he must be aware of the experience to be conceptualized, etc. The sequence of goals is cumulative in that each activity contains the previous ones. For example, intellectually relating the motive to one's values, self-image, and the demands of reality involves attention, memory of the experience, and a descriptive vocabulary. Furthermore, each step has distinctive criteria for success that can be used to assess progress.*

It may be helpful to briefly illustrate this sequence as it was implemented during the training program. To get and maintain attention throughout the course we decided to create moderate novelty *vis-a-vis* the norms, values, and procedures of schooling as the boys knew it. The course was held in a school, taught by regular teachers for set periods of time. This context was familiar. At each stage in the learning sequence, however, we departed moderately from traditional school routines. For three of the groups (not the Planning group) we used educational games to provide the experience base for conceptualization, rather than workbook exercises or written projects. Whenever possible we introduced "contests" in learning the conceptual vocabulary instead of orienting them to tests. We gave prizes instead of grades, e.g., penny candy, ice cream bars, cokes. (In the Affiliation group there were no competitive contests and rewards were always given to all students.) To help them relate their experience to values, ideal self-images, and reality demands, we provided lectures, among other methods. But the presentations were made by the star of the Harvard football team, and by a local black-belt judo expert. These men told how Achievement Planning or Actions were helpful to them. The "final exam" of the courses was a "Personal Change Project." We helped each person practice what he learned by coaching him in setting a meaningful goal that could be reached in six weeks. Each boy was given a plastic serial counter (like those used to tabulate golf scores or grocery bills) to keep track of his daily progress in money earned, basketball

*See session 5, "Side Trip—Internalization," in *Teaching Achievement Motivation*, A. Alschuler, D. Tabor, and J. McIntyre, published by Education Ventures, Inc., Middletown, Connecticut, 1970.

free-throw percentage, number of pages read, etc. We reminded
them to keep track of their progress on the graphs we gave them,
but since the project extended from the last week of the course
for five additional weeks, we had a popular radio disk jockey
remind the boys for us during the "bulletin board" portion of his
program. We provided the boys with a post card each week to send
in to us showing their progress. This was structured as a contest
between the four groups for prizes at an ice cream party put on by
the instructors five weeks after the course. This was one way we
tried to progressively shift responsibility to them for maintaining
what they learned.

Beyond these illustrative task-orientation activities we tried a
variety of moderately novel system maintenance procedures. We
continued to stress the reference groups through the special
insignia T-shirts and special group names (Jaguars, Thunderbirds,
Vampires). The low student-teacher ratio (approximately 7:1)
allowed more individual attention and warmer personal relationships. At one point we brought in a fellow researcher from St.
Louis, where similar research was being inaugurated. This gave
credibility to the competition between Cambridge and St. Louis
and reinforced the boys' sense of belonging to this group. To be
sure, we relied heavily on traditional classroom system maintenance procedures and rules as well, e.g., approximately one person
talking at a time, the teacher arbitrates disputes, etc. For the most
part, the tone of the classes was one of enthusiastic participation—
a very narrow ridge between deadening overcontrol and frenzied
lack of cooperation. Virtually all of these "treatment" procedures
were aimed at the successful management of the course as a
system.

Measures of Course Effectiveness. A wide variety of data was
collected from the boys, including pre-course testing, the change
project results, data from the two follow-up testing sessions 6 and
9 months afterwards, and finally the school file data for the entire
school year. These data are described under the four general
headings below.

    1.   *Attending behavior*
        a.   Number of days attending the course and drop-

           outs.

    b.   Number of weekly "personal change project" post cards returned out of a possible 6.

    c.   Attendance at follow-up meetings 6 and 9 months after the course.

    d.   Degree of expressed interest in the course:

        The number of negative responses subtracted from the number of positive responses to 4 questions asked 9 months after the course.

        1.   "What did you think of the kids in your group?"

        2.   "What did you think of what you did?"

        3.   "Would you like to do something like that again next summer?"

        4.   "What did you think of your teachers?"

2.   *The Motive Syndrome*

    a.   Achievement and Affiliation Imagery.

        Three TAT stories were obtained before the course and again six months after the course. Because the stories were short, only motivational imagery for n-Ach and n-Aff was scored.

    b.   Feedback errors.

        In two risk taking games, like Ring Toss, Darts-Dice, and "The Addition Game," administered 9 months after the course, moves were scored for the total number of errors made in using feedback to maximize goal attainment.

    c.   Goal Setting Change.

        During the course and again 6 months afterwards, the boys wrote an essay on "What I want to do and be." Essays were given 1 point for each of the following:

        1.   specific goals

2.   moderate risk goals

3.   means stated for reaching goals.

Change in "Goal Setting" was calculated by comparing scores between pre- and post-course essays.

3.   *School Performance*

a.   Stanford Achievement Test (SAT) gains.

Appropriate levels of the intermediate and advanced SAT math and verbal tests were given the first day of the course and again 6 months after the course, i.e., 5 months into the school year. The expected gain on each test is 0.5. For both tests combined, the expected gain is 1.0.

b.   Grade Point Average Gain.

All English, social studies, math and science grades were converted to numerical scores and averaged for the year prior to and following the summer courses: A+ = 98, A = 95, A- = 92, B+ = 88, etc.

c.   Deportment.

The number of days absent and tardy each were summed for the year prior to and following the n-Ach course. The presence or absence of a poor conduct mark (C or below) was noted from the school files for the year prior to and following the course. From this, conduct was rated "worse," "same," or "improved."

4.   *N-Ach Related Behavior*

a.   Number of new jobs paid outside the home as of 6 months after the course.

b.   Travel-exploration: excursions initiated by boy rated from +3 to -3 on basis of distance, method, purpose, and frequency.

c.   Changes and new interests: sum of specific changes

and new interests mentioned in response to the following questions asked 9 months after the courses;

    1.   "Have you changed in any way lately?"
    2.   "Do you have any new interests?"
    3.   "Have you joined any clubs?"

d.   Self-image: The boys were asked to give instructions to an imaginary physical "double" so that the double would be just like them. The "instructions" were scored (+) whenever there was any concern with achievement, e.g., "you work hard," "you are good at . . . ," "you want to do difficult things." This was administered 9 months after the course.

e.   N-Ach techniques: The number of statements of n-Ach techniques endorsed by the boy as "like me." Eight of 30 statements were precoded as n-Ach techniques, e.g., "he plans a lot," "he works hard," versus "he believes luck is important," "he is friendly."

f.   N-Ach TV shows: Twelve TV shows were listed and 3 were precoded as most strongly emphasizing n-Ach. The boy was given a (+) if his first choice in his ranking of the 12 shows was an n-Ach show.

g.   N-Ach athletes: Six paragraph descriptions of fictitious athletes were created, 2 of which emphasized n-Ach most strongly; the others, n-Power, and n-Aff. The score for the boy was (+) if his first choice in ranking his preferences was one of the n-Ach athletes.

h.   N-Ach outdoor games and n-Ach indoor games: Six outdoor and 6 indoor games were selected. In each category there were 2 dominantly n-Ach, 2 n-Aff, and 2 n-Power games. The boy's score was (+) if his first choice was an n-Ach game.

i.   Internality: Rotter's 23 item scale to measure one's orientation to internal or external control of reinforcement was administered.

j.   N-Ach doodles: Two doodles were administered
      and scored for n-Ach on the "discreteness-fuzzi-
      ness" dimension as described by E. Aronson in
      Motives in Fantasy, Action and Society, Atkinson,
      J.W. (Ed.) Princeton, New Jersey: D. Van Nostrand
      Co., 1958.
k.   Overall Yield Score:* Results for each of the 11
      measures of n-Ach-related behavior were divided at
      the mean for the 2 groups being compared. Each
      boy received a (+) whenever his score was above
      the mean. Thus, each boy could receive an overall
      yield score ranging from 0 to +11.

Results

Our success in managing the course as a system can be
assessed in part through the several measures of attending behavior
we collected. We did not consider this an experimental independent or dependent variable, but instead as a pre-condition for the
successful completion of the experiment. Therefore, the four
groups should be comparable. There are no other appropriate
comparison groups to use in isolating specific sources of high or
low attending behavior since the first experiment differed in many
sample characteristics as well as treatment procedures. Therefore,
the meaning of the general level of attending behavior will have to
be judged on an *a priori* basis, e.g., a 50 percent dropout rate is
unacceptable. The average attendance for all 4 groups over the 10
sessions was 77 percent, ranging from 74 percent for the
Achievement Planning group to 84 percent for the Achievement
Full group, not statistically significant differences. However, there
were 8 boys who attended 5 or fewer sessions.** We considered

---

*An Overall Yield Score was not obtained for Motive Syndrome Yield
because they are measures of recall rather than of generalization. Nor was an
Overall Yield Score calculated for school performance yields because,
unfortunately, about one-half of the data were missing on about one-half of
the boys.

**Three from the Action group, one from the Planning group, three from the
Affiliation group and one from the Full Achievement group.

this an insufficient exposure to the course for a fair test of the training. They were dropped from subsequent data analysis. This is an effective "dropped out" rate of 15 percent. Three of these "dropouts" were due to prolonged illness and lengthy family vacations. In general, this overall rate contrasts sharply in quantity and kind with the spirited, rebellious dropping out during the first experiment. Even after 9 months, almost all of the boys indicated positive interest in the course; the modal reaction to the 4 follow-up "interest" questions was 4 endorsements.

Postcourse attendance behavior is somewhat less favorable. In the Personal Change Project, 50 percent of the post cards were returned over the 6-week period, ranging from 37 percent in the Full Affiliation group to 57 percent in the Action group, not statistically significant. Attendance figures for the 2 follow-up testing sessions are about the same, averaging 65 percent for all 4 groups combined: Full Affiliation group, 58 percent; Full Achievement group, 61 percent; Action group, 59 percent; Planning group, 82 percent. Overall there are no systematic significant differences in training. Attendance appears to be sufficiently high for meaningful training, but the attrition in the follow-up testing sessions, given the originally small sample sizes, makes it even more difficult to detect any but the strongest differences between groups in the effects of the courses.

Analysis of the long-term effects of the training is a two-step process. First we must ascertain that there are effects due to instruction in the achievement motivation syndrome. For this purpose the Full Achievement and Full Affiliation groups will be compared, since the courses are identical except for the motive syndrome taught. Given demonstrated differences in achievement-related yields attributable to instruction in the achievement motivation syndrome, it is then meaningful to ask whether the Planning or the Action components of the syndrome are most responsible for these long-term effects. Thus, step two of the analysis will compare the Planning and Action groups. Table 4.2 contains the results of the four types of training on the 21 dependent variables.

It is obvious at a glance that the number of statistically significant differences between the Full Achievement and the Full

Table 4.2

Long-Term Effects of
Motivation Training

Effects	Number and percent of boys above median score							
	Full Achievement Group (n = 14)		Full Affiliation Group (n = 13)		Achievement Action (n = 11)		Achievement Planning (n = 14)	
The Motive Syndrome								
Achievement Imagery	5/10	50%	3/7	43%	1/8	13%	6/13	46%
Affiliation Imagery	3/10	30	4/7	57	3/8	38	5/13	39
Fewer Feedback Errors	6/9	66	3/9	33	4/6	66	5/11	45
Goal Setting Change	3/6	50	2/7	29	4/5	80	4/11	36
School Performance								
SAT Math Gain	5/8	63	2/6	33	4/7	57	6/13	46
SAT Verbal Gain	5/8	63	2/6	33	4/7	57	5/11	45
GPA Gain	7/11	64	3/8	38	5/10	50	6/12	50
Fewer Absences	4/8	50	1/5	20	5/9	56	5/11	45
Fewer Tardies	6/7	86	—[1]	—	4/9	44	3/9	33
Same or Better Conduct	4/10	40	6/8	75	2/9	22	0/9	0
N-Ach Related Behavior								
New Jobs	6/9	66	6/7	86	4/6	66	5/14	36
Travel-Exploration	5/9	56	1/9	11	5/7	71	5/11	45
Changes & New Interests	4/9	44	5/9	56	3/7	43	4/11	36
Self-Image	5/9	56	5/9	56	2/7	29	8/11	73
n-Ach Techniques	8/9	89	6/11	55	5/7	71	6/10	60
n-Ach TV Shows	2/9	22	3/9	33	4/7	57	2/10	20
n-Ach Athletes	7/9	78	2/9	22*	4/7	57	3/11	27
n-Ach Outdoor Games	4/9	44	4/11	36	5/7	71	6/11	55
n-Ach Indoor Games	9/9	100	4/11	36**	6/7	86	7/11	64
Internality	5/9	56	4/9	44	6/7	86	6/11	55
n-Ach Doodles	6/9	67	4/9	44	5/6	83	3/11	27
Overall Yield Score	7/9	77	1/9	11**	4/7	57	2/11	18

* = p $<$.05; ** = p $<$.01; Chi-square tests, corrected for continuity, one tail.

1.   Data were available on only 1 of 13 boys.

Affiliation groups does not depart from what would be expected by chance in 21 comparisons. From this point of view we cannot place much confidence in any *one* of the long-term effects. The results of achievement motivation training are not narrow and highly focused. However, the Overall Yield Score is a much better index of change since it combines the alternate manifestations of achievement motivation. As such it is closer to the nature of the motive itself, a generic concern with excellence with a wide variety of applications. Of the 14 Full Achievement boys, 5 did not attend the follow-up testing sessions. Four of the 13 boys in the Full Affiliation group did not attend the testing sessions. Of the remaining 9 Full Achievement boys, 7, or 77 percent, had an Overall Yield Score of 6 or more, while only one of the 9 Full Affiliation boys had a score of 6 or more. (Mann-Whitney test $Z = 2.96$, $p < .022$.) In other words, the training significantly increased n-Ach-related behavior outside the school over a nine-month period following the course. This result is in accord with common sense and with the intentions of the training. We helped students apply what they learned in a variety of areas meaningful to them. Given this intended diversity of outcomes and the generic nature of a motive, a broad measure of the course's impact is more appropriate than any single index of change.

The pattern of results for the Planning and Action groups is consistent and clear. As with the first set of comparisons, no highly significant statistical differences exist on individual measures. However, comparing the two groups on the Overall Yield Score by the Mann-Whitney test results in a Z score of 1.68, $p < .05$ (1 tail) in favor of the Action group. As indicated in Table 4.2, 4 of the 7 Action boys (57 percent) scored 7 or above while only 2 of the 11 Planning boys (18 percent) scored 7 or above on the Overall Yield Score.* By inference, it appears that the training in risk taking, use of feedback to set challenging goals, and taking initiative and personal responsibility is what makes the critical differences in achievement motivation courses for boys like those

---

*Four members of the Action group and 3 members of the Planning group did not attend the follow-up testing sessions. This reduced the effective sample sizes to 7 and 11 respectively.

in this sample. This inference is supported by two further comparisons. Using the same median split on the Overall Yield Score (6 or more), the Full Achievement group is not significantly different from the Action group (7 of the 9, or 77 percent versus 6 of the 7 or 86 percent above the median respectively). In contrast, the Planning group is significantly lower than the Full Achievement group: only 6 of the 11 (55 percent) score 6 or more on the Overall Yield Score (Mann-Whitney test Z = 1.94, p <.03, 1 tail). In other words, leaving out instruction in Achievement Planning does not decrease the overall yield, whereas leaving out the training in Achievement Action Strategies does significantly decrease the yields for this age group.

Since the several samples were not perfectly matched to begin with, it is important to get at least a brief check on these conclusions to see if background factors may influence the outcomes. The Overall Yield Score and the Stanford Achievement Test score gains (mathematics and verbal subtests combined) were used as the most important outcome variables against which to assess the influence of pre-course background variables. All four groups were combined into one sample for this analysis. Total gains in SAT and Overall Yield Scores were *not* significantly correlated (1) with the initial SAT scores, (2) with the difference between initial SAT scores and actual grade level, (3) with socioeconomic status, (4) with initial n-Ach score, nor (5) with the age of the boys. With respect to this last variable, however, if we look only at the two groups that had training in Achievement Planning, where we predicted age would make a difference, it is almost significantly related to total SAT gains and Overall Yield Scores. Six out of 8 boys 12 years or older gained at least 1.1 years on the SAT's, whereas only 4 out of 12 boys under 12 years gained that much on the SAT's (χ^2 = 1.87 corrected for continuity, p <.10, 1 tail). The same distribution and Chi-square is obtained for the Overall Yield Score. It appears that age of the boys, as a rough indicator of intellectual development, may be important in determining the efficacy of training oriented to changing patterns of thought.*

---

*These results probably are attenuated by the restricted range in ages. Thus, I thought it appropriate to report this nearly significant trend.

Discussion

The results of the experiment confirmed the major hypotheses and, overall, are grounds for being optimistic about increasing adolescents' motivation. Yet the findings are as imprecise and puzzling as they are encouraging. For example, attending behavior was undeniably better by all indices than our flagrant failures in the first course. We tried very hard to keep the boys coming; we put on a good show with a lot of "pizazz." They responded by arriving early, staying late, wearing their special T-shirts every day, until the insignia were hard to see from fading or dirt. We even had to turn away boys from Boston who came knocking at the doors to get into the "good thing" they had heard about. But these hard and soft data do not reveal our continuing puzzlement over why all this occurred. Was it because they were younger, less dropout prone, with something interesting to do during the long, idle summer? How much of our "success" can be attributed to the novelty of our pedagogy? Identifying the sources of our holding power is important for a very practical reason: students must be attending to learn. However, few teachers can or will spend enough energy to generate all of the novel attractions we were able to create with generous financial backing. Therefore, we need to be equally successful in the recruitment of attending behavior, but more efficient, if the course is to be taught and maintained in a normal school setting.

The long-term success of the courses is equally good and difficult to interpret. Teaching the achievement syndrome resulted in broad yields reflecting a variety of aspects of an orientation to achievement—TV preferences, favorite indoor games, doodling, more efficient use of feedback, etc. Does this mean that the courses resulted only in a subtle pervasive disposition to respond more readily in achievement and major yields for individuals that our measures did not pick up? Much of the difficulty in answering this question stems from the nature of the measures we used, i.e., "narrow bandwidth-high fidelity." The yields we measured were predicted in advance and measured as precisely as we could assess them. But, it is entirely possible that we missed the most important yields, and that the boys could have told us the big things to look for if we had asked them during the two follow-up testing sessions. Certainly this type of data, though less precise, would give us more information about where they consciously applied what they learned.

In a third way, the results are tantalizingly incomplete. Research on the value of educational simulations (Boocock and Schild, 1968) has to some degree missed the point by not assessing motivational yields along with the intended increases in information. In fact, it may be more accurate to view educational simulations as convenient tools for piggy-backing motive arousal methods in normal classrooms, and look for increased long-term *motivational* change as the legitimate, intended outcome of game simulations. Unfortunately, our data are less clear about why this should be so. Theoretically and empirically, age seems to be a factor. Under 14, the training in action strategies was more efficacious, and as the boys got older the training in new thought patterns seemed to be increasingly efficacious. But it may be that the novelty of learning from games, rather than this action-mode of learning itself, is crucial. In classrooms heavily dominated by cognitive exercises, "instruction," and question-and-answer learning, perhaps the improvisational freedom and yet purposeful learning afforded by educational games make them literally "memorable" events. How much should the teaching strategy be oriented to the dominant learning mode of the age group? How much should the teaching strategy provide variation and contrast with traditional learning procedures? It may be possible to approximate answers by comparing the efficacy of Planning and Action inputs with an older group. If the "action training" is more efficacious, even though the students are capable of benefitting from training in new thought patterns, then "variation and novelty" probably are more important. If, on the other hand, training in new thought patterns is more efficacious, even though it is similar to traditional learning methods, then coordinating the teaching strategy with the dominant learning mode of the age group would be more important.

This second experiment made progress in adapting n-Ach training for adolescents, and in showing that adolescents' motivation can be increased for relatively long periods through short training courses. The discussion of Experiment 2 suggests that further progress can be made (1) by conducting the next experiment within the constraints of normal schooling, (2) by including a more extensive open-ended data collection procedure, such as a semi-structured interview, and (3) by giving a similar set of Planning and Action comparison courses to an older age group. This will allow us to be more precise in defining what combination of personality characteristics (age, sex, etc.), course procedures (actions, strategies, planning pattern, novelty), and social contexts (school, leisure, sports, work) maximize the course yields.

5.

The Usefulness of
Achievement Motivation Training[*]

From the beginning we assumed that the eventual implementation of our methods on a wide scale would depend as much or more on the availability of curriculum materials as on the validity of our methods. With each new age group, therefore, we developed additional instructional games, exercises, and role plays that would embody concretely the theoretical ideas we were testing. With our success in maintaining the attendance during Experiment 2, it became apparent that equally effective, but more practical, methods would have to be developed by conducting this experiment *in* school during the normal school year. We decided to incorporate whatever existing procedures and sanctions there were in this average suburban high school for maintaining the physical presence of their pupils, e.g., keeping attendance records. We still had to solve the psychological attendance problem: How do you keep 30 students engaged in learning when the terrible acoustics make it physiologically difficult to hear, and when students are accustomed to about 50 percent "down time" in a class, i.e., "you only need to be up half the 43 minutes to get all the teacher has to say." Our goal was to adapt our procedures to the typical constraints of time, but to provide sufficient variations and contrasts to elicit and sustain a high percentage of learning, or "up time."

*I wish to thank the following people, whose efforts made this experiment possible: Antoinette DiLoretto, John Lennon, Diane Tabor, and Steven Rodewald.

Our working contexts were several 10th grade "Elementary Business Principles" classes in the Vocational Education Department. The course title is a euphemism for "basic math for non-college bound students who did poorly in math in 9th grade." By virtue of their "achieved status" (relatively low grade point averages) and "ascribed status" (predominantly lower-middle and upper-lower class), the large majority of these students were preparing for jobs rather than college. We argued that "achievement motivation training" probably was as appropriate an interpretation of "Elementary Business Principles" as basic math. On this basis we were allowed to give n-Ach training as part of this regularly scheduled semester course.

It also seemed likely to us that the course would, in fact, be particularly relevant for those students who have more immediate concerns about succeeding outside of the school. From our point of view this increased the likelihood that we might discover a consistent pattern of non-school course yields, at least among the boys in the class. Lesser (1963), in his review of research on n-Ach in women, reports a consistent pattern of null findings, except for career-oriented women or in sub-cultures where an achievement orientation for women is socially endorsed. The girls in our classes were oriented to careers, if at all, only as an interim occupation until they got married and raised a family. Thus, we expected the n-Ach course to be less meaningful for them and consequently to result in fewer long-term non-school yields. Lesser also reports other relevant data: that high school girls achieve by means of conforming to what is expected of them in structured situations, while boys prefer to achieve in independent situations. Lesser concludes that girls' achievement strivings are motivated more by the desire for social acceptance and approval than by the need for personal accomplishment. Therefore, we predicted that the results of the n-Ach course for girls would be less evident outside of school than in school, where the more highly structured situation defines the means for approval and social acceptance. And, because n-Ach is more relevant to the social roles of boys, we believed the effects of the n-Ach course would be more pronounced for them, compared to the girls, both in and outside of school.

Procedures

Sample. The sample consisted of a 10th grade "Elementary Business Principles" class, all of whom had received a C or less in 9th grade mathematics. The comparison group consisted of a 10th grade "Bookkeeping" class similar to the experimental class except that they all had received an A or B in their 9th grade vocational math course. Relevant comparison statistics are presented in Table 5.1.

The average age of these students is about 4 years older than those in Experiment 2. Their vocational orientation and capacity for formal operational thinking both should be considerably more well-developed. SES, IQ, the Nelson-Denny Reading Test Results, and 9th grade GPA all are below the school average. As would be expected on the basis of admission to the "Bookkeeping" class (A or B in 9th grade math) there is a significant difference in GPA for both boys and girls, favoring the control group. For the girls this may be offset in part by a significantly higher IQ in the experimental group. Because these groups are not perfectly matched (although on the whole they are quite well matched), differences in course yields will have to be checked against these background variables.

Treatment. The course was conducted three periods a week during the last half of the first semester. The experimental group received approximately 22 hours of training, taken out of the time they would have been learning other aspects of "Elementary Business Principles." The training consisted of inputs for all six phases of the learning sequence described earlier in Experiment 2 and extensively in *Teaching Achievement Motivation* (Alschuler, Tabor and McIntyre, 1970). The training differed from the previous experiment in several respects. Since all participants were in school, they could not volunteer for the course. Thus, our "recruitment" pitch stressed the prestigious and innovative nature of the course, e.g., "We are asking your help in adapting this businessman's course for Business Education students. This is a pilot project which, if successful, will be published and used extensively elsewhere in the country, etc." In this way we tried to avoid their seeing the course as remedial. We also said the course was not mandatory, in the sense that we would arrange study halls

Table 5.1

Background Characteristics of Experimental and Control Subjects

Variables	Boys		Girls	
	n-Ach (n = 8)	Bookkeeping (n = 12)	n-Ach (n = 14)	Bookkeeping (n = 14)
Age[1]	15.8	16.5	15.8	16.0
Socio-economic Status[2]	3.7	4.2 (n = 11)[6]	4.5 (n = 13)	4.3
IQ[3]	100.0	100.5 (n = 11)	105.0 (n = 11)	99.4*
Nelson-Denny Reading Test[4]	9.4 (n = 7)	9.3 (n = 10)	10.0 (n = 12)	9.5 (n = 11)
Ninth Grade GPA[5]	1.59	1.94	1.74	2.16*

* $p < .05$, based on Mann-Whitney Test

1. "Age" is calculated as of the end of the 10th grade.
2. Scores based on Hall, J., and Jones, D.C., Social Grading of Occupations, *British Journal of Sociology* 1950, (1).
3. OTIS intelligence test administered during the 8th grade.
4. Means and ranges are in grade level equivalents, i.e., 10.2 is the second month of the 10th grade.
5. 4 = A, 3 = B, 2 = C, 1 = D, 0 = F. Grades in major courses were summed and divided by the number of courses for the GPA. Withdrawals due to poor grades were counted as F's.
6. When the statistic is based on missing data, the effective sample size is given in parentheses.

for those who did not wish to participate. The activity portions of the course in general were purposefully less noisy. There were no special prizes, T-shirts, insignia, nor ice cream parties, out of deference to the tolerance limits of neighboring teachers and wary administrators.* The same basic games were used along with a variety of relatively novel paper-and-pencil self-study exercises (see "Who Am I," Alschuler and Tabor, 1970d). We maintained the student-teacher ratio at about 8:1. This allowed us to do considerably more individual work at the end of the course helping students identify meaningful goals and start their "Personal Change Projects" (see "Aiming," Alschuler and Tabor, 1970f). In sum, there were fewer noisy group exercises, more group discussion, paper-and-pencil work, and individualized help.

Measures. Since we were not particularly interested in the short-term arousal of n-Ach, we decided to concentrate on the long-term effects of the course. Our In-School measures consisted of Grade Point Averages for the year prior to and the two years following the course, as well as students' Deportment records (absences, tardiness, and dismissals) for the same period of time.

From our point of view, the best measures of internalization are long-term operant outcomes. We were more interested in internally cued operant behavior than in externally cued respondent behavior. By analogy, school behavior is heavily cued by a highly structured learning environment. The intended respondent behavior is measured and reinforced by grades or extinguished by expulsion. A better measure of the degree to which n-Ach has been internalized is to see how much internally cued, operant n-Ach behavior occurs. This means we must assess behavior in relatively unstructured, "lightly" cued situations where the range of possible behavior is extremely wide. For example, in a student's life, the summer allows for more operant behavior than the school year, and leisure time even more than work time. Thus, in our follow-up data collection we focused on what students did during the second summer after their n-Ach course, approximately 18

---

*In an act of pure good faith and fortitude, the superintendent allowed us to conduct this training in his school. The public disaster of our first experiment in his district was still vivid in his memory.

months after their motivation training. This was sufficient time for internalization to take place and for the ubiquitous decay curve to take effect. By waiting so long and looking where there was least external pressure for achievement strivings we created an extremely tough test of the efficacy of our training.

The n-Ach course, by design, helps each student explore his own unique equation with achievement concerns. Although the general class of achievement goals, planning, and strategies can be rigorously and reliably defined, the number of possible specific instances makes it difficult to predict in advance what unique applications an individual will make. A semi-structured interview is admirably suited to this situation, since its flexibility (compared to paper-and-pencil surveys) allows the interviewer to find out from the student what unique use has been made of the course. A reliable coding system can be developed to assess the extent of achievement strivings in these reported activities. Prototypes for this type of coding system exist in McClelland and Winter's Entrepreneurial Acts Score (1969) and in Andrews' Entrepreurial Activities Rating (EAR) (1965). Interestingly, Andrews found that the n-Ach of Harvard freshmen measured by the TAT correlated more highly with non-academic initiative and personal responsibility, as measured by his EAR, than with grades during the freshman year.

More specifically, the interviewer asked what they did during their summer: (1) What, if any, *work* they performed, how much they were paid, how they got the job, why they got the job, what they learned from it, and whether they planned to continue with that work. (2) What did they do during their *leisure* time—sports, hobbies, travel? How did they get started, why, how did it turn out, did they have any further plans for the activity? (3) What *plans for the future* did they have, how specific are the plans, had they taken any steps to reach those goals? (4) Was the n-Ach course useful? (Or, for the control subjects, the Bookkeeping course.) How was it useful specifically? In each of these four areas a four-point scale was developed, roughly following the scoring of TAT n-Ach.

Unrelated Imagery (-1): The student has no plans or activities with the potential for achievement strivings. In most cases the main potential is for n-Affiliation.

Task Imagery (0): The student has plans or activities with achievement potential, but they are pursued with little evidence of any n-Ach. Instead, the student seems to be responding to external cues such as the pressure of parents or friends.

Act (+1): This category is scored if the student has completed actions toward a post or future goal.

Future Goals (+1): This category is scored when a student states a serious interest to reach an achievement goal, and he states what he plans to do and why.

A complete account of the interview schedule, the scoring system with examples, and practice protocols may be found in *Teaching Achievement Motivation* (Alschuler, Tabor, McIntyre, 1970, Appendix D, pp. 170-193). The reliability of the scoring of these interview protocols was 86 percent between two coders.

Results

In order to determine the effects of training on Grade Point Averages (GPA) in 10th and 11th grade, the initial differences in GPA must be controlled. Analysis of covariance is the appropriate statistical technique. Changes in GPAs from 9th to 10th and from 9th to 11th grades were analyzed separately for boys and for girls, thus making four Analyses of Covariance. Of these four, the results are significant only for the difference in GPA gains in 10th grade for the boys. The mean GPA in 10th grade, adjusted for 9th grade averages, was 2.11 for the fully trained boys and 1.73 for the untrained control boys ($t = 1.79$, $p < .05$, 1 tail). On the average, training increased the boys' GPA by about 1/3 of a letter grade by the end of the 10th grade, a full semester after the end of the n-Ach course. Apparently, the effect of training on academic performance is relatively limited in time and limited to the boys.

As for deportment, the n-Ach course did not produce

significant decreases in the number of absences between the 9th and 10th or the 9th and 11th grades for the n-Ach boys or the n-Ach girls compared to the control boys and girls. There are non-significant trends for the n-Ach boys and the n-Ach girls compared to the control groups towards fewer times tardy during the 10th and 11th grades. When both experimental groups are combined, this trend almost reaches significance; 12 of 18 experimental subjects had the same or fewer tardies in the 10th grade compared to only 11 of 24 control subjects ($\chi^2 = 1.80$ corrected for continuity, p $<$.10, 1 tail).* These trends are maintained in the 11th grade; 10 of 18 experimental subjects have the same or fewer tardies, whereas only 9 of 24 control subjects reduce the number of tardies in the 11th grade ($\chi^2 = 1.35$, corrected for continuity, p $<$.15, 1 tail). Approximately similar results occur in the number of dismissals. During 10th grade, all 8 of the experimental boys had the same or fewer dismissals from school, compared to only 7 of 11 control boys during the 11th grade. The differences between the experimental and control groups in the reduction of dismissals is not significant for the 10th or 11th grade. "Dismissals" in this school are for legitimate, formally acknowledged reasons. "Expulsions" are erased from the records at the end of each year so that the student can start the next year with a clean slate. Thus, these deportment measures more accurately are "attendance" records. In general, it seems that the n-Ach course had minor, if any, effects on attendance.

The results of the follow-up interviews are presented in Table 5.2. The results for the boys 1½ years after the course are encouraging but a bit equivocal. On the one hand, they appear to engage in more work and leisure activities that they describe as constructive, purposeful, and achievement oriented. At the same time, this difference is not reflected in the degree of specificity of future planning. The control boys actually earn significantly more

*The effective sample size of the experimental group was reduced from 22 to 18 for the following reasons: (1) One boy dropped out of school halfway through the 10th grade and one girl dropped out at the beginning of the 11th grade, and (2) two girls did not attend the school in the 9th grade. These missing data on 4 subjects make before-after comparisons impossible.

Table 5.2

Results of the 18-Month Follow-Up
Interviews for Experimental and Control:
Boys and Girls

Achievement-Oriented Non-School Yields	Boys		Girls	
	Experimental (n = 8)	Control (n = 12)	Experimental (n = 14)	Control (n = 14)
Summer Income	431	594*[1]	385	352
n-Ach Oriented Work	0.88	0.33	0.36	0.29
n-Ach Oriented Leisure	1.00	0.33	-.36	0.00
Extent of Future Plans	1.25	1.25	1.29	1.07
Reported Usefulness of Course	1.13	0.25*	.64	-.63**

1. $* = p < .05; ** = p < .01$

p values are based on Chi-square tests corrected for continuity. In a few cases, Fisher Exact tests were used. The p values are one-tailed. For each of the four interview categories, the distribution of scores was divided as close to the mean as possible. In each case this was -1, 0 vs. +1, +2.

than the experimental boys. The boys, and the experimental girls also, report that the n-Ach course was very useful to them and describe specific changes they have made as a result of the course. A few quotations will suggest the flavor and range of these applications.

"I worked my way back into the college program."

"Once I thought about giving up basketball. Now I play with varsity players, and I learn from them."

"I used to get in lots of trouble. But I sat down, thought things out and now I don't get in as much."

"It made me get interested in broadcasting, a field I like, and made me plan to go to college to specialize in it. I've been covering school football games for the Globe."

"I want to own three or four barrooms. I've been setting my plans down on paper."

Few such changes are attributed by control boys and girls to the Bookkeeping course they took.

It is possible that the single most precise and direct route to discovering the effects of the course is to ask the students how useful the course was to them. It is also possible that these students simply told us what they thought we wanted to hear. If the answers to this interview question are valid indices of course success, they should correlate with the other results of the training. In fact, the reported usefulness of the n-Ach course correlates with the change in GPA from 9th to 11th grades (p $<.008$), the change in the number of dismissals from 9th to 11th grades (p $<.007$), n-Ach-oriented summer work (p $<.15$), n-Ach summer leisure (p $<.007$), and future plans (p $<.15$).* This pattern of relationships supports the notion that the "use of n-Ach course" answers are good indicators of the course yields.

*For each of these yield variables, the distribution of scores for the entire sample of n-Ach course subjects was divided as close to the median as possible

Using this yield measure, it is possible to carry the analysis of results one step further. Perhaps some background variables like SES or sex dispose a person to benefit more or less from this type of training, just as "being in charge" was a pre-condition for the effectiveness of n-Ach training for adult businessmen. In fact, however, the relationship between the reported usefulness of the n-Ach course does *not* approach significance for any of the following background variables: sex, age, SES, IQ, Nelson-Denny reading test score, or 9th grade GPA.* The restricted range of scores for all but the sex variable may account for the absence of significant relationships like those found by Kolb (1965) between SES and GPA gain. However, inasmuch as only 33 percent of the students in the n-Ach course reported that it was extremely useful (+2), and 66 percent useful to some degree (+1 or +2), it seems worthwhile to search for other factors in the course, or perhaps psychological differences before the course that could increase the course yield.

Discussion

The choice of a Business Education class in which to give an achievement motivation course appeared to be ideal, since the manpower allocation, the level of SES, school performance of the students, and the explicit orientation of the course all seemed to increase the likelihood of producing and identifying a significant pattern of non-school yields. Basically the results confirm but do not clarify the results from the previous experiment. The n-Ach course does improve the academic performance over a two-year period, more for the boys than the girls. Attendance improves over a two-year period, again more for the boys than the girls. Finally, the interviews revealed a variety of fairly idiosyncratic applications during the second summer after the n-Ach course. These long-term non-school applications, viewed as a whole, are broad and specific as in the previous experiment, with no distinct clustering.

to form four-fold contingency tables. The p values are based on Chi-square tests corrected for continuity and sometimes on Fisher Exact tests. The p values are one-tailed.

*See previous footnote.

Remarkable as it may be for 22 hours of motivational training to produce such a wide range of results 18 months later, it is nonetheless problematic that the conditions which maximize the course yields remain so elusive.

Some progress has been made. Girls benefit from the course more in school than outside, but in both areas consistently less than the boys. No other single background factor appears to predetermine the effectiveness of the n-Ach training. However, at least two further possibilities need to be examined. As indicated in the previous experiment, the interaction of age and training emphasis (action vs. planning) may significantly affect the degree, if not the location, of the course yields. Second, there may be some pre-course psychological dispositions that influence the effectiveness of the training. Given these variations in pre-course and course variables, it may be possible to detect more distinct patterns of yields. However, the non-school yield measure needs to be augmented by including a wider variety of more precise yield measures. This should increase the possibility of identifying yield patterns, since the interview only provides four four-point scales. Given these intentions for the next experiment, this experiment can be seen as a useful bridge.

6.

Personality and Course Factors That Maximize the Yields of Achievement Motivation Training

This experiment explores the questions raised in the previous two experiments. What combination of personality factors and types of training maximize n-Ach course yields in school and outside of school? In addition to the standard demographic background variables, a variety of pre-course psychological measures were collected to assess relevant personality factors that might be related to the efficacy of n-Ach training. Two types of n-Ach training were provided: one n-Ach course, minus the action inputs, emphasized achievement planning and the other n-Ach course, minus the achievement planning, emphasized achievement action strategies. These are the same basic variations studies in the previous experiment but given to an older sample, namely, 10th grade business education students. These types of courses allow us to address the question of whether n-Ach inputs that maximize the course yields are related to age. We assumed that these older students would find it more meaningful than the younger students to think about their own thoughts and envision a specific future. These cognitive abilities develop during the period of formal operational thinking, according to Piaget. For most students this has begun roughly by the age of 14. Thus, we predicted that training emphasizing achievement planning would be more effective at this age. To assess the yields from training as precisely as possible, an additional set of measures of predicted non-school results was devised and administered.

Procedures

Sample. The students in this experiment were drawn from the same general population in the same school as in the previous experiment, i.e., boys and girls in two classes of 10th grade "Elementary Business Principles." Besides collecting background information from the school files (age, SES, IQ, Nelson-Denny Reading Test scores, and 9th grade GPA), we administered several psychological tests to assess further the comparability of our samples, and also to use as possible within-group predictors of gains. Specifically, the TAT (four pictures) was given to measure pre-course levels of n-Ach, n-Aff, and n-Power.* We also obtained four questionnaire measures of attitudes hypothesized from theory and empirical research to be important.

Value of Achievement (v-Ach). Items in this scale, developed by deCharms, Morrison, Reitman, and McClelland (1955), reflect Achievement values such as the importance in life of accomplishing things that are difficult. A high score on this scale means that the person endorses these values. Interestingly, there is rather consistent evidence that this measure does not correlate with the TAT measure of n-Ach (McClelland, *The Achieving Society*, 1961; Atkinson [Ed.], 1958). Nonetheless, it is possible that this attitude constitutes a favorable disposition to learn from a course publicly described and designed to help people implement these achievement values.

Internal-External Control of Reinforcement (I). "Internal control of reinforcement" is the generalized expectancy that reinforcement is contingent on one's own behavior. In contrast, people who believe that what happens to them is more the result of fate, chance, luck, and events beyond their control have a generalized expectancy of "external control of reinforcement." Such a person is less likely to benefit from a course that presupposes the belief that one can achieve through energetic and planned actions. In empirical research, Crandall *et al.* (1965), Lefcourt (1966), and McGhee and Crandall (1968) have demonstrated positive relationships between "internal control of reinforcement," achievement striving, and academic performance in

*Scores on these motives were obtained using the system described in Atkinson (Ed.) *Motives in Fantasy, Action and Society*, Princeton, New Jersey: D. Van Nostrand, Inc., 1958. The coder established satisfactory reliability as measured by the test stories in Atkinson's book.

children. In a nationwide study of educational opportunity, Coleman (1966a) found that the single best predictor of academic gains was a three-item scale taken from Rotter's (1966) I-E scale (see also Rotter, Seeman and Liverant, 1962). Thus, besides being a possibly important predeterminant of the effectiveness of n-Ach training, increases in "internality" would be a valuable outcome of training. Systematic training in identifying and producing effects by one's own behavior may increase "internality."

Debilitating Test Anxiety (DA). This scale, developed by Alpert and Haber (1960), has been used by Atkinson and Feather (1966) as their principal measure of the tendency to avoid achievement-oriented situations. According to extensive research by these authors, one's orientation to achievement situations is the result of one's tendency to approach (measured by TAT n-Ach) minus one's tendency to avoid (measured by DA). Thus, a high DA score might mitigate efforts to teach achievement strivings. On the other hand, if the n-Ach training is successful, we might expect DA to decrease.

Self-Esteem (SE). Coleman (1966a) reports that "Self-Esteem," like "internality," is highly related to gains in school achievement. Although it is difficult to know whether this results from or is a cause of school achievement, it is nevertheless an important pre-course variable to hold constant. Like the other attitudes, an increase in SE would be a notable and worthwhile result of n-Ach training. The scale used was developed by deCharms and Rosenbaum (1962).

Comparisons between the two groups receiving n-Ach training on all of the pre-course variables are presented in Table 6.1. As Table 6.1 indicates, the two groups of boys and girls are extremely well matched on all the measured variables. None of the statistical differences between the groups of boys or girls is significant.

Treatment. The courses given to these students were identical to the full n-Ach course given to the students in the previous experiment with the following exceptions: (1) One group did not receive any of the inputs designed to teach achievement planning (the Action group) while the other group did not receive any inputs designed to teach achievement action strategies (the Planning group). (2) Somewhat less time was spent in individual consultations with students on their "personal change projects" at the end of the course. (3) As a result of these two course reductions, the total class time of instruction was about 11 hours (15 sessions of 43 minutes) or approximately half the time of the "Full course." The student-teacher ratio was maintained at about 20:2. The course. was given to both classes in May 1967, during the spring of their 10th grade year. Contact with these students during the follow-up meetings occurred in February and March 1968, about 1 year after the course, and again in the late fall of 1968, 1½ years after the course.

Measures. Our measures of "School Yields" consisted of increases in Grade Point Averages from 9th to 11th grade and decreases in absences, tardies, and dismissals from 9th to 11th grade. In addition to these separate measures, an "Overall School-Related Yield Score" was derived by dividing each distribution at the mean, and giving each individual a (+) for each of his scores at or above the mean, i.e., the possible range on this Overall School-Related Yield Score is 0 to 4.

To assess the perceived impact of the n-Ach course on individuals we conducted telephone interviews 1½ years after the course. These were scored in the same way as described in the previous experiment.

As in the second experiment we collected a wide variety of additional "Non-School Yields." These twenty additional measures were obtained approximately one year after the course. The four pre-course attitude measures were re-administered along with a measure of the "realism of vocational risk taking" based on one developed by Mahone (1966). From a list of 50 occupations, students chose the one closest to their own vocational choice. Students also indicated the percentage of people they believed had less ability than they, and the percentage of people who did not have enough ability to do their chosen job. This allowed us to derive a discrepancy score between their perceived ability and the ability they believed was required by the job. This discrepancy score was our measure of the realism of their vocational aspirations.

To assess other non-school yields, we constructed an Activities Survey. We wanted to identify more precisely some of the

Table 6.1

Background Characteristics of Subjects
Receiving n-Ach Training

Variables	Boys		Girls	
	n-Ach Planning (means for n = 12)	n-Ach Actions (means for n = 12)	n-Ach Planning (means for n = 6)	n-Ach Actions (means for n = 9)
Age[1]	16.1	16.4	16.1	15.8
Socioeconomic Status[2]	3.6 (n = 11)[3]	4.8 (n = 11)	5.2	4.6
IQ[4]	104.6 (n = 11)	104.0 (n = 11)	100.5	101.3
Nelson-Denny Reading Test[5]	9.2	10.0 (n = 11)	9.1 (n = 5)	9.3
Grade Point Average[6] (9th Grade)	1.59	1.35	1.33	1.61

N-Achievement	2.0	1.3 (n = 10)	3.2	3.9 (n = 8)
N-Affiliation	1.1	2.3 (n = 10)	1.3	3.0 (n = 8)
N-Power	1.8	2.4 (n = 10)	2.7	2.6
V-Achievement	1.3	1.0	2.0	2.1
Internality[7]	4.3	3.7	2.0	3.3
Debilitating Anxiety[8]	2.3	-1.3	-1.7	-3.6
Self-Esteem	0	1.5	0.7	3.3

1. As of the beginning of the n-Ach course.
2. SES is based on Hall, J. and Jones, D.C., Social Grading of Occupations, *British Journal of Sociology*, 1950 (1).
3. When comparison statistics are based on missing data, the actual sample size is given in parentheses.
4. Based on the OTIS IQ Test administered in 8th grade.
5. Scores are given in grade level equivalents, i.e., 10.2 equals the second month of the 10th grade. The test was given in October of the 10th grade.
6. A = 4, B = 3, C = 2, D = 1, E = 0. Grades for major courses were summed and divided by the number of courses to obtain the GPA.
7. A high score here means high on internality.
8. A high score here means low on debilitating test anxiety.

possible changes in the areas probed broadly by the interview, i.e., work, leisure, sports, and hobbies. No existing measure was appropriate for our needs. The various indices used in this experiment will be described only briefly here:

Work: We asked each subject how much he or she earned during the summer of 1967, how much the subject earned during the school year, and probed for evidence of initiative in finding and landing the job. We also found out how much the subject earned during the summer of 1968, and calculated the increase or decrease over the previous summer.

Leisure: We tried to sample the subjects' use of leisure time by obtaining an hour-by-hour record of what they did the last Saturday. This record was scored for when they got up, the number of operant hours (awake, non-meal hours), the number of hours spent in purposeful activities alone, and purposeful activities with others. We also asked if they had made any special independent trips and, if so, how far they went.

Sports and Games: From a list of about 30 sports (separate lists for boys and for girls), subjects were asked to indicate which ones they do three or more times in each two-week period during the appropriate season. This was scored for the total number of activities, and the number of pre-coded achievement-oriented, individualistic, competitive sports they checked. The coding was based on Kulakow's scoring system (McClelland, 1961, pp. 323-324).

Hobbies: From a list of about 30 hobbies (again separate lists for boys and for girls), subjects were asked to check the ones they did three or more times during a normal two-week period. These responses were coded for the number of pre-coded achievement-oriented hobbies. This coding was based on Kagan and Moss' (1962) finding that boys who have more mechanical hobbies show higher levels of achievement imagery in their TAT's as adults. The result is the opposite for girls. The number of mechanical hobbies is negatively correlated with achievement imagery; for girls the scoring was reversed.

The final portion of the first follow-up session was devoted to interview questions. Students were asked to describe the two most important things in their life. These answers were coded from -1 to +2 using the same system as in the interview for "future plans."

As with the set of school yields we also derived an "Overall Non-School Yield Score" from the measures described above. For each measure the distribution of scores was divided at the mean. An individual's Overall Non-School Yield Score consisted of the number of times his scores were at or above the mean.

Results

None of the results on the four individual school yields nor on the Overall School Yield Score are significantly different for the Action and Planning groups, either for the boys or for the girls. None of the results for the 20 individual Non-School Yields are significantly different for the Action and Planning groups for the boys or for the girls. However, as in the previous experiment, there is a significant difference between the Action and Planning groups for the boys on the Overall Non-School Yield Score. Nine of 12 boys (75 percent) in the Planning group earned an Overall Non-School Yield Score of 9 or more, while only 4 of 13 boys (31 percent) in the Action group earned a score of 9 or more (χ^2 = 3.39, p <.05, 1 tail). As in the previous experiment, the results of the training are reflected in a broad array of specific instances rather than being concentrated in a few narrow areas of large change. This is consistent with the nature of the motive itself; it is a generic concern, not a highly focused specific interest.

The meaning of this difference between the Action and Planning groups is clarified further by comparing the Overall School Yield Scores of each against the results for the fully trained boys in the previous experiment. A slightly abbreviated Overall Non-School Yield Score had to be used, since only 15 of the 20 measures had been obtained for the fully trained boys.* In all other ways the Overall Non-School Yield Score was derived in precisely the same way. Five of 7 fully trained boys (71 percent), 8 of 12 boys in the Planning group (67 percent), and 4 of 12 boys in the Action group (33 percent) obtained a score of 8 or more on this abbreviated Overall Non-School Yield Score. Only the difference between the fully trained group and the Action group is significant (Mann-Whitney test, $Z = 1.96$, p $<.05$, 1 tail). In other words, omitting instruction in Achievement Planning decreases the long-term yield score for boys of this age group. Whereas, apparently, 11 hours of training that omits instruction in achievement action strategies is nearly as effective for boys of this age group as a full 22-hour course. Since there are no significant differences for the girls on the abbreviated Overall Non-School Yield Score, this difference in training appears to be more important for boys than for girls.

None of the four scores derived from the telephone interview show significant differences between the Action-oriented and Planning-oriented training groups for the boys or for the girls. The single best interview score, however, the reported usefulness of the n-Ach course, does indicate that the training as a whole was more effective for the boys than for the girls: 10 of 24 boys (42 percent) earned a +2 rating, while only 1 of 14 girls (7 percent) earned a +2 rating ($\chi^2 = 3.58$, corrected for continuity p $<.05$, 1 tail). Further, the percentage of "+2 usage" for the boys and girls combined (29 percent) is quite comparable to the fully trained group, previous experiment (33 percent). This comparison shows again that even as few as 11 hours of specialized motivation training can produce significant long-term gains in motivation.

It is somewhat puzzling to note that the Overall Yield Score from the measures does not correlate significantly with the reported "Usefulness of the Course" reported six months later, a year and a half after the course. It may simply be yet another

*The four attitude scales and the measure of "realism of vocational risk taking" were not collected.

example, among numerous others in the research literature on Achievement Motivation, where an operant measure of a motive (the interview) does not correlate with a respondent measure (the sum of the test scores). Or, it may be that the two yields are equally legitimate but independent types of course yields, the Overall Yield Score reflecting a general disposition to respond in an achievement-oriented way as reflected in a variety of test situations, as opposed to the reported usefulness of the course in planning and conducting at least one single, major project. Or, finally, it may reflect accurately changes in the students between one year and 1½ years after the course. Unfortunately, our data is insufficient to allow a clear understanding of this null relationship between these two measures.

In addition to comparing the relative changes between groups, it is important to assess the significance of pre-post absolute changes in the yields. With regard to the change in GPA, if we take the mean changes in GPA from 9th to 11th grade for the control boys and control girls in the previous experiment as a base rate, only 14 of 24 boys and 10 of 15 girls exceed this average. Both results are in the predicted direction but are not significant. These results are virtually the same when boys and girls are broken down into Planning and Action sub-groups. The absolute changes in the four measured attitudes are not statistically significant for the boys or the girls with the sub-groups combined or analyzed separately.

Another purpose of this experiment was to assess the effects of several psychological background factors on the results of n-Ach training. Of the four pre-course attitudinal measures, only initial v-Ach for all the boys is significantly related to the reported usefulness of the course (χ^2 = 3.58 corrected for continuity, p <.05, 1 tail). None of the other relationships to reported usefulness or to the Overall Yield Score are significant. The effects of two additional combinations of background variables can be evaluated. As indicated in Chapter 2, Parsons (1959) argues that by the 10th grade lower SES-low achieving students have been tracked and oriented to non-college vocational goals. Thus, we might expect low SES-low GPA students to make more use of the n-Ach course than the high SES-higher GPA students in this sample. However, there were non-significant trends in this direction for the boys, girls, and for both sexes combined when the data were divided in this way and examined. A second prediction can be derived from Atkinson and Feather's theory (1966) that the resultant disposition to act in achievement-oriented ways is the sum of the tendency to approach such situations (measured by TAT n-Ach) and the tendency to avoid such situations (measured by the scale for Debilitating Anxiety). Thus, we would expect students initially high in n-Ach and low in DA to profit more from an n-Ach course than students initially low in n-Ach and high in DA. However, our data do not support this hypothesis either. In sum, neither of these complex predictions, none of the simple relationships assessed in the previous experiment (age, SES, IQ, Nelson-Denny Reading Test scores, and 9th grade GPA), and almost none of the attitude scores predicted the effects of n-Ach training for the students. In contrast, there are consistent sex differences in the yields, and for the boys, initial v-Ach appears to predict the usefulness of n-Ach training.

Discussion

These results are most meaningful when viewed in the context of results from the other experiments. We now have evidence that achievement motivation training can be effective over a wide age range—from adults to junior high school students—provided appropriate adaptations are made to sustain the attendance and attention of the particular age group. This appears to be a simple pedagogical problem of creating moderate novelty relative to the existing teaching methods, settings, norms, and values in the schools. The need for relativism means that no specific technique will be equally effective in all training contexts. This is a clear caveat for teachers not to make direct transfers of techniques described elsewhere (Alschuler, Tabor and McIntyre, 1970) into new situations without considered appreciation of the existing social norms, values, and procedures. What is moderately novel in one situation may be innocuously funny or destructive in another situation.

The yields of n-Ach training are broad, extending from increases in GPA for boys to special projects conducted outside of school as reported in the telephone interviews. The range of course yields also is evident in the significantly increased Overall Non-School Yield Scores for the boys. Within this array of specific yields composing the Overall scores, no one application occurs with sufficient frequency to be predicted for an individual or group in advance. This is consistent with the theory and practice of n-Ach training. N-Ach is a well-defined generic concern that can be manifested in a wide variety of contexts. The training teaches what the motive is, and helps students apply it in ways that are particularly well suited to their individual life situations.

The most efficient way of identifying these course-related yields is to ask students what use they have made of the course. We obtained consistent yields of about 30 percent at the +2 "use" level, and another 30 percent at the +1 "use" level. These figures now constitute rough base rate yields against which the effectiveness of future combinations of course inputs can be assessed. Using this yield measure, cost-effectiveness studies can be conducted and "instructional objectives" can be stated (e.g., at least 33 percent at the +2 "use" level over a two-year period) without coercing students into making restrictively narrow and personally inappropriate applications.

To a certain degree the factors that maximize course yields remain elusive. Of all the *pre-course* variables assessed, only sex, and for boys, initial v-Ach, predicted the degree of reported usefulness. One can restrict n-Ach courses to boys and thereby increase the group percent of +2 usage, but this merely excludes potential failures instead of developing more effective training procedures. Furthermore, girls do benefit from the course to a certain degree, especially in school-related situations. As for v-Ach, apparently it serves a gate-keeping function. Only those boys benefit from n-Ach training who value achievement goals prior to the course. Perhaps the boys with initial low v-Ach do not benefit as much because the training does not help them move towards goals they value. This finding constitutes an empirically supported answer to concerned parents and administrators who fear that the course will dramatically transform their child into a greedy businessman, grasping entrepreneur, and thoroughly unpleasant person. Our data show that no such extreme changes occurred and that the courses affected only those boys for whom Achievement was already a strong value. This v-Ach finding has the further implication that if the results of n-Ach training are to be increased, maybe the place to start is before the course by increasing individuals' value of achievement.

Of the essential n-Ach *course* variables studied, there is an important interaction with age. For boys below the age normally associated with the initial acquisition of formal operational thinking, the presence of inputs designed to teach the n-Ach Action strategies is essential to maximize the yields. This would roughly correspond to the junior high school age group. By the time students are in senior high school, they are better able to think about their own thoughts and can construct for themselves a more meaningful set of future goals. Our data show that teaching achievement planning is more important for this age group, particularly for the boys, since the course as a whole is more effective for them.

These findings are optimistic. Relatively brief instruction (as little as 11 hours) appears to generate a wide variety of yields for a wide variety of students over a long period of time. These results stand in marked contrast to the long history of attempts to influence the motivation of adolescents in any significant way within a practical time period and cost. The surprising generality of these methods do carry with them certain limitations. Because of this very same diversity of yields, it is inappropriate for a teacher to give an n-Ach course to his students with the expectation that it will boost all of their performances in the teacher's specific class. At a more theoretical level, this diversity and its lack of relation to pre-course yields does not allow precise statements to be made about solutions to the larger system maintenance problems. For example, we *cannot* say that high-SES students apply the n-Ach course in school rather than outside of school because n-Ach increases entrepreneurial role responsibility and commitment to their allocated social manpower roles. It may be that solutions to the potential conflicts like those between n-Ach and the larger social system of which the student is a member (school, family, industry) are worked out in part during the individualized goal setting projects at the end of the course.

Difficulties are anticipated and methods of overcoming them are devised. Training in the use of feedback to modify plans and goals attempts to internalize a self-adjusting cybernetic system to deal with these types of conflicts in the larger social system. It is not possible on the basis of data from these experiments to specify any more precisely the principles of system maintenance during the course, or for adjusting the course to reduce conflicts between the students' intensified n-Ach and the values, norms, and rules of their ongoing, larger social systems.

In one sense, we could consider the problem of long-term system maintenance solved, since the various yields do last for a reasonably long time. However, the +2 yield percent is only about 33 percent, leaving room for improvement and many questions as to why only 33 percent say they benefitted greatly. Having explored the factors before the course and within the course that contribute to these yields, it seems appropriate in the next set of experiments to go beyond the course to examine the contribution of the subsequent environment to these yields. It seems obvious that the yields could be increased and potential conflicts with the larger social system resolved if we could also alter portions of the social environment to support and encourage n-Ach. Since Lewin, it has been a fundamental axiom of the behavioral sciences that behavior is a function of personality factors and the environment. The contribution of the environment to the maintenance of strengthened n-Ach behavior needs to be studied in greater detail to discover how system conflicts can be minimized and course yields maximized.

PART THREE
Achievement Motivating Systems

7.
Socialization
and Classroom Structure*

Schooling, through its sheer consumption of conscious time, is a potent force in shaping students' values, norms, and motives. These implicit results of schooling are no less important than preparing students for a specific vocation. The problem does not lie in obtaining agreement that schooling does and should shape essential cultural orientations, but in identifying how these orientations can be taught consciously.

Dreeben (1968) attempts to explain how certain structural properties of schooling contribute to the learning of norms:

> Whatever pupils learn from the didactic efforts of teachers, they also learn from their participation in a school setting. Implicit in this statement are the following assumptions: (a) the tasks, constraints, and opportunities available within social settings vary with the structural properties of those settings; (b) individuals who participate in them derive principles of conduct based on their experience coping with those tasks, constraints, and opportunities; and (c) the content of the principles learned varies with the nature of the setting. To the question of what is learned in school, only a hypothetical answer can be offered at this point: pupils learn to accept social norms, or principles of conduct and to act according to them.

*Portions of this chapter appeared previously in Chapter 3 of *Teaching Achievement Motivation*, Alschuler, Tabor and McIntyre, Education Ventures, Inc., 1970, and are used with permission of the publisher.

Dreeben performs an analytic exegesis to show how the structure of schooling teaches four norms that have particular relevance to economic and political participation in industrial societies: Independence, Achievement, Universalism, and Specificity. A summary of how Achievement norms are taught will illustrate the general line of his argument. By an Achievement Norm Dreeben means, "to perform tasks actively and master the environment according to standards of excellence." Classrooms are organized around a set of activities for which the teacher compares and evaluates the quality of students' performance. The evaluation process, no matter how it is done, forces students to cope with their success *vis-a-vis* peer-equality in non-academic areas, or to cope with their failures as assaults on their self-respect. Because of ubiquitous evaluation procedures, students come to expect and accept work in an achievement frame of mind. Through successes and failures in class, sports, music, dramatics, and art, students learn a variety of ways to cope in achievement-oriented situations.

For our purposes, Dreeben's approach is provocative and useful in focusing the search for situational methods on the structural properties of the teaching-learning process. Dreeben also underscores the cultural perspective: the norms, values, and motives taught in school shape the dominant cultural orientations. This helps set the tasks for this chapter: (1) to identify the structural properties in classroom learning that teach achievement, affiliation, and power motivation, (2) to examine the cultural relevance of these structural properties, and (3) to assess the feasibility of consciously altering these properties to teach culturally relevant motives in classrooms.

Classroom Structure and Motivational Games

The motivational goals, thoughts, actions, and feelings of students are determined in part by the classroom structure, i.e., the rules for what students can and can't do, the incentives for doing well, and penalties for doing poorly. It is as if these rules, incentives, and penalties defined a learning game—with players, a point system, obstacles to be overcome, and decisions to be made. Using this analogy it is possible to develop a structural model of what types of games teach achievement, affiliation, and power motivation.

Four characteristics distinguish a game from other forms of activity: (1) the rules that govern the activity are agreed upon in advance by the players; (2) the rules describe classes of acceptable and unacceptable behavior within which players exercise choice of actions; (3) there are obstacles to be overcome; and (4) a scoring system is specified. In general, games are more organized than "play" or "pastimes," but less organized than "rituals." In "play" and other activities which merely "pass time" there are no rules, no necessary obstacles to be overcome, and no scoring. In "rituals" (greeting formalities, graduations, funerals, etc.) the specific actions rather than classes of acceptable and unacceptable behavior are defined. Also there is no scoring present. In general, games are more flexible than "rituals" and less open-ended than "play" and "pastimes."

By this definition, most normal classroom teaching is not a game. Usually the rules are not well specified in advance. When rules are extremely vague, classroom activity often becomes a pastime, literally a way to pass time between more meaningful activities. This forces students to "test limits" in order to discover the unstated rules and boundaries. Limit testing is necessary for would-be game players, but from the teacher's point of view it is a discipline problem and a waste of valuable learning time. Nor is classroom teaching a game when teachers over-specify the minute activities to be performed. This ritualized learning is clearest in older "learning by rote" methods, but is present today in slightly altered forms, e.g., making specific problem assignments in mathematics and learning through programmed texts.

To arouse students' motivation more systematically in the classroom, *learning should have the formal properties of a game,* i.e., rules that are clearly specified in advance, and defined classes of behavior, obstacles to be overcome, and a well-specified scoring system. It is then possible to vary these properties to arouse the desired motives. The first task is to decide whether to stimulate concerns about excellence, friendship, having influence, or some combination of these motives. The desired motives can be stimulated by creating rules which change the nature of the scoring system, the types of obstacles to success, and the locus of decision-making.

1. *Scoring Systems*

There are three main types of scoring systems in games: Zero-Sum, Non-Zero-Sum, and Shared-Sum. Zero-Sum scoring systems have a fixed number of points. When one player makes points, another player automatically loses points, the sum total number of points thus remaining a constant zero. Arm wrestling, cup play in golf, betting games, chess, grading on the curve, "Pull-over" games—all have Zero-Sum scoring systems. In Non-Zero-Sum games the number of points is not constant. Each player is free to earn as many points as he can, independently of how many points the other player makes, e.g., archery contests, medal play in golf, preset academic grading standards, and Boy Scout merit badge progression. In Shared-Sum scoring systems, a score by one player is a score for all players on his team. Almost all team sports have Shared-Sum scoring systems.

Zero-Sum scoring systems structurally define power goals, since points are awarded only when one side forces the other side to yield or when one side demonstrates superior power, influence, or control. Inevitably, in Zero-Sum grading systems, students are in direct competition with each other. Grading on the curve or by rank ordering scores are Zero-Sum scoring systems, since judgments about a student's performance are determined only by comparison to others. One highly effective strategy for doing well in Zero-Sum games is to sabotage other players. Weakening your opponent, e.g., destroying other students' notebooks, is just as effective as strengthening yourself.

Non-Zero-Sum scoring structurally defines achievement goals, since it gives greatest value to independent, self-reliant accomplishment. Contrary to Zero-Sum games, Non-Zero-Sum games can be played alone, without direct competition with others. In such games, sabotage is not a useful strategy for earning points.

In Shared-Sum games, affiliation is made salient, since making points is a key method of establishing, maintaining, or restoring friendly relationships among team members. Academic situations rarely are Shared-Sum games, thus missing the potential facilitating effect of high affiliation motivation.

2. *Obstacles to Success*

In all games, points are made when obstacles are overcome. The motivational goals of every game depend on the nature of the obstacles to making points. For example, the need for affiliation (n-Aff) is not particularly valuable to a boxer, since the obstacle is the opponent's strength and skill. The boxer must demonstrate his influence over his opponent, not his ability to get along harmoniously. In general, when the obstacle is the opponent's potency, the need for power (n-Power) is a valued asset. N-Ach is valuable when the obstacles are within the player himself. In target shooting, for example, the standards are fixed and inanimate. In order to score, the player must overcome a variety of inadequate personal resources and skills (e.g., shyness, lack of coordination, etc.). In some games, the obstacles are both the opponent's and the player's skills, as in fencing, ice hockey, and football. These games call for both power and achievement concerns. Obstacles to scoring also can exist in a team's lack of cooperation or inadequate combined strength. In such games, the desire to perform in an effective coordinated manner is necessary, i.e., n-Aff is important. Most complex team games have power, achievement, and affiliation obstacles, thus calling forth triple motivation.

Many adolescents find sports more interesting and involving than studying, perhaps because all three motives are so clearly and strongly invoked by complex team games. From this perspective, the classroom is neither complex, a team effort, nor a game. When students respond to their natural affiliation needs in the classroom, more often than not they are obstructing the teacher's goals. There is a curious logic in such student response: When a teacher creates an n-Power classroom, the obstacle to success is in the teacher, his standards, his assignments, his disciplinary and rewarding power. As we have seen, sabotage is an appropriate strategy in power situations. What more effective way is there for students to demonstrate potency than to gang up on the teacher, to jointly sabotage the teacher's efforts? There is greater strength in friendly team effort, and often it is more fun.

3. *Locus of Decision-Making*

Motivation is a process of decision-making. The goals which define different motives define how decisions are made. Obviously, the object of the power motive (n-Power) is to make decisions for others, the object of the achievement motive (n-Ach) to make decisions for oneself, the object of the affiliation motive (n-Aff) to make decisions agreeable to the majority of members. Similarly, the motivational character of games can be inferred from the decision-making process built into them. In football, the quarterback is encouraged by his position to demonstrate both achievement and power motivation. For the rest of the football players, compliance is required for the sake of affiliation and team power. In the classroom, carrying out the assignments often is less palatable, since it serves neither power nor affiliative goals agreed upon in advance. Often students' compliance serves only the teachers' achievement goals and the students' interest in avoiding punishment.

The table below summarizes the scheme for analyzing the motivational structure of games.

Table 7.1

Motivational Structure of Games

		n-Achievement	Motives n-Power	n-Affiliation
	Scoring System	Non-Zero-Sum	Zero-Sum	Shared-Sum
Dimensions of Games	Obstacles to success	Personal and environmental	Opponent	Lack of cooperation, e.g., friction, conflict, distance, tension
	Locus of decision-making	Individual player	Captain or leader	Team

Socialization Games and
Cultural Motives

Piaget (1962) argues that the games children play serve as opportunities to standardize the meaning of words (e.g., debates over the rules), thus helping to socialize thought. Role reciprocity in games serves as an experience base for the concept of inverse relationships, which is abstracted as a cognitive operation in subsequent stages of intellectual development. As counterpoint to Piaget's theorizing, Berne (1964) suggests that human relationship games learned by the child at home serve as prototypes for relationship games we play as adults.

The empirical case for the relationship between children's games and dominant cultural motives is made by Roberts and co-workers in a series of articles (Roberts, Arth and Bush, 1959; Roberts and Sutton-Smith, 1962; Roberts, Sutton-Smith and Kendon, 1963; Sutton-Smith, Roberts and Kozekla, 1963; Sutton-Smith and Roberts, 1963; Roberts, Hoffman and Sutton-Smith, 1965). As developed by Roberts *et al.,*

> The theory implies (1) that there is an overall process of cultural patterning whereby a society induces conflict in children through its child training processes; (2) that society seeks through appropriate arrays and varieties of ludic modes (game playing) to provide an assuagement of these conflicts by an adequate representation of their emotional and cognitive polarities in ludic structure; and (3) that through these models society tries to provide a form of buffered learning through which the child can make acculturative, step-by-step progress toward adult behavior (Roberts and Sutton-Smith, 1962).

In other words, games model central issues in societies. In game playing children have the opportunity to face these issues and practice solutions. In this way they are gradually prepared for the societal conflicts which they will face as adults.

Roberts' first step in substantiating this theory was to describe three types of games: skill, strategy, and chance. Skill games must involve skill and may or may not involve strategy or chance, e.g., marathon races, hockey, hoop, and pole games. The defining property of skill games would categorize them, in general, as achievement games in our scheme. However, prize fighting is a skill game which involves power motivation. Thus, skill games are somewhat broader than pure n-Achievement games as previously defined. In games of strategy, physical skill must be absent, chance may or may not play a part, but obviously, strategy must be present. Roberts *et al.* (1959) list chess, go, poker, and the Ashanti game of wori as examples, all of which we would classify as primarily n-Power games because of their inevitable Zero-Sum scoring systems. Again, the translation is not perfect. "Strategy" games can have n-Ach involved secondarily. The relationship between strategy games, n-Power, and acculturation is evident in the following comment:

> In a game of strategy, for example, he (the player) can practice deception against his powerful opponent and can even "kill" him, but in addition he can also command his own forces, as he is commanded by those whom he normally obeys (Roberts and Sutton-Smith, 1962, p. 183).

In chance games, chance must be present, skill and strategy must be absent. Our scheme excludes games of chance because they are not theoretically germane to n-Ach, n-Aff, or n-Power.

In Roberts' attempts to validate his general hypothesis (Roberts, Arth and Bush, 1959) the researchers found that the presence of power games in societies was positively related to the degree and complexity of political integration. The number of chance games in cultures was positively related to the belief that the gods are non-aggressive and benevolent. Subsequent cross-cultural research by Roberts and Sutton-Smith (1962) showed that the frequency of skill and strategy games in societies was strongly related to emphasis in child rearing practices on achievement and obedience, respectively. The frequency of chance games was related to stress on performance of routine duties and punishment for initiative. These last two child rearing practices theoretically should inhibit the growth of n-Ach. Altogether, the data from Roberts and co-workers strongly indicate that games both teach and reflect central motivational concerns in societies.

The relevance of children's games in the socialization process lies in the degree to which they simulate, albeit simplistically, the dominant cultural processes and goals. An analysis of the social structure status system provides good clues for what types of children's games are most relevant, since the status system can be seen as the adult game for which children practice. Robert LeVine (1966) has conducted an illustrative analysis of the status systems of three Nigerian groups, the Ibo, the Hausa, and the Yoruba. Like McClelland (1961), LeVine makes a "culture lag" hypothesis, namely, that cultural changes in motivation will be reflected in national statistics, such as rate of economic activity, up to two generations after these motivational shifts occur. LeVine differs from McClelland in looking to the social structure rather than to folklore for evidence of these shifts. LeVine assumes further that as the status systems change they require and recruit new motives. Thus, an analysis of the status systems of the Ibo, Hausa, and Yoruba in the later 1800's should predict differences in the strength of different motives in schoolboys today.

In his book, *Dreams and Deeds* (1966), LeVine presents data confirming his theory. The following is a summary of LeVine's description of the nineteenth century status system of the Hausa and the Ibo. The history of the Hausa shows the existence of a "short-term autocracy" political system in which the kings of the empire ruled vassal states. The kingship was rotated among three ruling dynastic lineages. With each rotation went the right to patronage; some office holders were discharged and others of the king's choosing were installed. Office holders usually had responsibility for fiefs they administered and from which they collected taxes, keeping a portion for themselves. During the tribal wars, office holders raised troops from their fiefs and in return received booty and captive slaves from the king.

So long as an office holder retained the favor of the king through demonstrations of loyalty and obedience, he was allowed to overtax and keep the surplus himself as well as to exceed his formal authority in a number of other ways. Thus, the system has a despotic character, turning on relations of dependence and power between subordinates and their superiors (LeVine, 1966).

As a result, the principal way to rise socially was to become the client or follower of a person of greater status, to demonstrate worthiness by being loyal and obedient, and to collect additional followers for the patron. In these ways the fortunes of the patron were enriched and the follower's nomination to office was made more likely. Obedience led to office, and office led to wealth.

Clearly this system of status mobility placed a premium on loyalty, obedience, and sensitivity to the demands of those in authority over a man; excellent performance in an independent occupational role, self-instigated action toward goals that did not benefit the competitive chances of a man's patron, did not yield the man access to the major status rewards of the society and might conceivably damage his career (LeVine, 1966).

Implicit in this status system is the belief that there is a fixed and limited amount of goods. Access to those goods was dependent on the relative strength of the patron. Attaining and falling from office depended on compliance, submission, and subservience to the patron. The status system scoring was Zero-Sum and generated power-compliance motivation. Obstacles to success existed primarily in the strength of other patrons. One way to change the balance of power was to collect new clients for a man's own patron. Innovation per se and developing one's own unique skills were not valuable. Obviously, also, the locus of decision making was with the patron, not with the client.

Often, "loyalty, obedience, and sensitivity to those in authority" are valued tactics of our "brightest" students, who believe we have the answers necessary to doing well on semester tests and College Board examinations. They slavishly adhere to our requests so that we will patronize them with good grades and good recommendations. Student-instigated action toward goals that are not consistent with our own might conceivably damage their chances for the classroom status rewards.

In contrast to the Hausa, the nineteenth century history of the Ibo reveals more than 200 politically independent tribes, each with its own status system. In general, the tribes reached decisions through councils of elders who were highly responsive to the needs and wishes of tribesmen. In addition, most tribes had title societies that men could enter upon acceptance by members, payment of entrance fees, and provision of a feast for the members. The feast, more than the other two requirements, effectively confined entrance to those of some financial means. Membership entitled a man to share other entrance fees, prestige, and, in some areas, political power as well. Most of the titles were not inherited, but were open to men who could earn them. Since there were many routes to earning the necessary fees, the status system encouraged men to determine for themselves what personal skills and knowledge would be most useful. This encouraged men to make carefully calculated estimates of their abilities and to pursue their individual entrepreneurial goals.

> Occupational performance was the primary locus of
> social evaluation and performing well enough as a
> farmer, trader, or fisherman to obtain a title . . .
> required the continual application of his own efforts in
> the service of his individual goals (LeVine, 1966).

Higher status and power were granted on the basis of individual economic achievement, whereas among the Hausa the reverse was true. Higher status brought greater wealth. The clearest overall difference between the Ibo and the Hausa status systems was the political orientation of the Hausa and the occupational emphasis among the Ibo.

Although not formulated in this way by LeVine, the Ibo system implied that there was an unlimited amount of goods, and that goods, whether political influence or money, could be shared (e.g., sharing the entrance fee with titled elders). It was a Non-Zero-Sum and Shared-Sum scoring system in which the obstacles to success were within the individual. Decisions were made either by the individual himself or by a group of equals.

N-Ach and, secondarily, n-Aff were the most valuable cultural motives. These differences in motives and social systems indicate a few of the ways the Hausa and Ibo are likely to misunderstand each other. The Hausa are likely to view the Ibo as upstart radicals who threaten the social order by their self-reliance, independence, and lack of compliance. The Ibo see the Hausa system as cramping individual initiative and as an equal threat to their own social structure.

Foster's analysis of traditional peasant societies (Foster, 1967) gives weight to the implication that people can be taught to view their culture as a Zero-Sum or Non-Zero-Sum system. Foster proposes that a universal characteristic of peasant societies is their belief in "the limited good." Whether it is land, wealth, friendship, honor, health, manliness, or power, these goods are assumed to be fixed, finite, and usually in short supply. Life is a Zero-Sum game. With respect to land in peasant societies this seems accurate and obvious. Other implications are not so clear. If good is limited within the society, new resources can be added only from outside the society, e.g., lottery winnings, Peace Corps volunteers. Foster suggests that this view is the reason behind extensive lottery betting in many peasant societies. Peace Corps volunteers who do not appreciate this Zero-Sum view of the world can get into trouble. When they enter a village they are likely to try to make friends with the first people they contact, often their neighbors. However, since the volunteers are a scarce new resource, their alliance with one family can be seen by the others in the village as a disruption of the distribution of goods. Thus, in making the first friend, many potential future friends are alienated.

Other examples further illustrate the belief that life is a Zero-Sum game. If one family happens to have a large crop one year, it is assumed to be at the expense of others or by special conniving. In order to placate these suspicions and fears, the fortunate family must immediately use up the additional crop in a feast for the village. This distributes the gains equally and maintains the status quo. The excess is neither stored, bartered, nor saved. Postulating a belief in Zero-Sum scoring helps explain this economically irrational behavior. Similarly, fertilizing a field to increase crop output is a threat to the balance of the social order, and represents deviant beliefs. In many Latin American peasant societies, even blood is believed to be non-regenerative, thus in fixed supply. Bleeding injuries are thought to permanently decrease the amount of a person's blood. Given this dominant cultural belief in limited goods, the ideas of improvement, increase, and investment with returns are all threats to the existing order.

Classroom Motivational Games

Having established the relevance of this particular model of motivational games to important cultural orientations, there remains the problem of establishing the feasibility of restructuring classroom learning to simulate motivational processes and thereby consciously facilitating the socialization process. The first source of encouragement for restructuring learning comes from the burgeoning use of simulation games in classrooms as units within traditional courses. The vast majority of these games are used either as an alternative tactic for teaching specific subject matter or to provide experiences in the complexities of specific social roles and situations. Proponents of learning through games say that such activity provides vicarious experience and increases a player's sense of efficacy (Boocock, 1966). However, a review of the studies comparing learning through simulations versus other methods of learning comes to the following conclusion:

> Without exception no evidence was uncovered support-
> ing the contention that participants learn more facts or
> principles than they would by studying in a more
> conventional manner (Cherryholmes, 1966, p. 5).

Cherryholmes also concludes that in every study there was striking evidence for increased student interest, involvement, and motivation. Still, many questions remain unanswered. What motives are increased? What kind of rules increase which motives? How can a knowledge of motivational games be applied to the classroom more systematically? Can the classroom itself be structured as a game?

A second source of encouragement stating the need for

restructuring learning comes from James Coleman's (1959) empirical study of "academic achievement and the structure of competition." In his study of values among students in nine public high schools in the midwest, Coleman found that few of the things students like to do have any relation to what goes on in school. Outdoor sports, being with the group, and hobbies were the favorite activities of over 70 percent of the 8,150 students in the study. As for academic activity:

> Despite wide differences in parental background, type of community, and type of school, there was little difference in the standards of prestige, the activities which confer status, and the values which focus attention and interest. In particular, good grades and academic achievement had relatively low status in all schools. If we add to this the fact that these responses (to the research questionnaire) were given in school classrooms, under adult supervision, and to questions which referred explicitly to the school, then the true position of scholastic achievement in the adolescent culture appears even lower. In fact, there is a good deal of evidence that special effort toward scholastic success is *negatively* valued in most teenage groups.

Coleman asks whether it is possible to reverse this low status position of academic excellence and make it as desirable as sports, hobbies, and being with others. His suggested solution is premised on an analysis of the structure of competition in schools, i.e., the collective student response to institutional demands for high quality academic performance.

> Grades are almost completely relative, in effect, ranking students relative to others in their class. Thus extra achievement by one student not only raises his position, but in effect lowers the position of others. Response of the group is purely rational. By holding down efforts and achievements of those who might excel, the general level of effort required to keep the average position is

reduced. The group's effort can be seen as one of combining to prevent excessive competition, and is precisely parallel to the trusts and combines in industries, which attempt by price fixing and other means to prevent excessive competition. The structure of the situation is the same in both cases.

It is as if students were operating in a game with a Zero-Sum scoring system with consequences analogous to those in peasant societies described by Foster.

Coleman's suggested solution is to make academic performance more like inter-scholastic athletic competition, where outstanding performances make a person into a "star," applauded by his fellow students, rather than "a damned curve buster" who is ridiculed, kidded, or excluded from the group.

Team competition incorporates a Shared-Sum scoring system that taps existing student needs to be "with" others. With a Zero-Sum scoring, students band together to beat the system, whereas a Shared-Sum scoring system allows students to band together to do well. If we conduct a quick mental inventory of all the situations that require team effort in sports, industry, research, or managing a family, the striking fact about school is the comparative absence of sanctioned rewards for team learning.

It would appear to be a comparatively simple matter to capitalize on the increasing legitimacy of educational games by expanding this orientation—first, to view an entire academic course as a game, and second, to have these games serve socialization functions in teaching valuable motives. These rather grandiose notions in fact involve deceptively simple, surprisingly inexpensive changes in classroom procedures. The two experimental studies to be reported next demonstrate the feasibility of accomplishing these aims.*

---

*Both of these examples are offered for illustrative purposes only. They were inaugurated by the teachers as solutions to practical problems they faced, prior to any active involvement of the author. Thus a number of important research "controls" could not be introduced ex post facto. The research questions raised by these pilot studies are identified later in this chapter and are answered systematically in the next two chapters.

Two Studies

A high school typing class

In many high schools, business education classes are considered low level subjects for non-college bound students who must prepare in secondary school for jobs after graduation. For students with little interest in school, these classes often are used as an institutionalized dumping ground. Severe discipline problems are more frequent than in the prestigious college preparatory classes. As a result, the most well-prepared, experienced business education teacher can face overwhelming classroom problems. This was true even for Dr. Antoinette DiLoretto, head of the business education department at a large suburban high school and the author of several published texts on typing. In 1965-66 she taught an office practice-typing class for three quarters of the four-quarter school year. Frustrated by the low interest and involvement her students had shown, and inspired by an n-Ach course she took with several other teachers, Dr. DiLoretto decided to structure the typing class differently. The new structure was initiated toward the end of the first quarter in the 1966-67 school year. She replaced what had been a power-compliance oriented structure with a structure that encouraged affiliation and achievement motivation.

In the 1965-66 class, as in most typing classes, increased skill in typing was defined as progression through the text, and practice was assumed to be the only major obstacle. More practice would increase the gross number of words typed per minute (GW/M), and decrease the number of errors (E). Both of these elements were reflected in the final net words per minute (NW/M : NW/M = GW/M - [2 x E]). In 1965-66 the only way of improving was practice, practice, and still more practice.

In 1966-67, as in the previous year, either GW/M could be increased or E decreased. However, the number of tactics for accomplishing those goals was radically increased. Under the new structure, all typing test material was inspected before one took the speed test. Difficult strokings were identified by the group and solutions discussed. Also, the students were encouraged to search for personal obstacles (e.g., heavy clanking rings, mental blocks, sitting position, etc.). A variety of new tactics were discovered when the new obstacles were identified. The increased focus on personal obstacles and new tactics meant that achievement motivation should have been increased and reflected in higher typing scores.

In 1965-66 the teacher herself decided the number of words per minute equivalent to each letter grade. This helped create the standard power classroom structure. In 1966-67, the teacher and the class *collaborated* to determine the NW/M that would earn different letter grades. This shifted the structure towards n-Affiliation and away from n-Power.

In 1965-66 all students' typing speeds were posted on a bulletin board once a month. Students did not set their own goals. The following year progress was recorded quite differently. Students made daily records of their speed growth on graphs. On the basis of their graphs, students set short- and long-term scoring goals. In the realm of testing, 1965-66 typing tests were given almost daily by the teacher, who determined their length. Every week only the best score of the week was counted toward the student's course grade. In 1966-67, students decided when they would take a test, and determined the length of test appropriate to their chosen goals. They also decided whether or not to have the teacher record their scores. However, for grading purposes, students had to turn in at least one score each week. All of these changes shifted the locus of decision-making from the teacher to the students and shifted motivational structure from power to achievement.

In summary, students had opportunities to take greater personal responsibility for setting moderate-risk goals. They explored to a far greater extent whatever personal obstacles they faced and whatever instrumental activity might help overcome them. The two typing classes had an equal amount of structure, but the restructured class in 1966-67 was more flexible and open to initiative. Students determined fair rewards for their efforts and cooperation was encouraged. The structure and climate encouraged students to think and act like people with strong n-Ach.

To determine whether the change in structure had any effects on students, Dr. DiLoretto compared the beginning and terminal typing performance of students in the two types of classrooms.

The students in her 1965-66 and 1966-67 classes were comparable in intelligence as measured by the OTIS, and in ability as measured by the Nelson-Denny Test. In both years the text, typing test material, typewriters, classroom, and teacher were identical. Only the learning "game" was defined differently.

In seven of the total 30 weeks of testing, there were between one and three students absent. There was no consistent pattern of absences among students.

At the end of the third week of the first quarter in the 1966-67 class, before the new structure was introduced, the average typing speed of the two classes was an identical 39 NW/M. By the end of the third quarter, the 1966-67 class average was 66 NW/M, 54 percent more NW/M than the 1965-66 class. Nine out of the 10 students tested in the 1966-67 class did better than all 11 students tested in the 1965-66 class. The lowest scorer in the 1966-67 class was tied with the highest scorer in the 1965-66 class at 50 NW/M. These are socially and statistically significant results. The students in the Power-oriented class seem to have lost interest toward the end of the third quarter with the advent of spring vacation and the end of the typing class. By contrast, it seems that interest and effort remained high during the same period in the class structured for n-Ach and n-Aff.

A 5th grade mathematics class

These dramatic results are somewhat hard to believe. Yet, structured changes introduced by another teacher in an elementary school mathematics class resulted in equally impressive learning gains and student interest. Elementary school mathematics classes can have problems similar to those common in business education classes. Although the students are younger and the subject matter different, classes structured for power seem to generate the same problems (e.g., listless compliance, passive resistance, and rebelliousness). In 5th grade it is especially popular to "hate math." These standard problems were encountered by James McIntyre, then in his first full year of teaching. For the following year he decided to restructure the class as a different type of "game" to meet the needs of the students and subject matter more appropriately. The net result was that students learned more and liked the process of doing mathematical thinking for its own sake.

The "Math Game" was modeled after the "Origami Game," designed originally as a device for teaching achievement motivation. The Math Game curricular content consisted solely of the textbook *Elementary School Mathematics* (1964). Students' activities were structured according to the following Math Game results.

Each student contracted with the teacher to produce a chosen percentage of correct answers in each chapter of the text. Contracts were made for one chapter at a time. The student chose his own deadline for completion of the chapter. The contract then was co-signed by the student and the teacher.

The score was kept with play money of various denominations. The student's success in learning math was indicated by the amount of play money he earned. Each student was given $2,000 to start playing the game. After signing the contract, the student paid a fee for franchise and materials. This fee was directly proportional to the percentage of correct answers for which the student bid: the higher the percentage, the more the student had to pay initially. In order to earn the maximum amount for his chosen percentage, the student had to meet his contract obligations, both in percent of problems correct and deadline. The amount of money he earned was directly proportional to the goal he set. The higher the percentage of correct answers he bid for and produced, the more money he earned. The schedule of payments was as follows:

Percent Tried	Cost	Return	Rate
100	$500	$2000	4-1
90	$450	$1350	3-1
80	$350	$ 700	2-1
70	$250	$ 400	8-5
60	$150	$ 250	5-3
50	$100	$ 150	3-2

There also were three ways for the student to lose money. Although contracts could be revised or extended at any time, as long as the deadline was not less than one week away, a flat $10 fee was charged. Second, students could lose money if they did not produce the number of correct answers for which they contracted, each missing correct answer costing one percent of the payoff. Were a student to contract for 70 percent in a chapter with 400 problems (i.e., 280 correct answers) and turn in only 270 correct answers, 10 percent would be deducted from his payoff. In this case the penalty would be $40, as the payoff on a 70 percent contract was $400. The students were under no restraint to stop working after reaching their percentage goal. They could protect their investment by doing more problems than contracted for. Thus, they could hedge against possible errors and not lose, as long as they had produced the required number of correct answers. The third way to lose money concerned deadlines. Since the student set his own time goals, the penalty for being overdue was severe. For each school day a chapter was late, 10 percent of the payoff was deducted. A student contracting for 100 percent correct answers (Payoff: $2,000) lost $200 for each day over the deadline.

In order to have an adequate self-assessment of daily work and progress, graphs were issued each Monday. The teacher specifically stated that he did not want to see them. They were entirely for the personal use of the students. An explanation of their use was given in the first session, and thereafter they were only mentioned by the teacher when he passed them out each Monday. The graph merely consisted of the number on the ordinate and the seven days of the week on the abscissa.

End-of-the-year rewards were given to the six highest money winners in the class. The rewards were of the class's own choosing, and the winners had their choice from the following list: rabbit, gerbil, slot-car kit, and jug of candy. In addition, an ice cream party was promised to all those who completed the book by the end of the school year.

The scoring for the Math Game was primarily a Non-Zero-Sum system, with the exception of the special prizes for the six highest money winners. The obstacles to scoring were quite clearly defined by ways to earn money and avoid loss (i.e., production of the number of correct answers contracted, no revisions of contract due dates, no overdue contract fulfillments). In each case the obstacles were within the player and required the player to develop action strategies characteristic of people with strong achievement motivation: accurate, moderate risk taking and the use of feedback to modify goals. Decision-making was almost entirely the personal responsibility of the students. They made their own assignments, determined their own pacing, worked through the book by themselves, and sought help from Mr. McIntyre and friends as they felt the need. Often the students conferred outside of class about possible new tactics for beating the game. In their lengthy talks and calculations of the odds, they learned a lot of practical mathematics. Mr. McIntyre was able to establish a warm, friendly role as coach, consistent with the leadership style of people who foster n-Ach climates. The role of the teacher as "king of the classroom" did not exist.

Since the full battery of Stanford Achievement Tests was given in the spring of each year, it was possible to make year-to-year comparisons in the students' mathematics gain scores. From March in the third grade to March in the fourth grade the average gain was 0.2 years, from 3.8 to 4.0. From March in the fourth grade to June in the fifth grade, the average gain was 3.0 years, from 4.0 to 7.0. This achievement spurt may be measured in a different way. All 14 of the students gained over one year in mathematics during the fifth grade, while only two of the 14 gained over a year in mathematics during the fourth grade—a highly significant difference. These gains in the fifth grade are striking, especially in view of how poorly the same students did the previous year with the same teacher and text series.

Other evidence, though less scientific, may be more persuasive to teachers; namely, what happened to the individual children? Did they become grasping entrepreneurs and cutthroat businessmen? Did they work solely for the rewards? What were some of the other by-products of this structure? Mr. McIntyre's impressions were very clear. Children who did nothing in mathematics in fourth grade, except under duress, suddenly began taking their books home on weekends. Very few deadlines were missed. Many students began assessing themselves more optimistically, yet realistically, and they performed up to those standards. One boy fidgeted through the entire year in mathematics in fourth grade. Threats and stern words could not focus his attention, nor could they keep him in his seat. His total output reflected a small portion of his ability. Within the new structure, however, he chose his first goal of 70 percent with two weeks to finish the contract. Within three days he revised his goal upward to 100 percent, paid the extra fee, and did all the problems with only 11 errors out of almost 400 problems. Another similar student, a girl, was considered by the teacher to be mathematically slow when in the fourth grade. She was consistently at the bottom of the class and seldom handed in assignments. Her 100 percent contract for the first chapter was the first completed, and she had only six errors. Her error total was the lowest in the class.

Four other girls in grade four had found math an excellent time to do other things, such as writing notes to one another and playing with clay. In grade five they still clustered around each other, but were quiet except during the loud disagreements over mathematics problems. Two boys performed well on occasion in fourth grade, but also were constant behavior problems. They worked so diligently together in fifth grade that the teacher often forgot they were in the classroom. Another boy needed more structure within which to work, but resented all structures adults imposed on him. By setting his own limits and working at his own speed within a structure that he felt was his own, his work in mathematics was free from the anguish that once accompanied it.

Once during the year, several students decided to take a vacation from math for two weeks. They came to class and were allowed to relax, so long as they didn't disturb others. They had budgeted their time for the year and realized they could afford the vacation. After two weeks they returned to the task and successfully completed the year's work.

It was the teacher's impression that in the first half of fifth grade, enthusiasm was generated more by the game than by intrinsic interest in mathematics. However, in the second half of the year, with the students buoyed by the new-found competence, the game, prizes, and play money became more or less irrelevant while the pace of work continued. Mathematics itself had become interesting.

As research studies, these two experiments leave much to be

desired. The sample sizes are small. Sample characteristics that might predispose them to benefit from this type of learning structure were not measured. There is no objective assessment of the reported classroom atmosphere. Most important, there were no measures of the changes in achievement, affiliation, or power motivation. For these reasons the "experiments" should be viewed as encouraging feasibility studies that need to be replicated carefully. In addition, it is important to examine the interaction effects of giving a motivation training course to students who then have the opportunity to practice what they have learned in a course structured to reward those motives. These questions are examined in detail in the next two chapters.

Motivating Students for a
Pluralistic Society

A belief that one, two, or three motives are most central and important obviously is oversimplistic, since we live in a complex, pluralistic society where a broad range of motives is needed. Unfortunately, at present only a few motives are encouraged in most schools. Ideally, there should be as much variety in the teaching-learning process within a single school as exists outside and after school, where students are variously "required," "ordered," "coached," "persuaded," "led," "followed," "threatened," "promised," "lectured," "questioned," and "left alone." Compared to this handsome array of naturally occurring learning processes, the typical range within a school often is embarrassingly narrow. To restructure the learning process in school is to re-motivate students, since motives are processes of goal-directed thinking, acting, and feeling. A wider number of motives can be taught through the ways students learn.

A variety of motivational structures in schools is necessary preparation for a pluralistic society. These options are important also because each structure and leadership style may have built-in limitations that can be compensated for only by the availability of alternative structures and styles. For instance, some teachers feel that fostering achievement motivation stifles creativity. Other teachers argue that helping students to become creative is nice, but that most students need to learn how to get along in a competitive world. The complementary differences between learning structures for n-Ach and creativity can be illustrated best by comparing the types of implicit contracts on which they are based. Achievement-oriented contracts, such as those in the Origami and Math Games, are modeled after industrial, product-oriented contracts. The yields, as well as the quality, quantity, production time, and purchase/sales prices, are specified clearly in advance. Such contracts as models for learning are most appropriate when the learning yields can be clearly specified. In contrast, creativity-oriented contracts are modeled after research, process-oriented contracts which require that the problem be stated, along with the methods of gathering information and how much time the creative researcher will spend on the problem. The solutions cannot be described in advance since the point of the investigation is to discover answers to the problems. If the problem is difficult and the desired solution creative, then quantity, quality, time, and cost of the solution cannot be guaranteed. Requiring the information in advance only inhibits the creative effort. It is as if students were asked to tell teachers what they will know before they started learning.

Interestingly enough, the leadership styles appropriate to these two motivational processes also have reciprocal advantages and disadvantages. A leader who wants to support truly creative efforts in students must suspend critical judgment, reduce the risks of failure, and be prepared to wait a long time for results that still may be failures. By definition, creative responses and solutions are rare events. Most likely, not all students will flourish in a class with so little structure, pressure, and lack of specificity of desired goals. In fact, many of those who flounder might be productive under a leader who created an achievement-oriented structure and style. However, other students will feel cramped, stifled, and bored by the demands of a situation pressing for achievement motivation: deadlines, careful plans for goals, quality controls, regular concrete feedback on progress, and realistically calculated risk taking. The central features of achievement motivation can be anathema to the truly imaginative, free-wheeling spirit of the highly creative individual.

This is not an argument for tracking students on the basis of need for creativity and need for achievement instead of IQ. Rather than sacrifice either type of learning, both can co-exist within schools. Learning structures can be developed to foster achievement and creativity and many other valuable motives within every school. In individuals, as in cultures and schools, many motives can co-exist and should be developed. Each individual needs many strong motives to function well and enjoy the opportunities presented by a pluralistic society. One way schooling can teach these motives is through the variety of learning structures provided for students.

8.

A Final Attempt to Maximize the Yields of Achievement Motivation Training for Adolescents*

It is axiomatic that practice facilitates learning. The problem in psychological education is to determine what kind of practice maximizes the long-term usefulness of what is learned. In laboratory studies, small variations in the nature, timing, and amount of practice can be carefully controlled. The daily exigencies of schooling do not permit such elegant research. Nor is it likely that any minor changes would alter dramatically the major impact of training two years following the course. Therefore we assumed that it would require a major new opportunity in which students could practice what they learned to noticeably increase the long-term course yield. In thinking through this research question, we became increasingly concerned about what happened to our students after the course was over, and what we could do to support what they learned.

It seemed unethical to us to increase students' concerns about striving for self-chosen types of excellence, and then return them to classrooms where this process was not systematically encouraged and consciously valued. We believed the least we could do was to adapt the way in which one of their courses was taught so that they could practice and benefit from the n-Ach course in

*A number of individuals assisted in conducting this research. I am particularly indebted to teachers at Broadmeadows Junior High School, Massachusetts: Harry Bede (principal), Althea Sawyer, Marilyn Robbins, Peggy Hoyle, Joe Long, Tom Callahan, Stella Krupka, Charles Hickey, Mary Bozolian, Jo Ann Conroy, Scott Newell, Tom Regan, and Pat Cheverie. Several others were invaluable in collecting and collating the research data: Diane Tabor, James McIntyre, Beverly Silver, Steve Rodewald, and Elizabeth Wilson.

school. We were supported in this concern for our students by the n-Ach course teachers, who also wanted to know how they could carry into their own classrooms some of the methods and principles that they were using in the motivation course itself. It seemed important to respect these concerns and to test the assumptions on which they were based. Our hypothesis, then, was quite simple. We predicted that those students who also had a chance to practice what they learned for one semester in an achievement-oriented mathematics class would report a year to two years later that the n-Ach course was significantly more useful to them than students who only participated in the n-Ach course.

This experiment also allowed us to enter the classic debate over what is the most effective teaching strategy. Broadly characterized, there are those who argue that the pace, content, and mode of teaching should respond to the' ebb and flow of students' interests. Pestalozzi, Rousseau, Dewey, Piaget, Neill, and, most recently, Silberman (1970), who advocates the English model of "open education," all share the conviction that learning proceeds best when the content is cued in by the individual's unique and changing needs. Problems in designing curricula are obviated in part by creating rich, flexible responsive learning environments. Students proceed at their own rate along self-chosen paths towards learning goals often not known in advance. The teacher is something more than just another resource in the environment and something less than leader, director, and expert. Through these means, advocates reason, learning ultimately is most productive and satisfying.

It is a classic debate because there have always been those who believe that teaching is most efficient when the outcomes are clearly specified in advance. This makes it possible for teaching to be thorough, systematic, and effective in channelling student interests through the predetermined subject matter goals. From this perspective, pedagogy is a problem of managing students' responses to teacher-determined learning goals. This was the predominant orientation during the Middle Ages, when education was rigorously focused on attaining a more nearly perfect and well-defined relationship to God. Teaching students to fear falling from grace was the principal vehicle for insuring that the teacher could direct students' learning. Surprisingly, the modern proponents of this orientation take their lead not from the clergy but from industrial psychologists like Mager (1962), who start with rigorous operational definitions of the instructional objectives. Whether through "contracts," learning by rote, traditional power-oriented teaching, or sophisticated multi-media and programmed instruction, these teachers all work for student mastery of specific subject matter.

In the field of psychological education the prevailing ethic of maximizing satisfaction is conveyed in the titles, tone, and substance of two recent books in the field: *Education and Ecstasy* (Leonard, 1968), and *Joy* (Schutz, 1967). The wisdom and efficacy of this orientation in this field, however, is empirically unsubstantiated. When we tried to predict whether the Satisfaction- or Mastery-oriented approach would most increase n-Ach, we were clearly uncertain. For each approach we could envision two opposite outcomes. It was possible that students in a Mastery-oriented n-Ach course would know more at the end of the course but dislike the learning process sufficiently to forget it faster and use it less. It was also possible that hard-won new skills and concepts would be more highly valued, retained longer, and used more than in a Satisfaction-oriented n-Ach course. On the other hand, we foresaw the possibility that students in a Satisfaction-oriented n-Ach course might learn objectively less but subjectively enjoy it and use it significantly more. Yet it seemed possible, too, that satisfaction during the course would be insufficient to sustain a carefully planned achievement project a year or so later. Overall, the classic debate seemed worth pursuing here, since virtually any significant difference in the outcome of the two types of courses would constitute useful information and be interesting. Even a "no significant difference" finding would be interesting, because it would fly in the face of the predominant practice and assumed superiority of Satisfaction-oriented teaching in the field of psychological education.

Procedures

Sample and design. The students in this study were drawn from the ninth grade at Broadmeadows Junior High School in a predominantly lower-middle and upper-lower class neighborhood in a suburb near Boston. To examine both basic questions in this experiment we needed a 2 x 2 design consisting of the following four groups: (1) students who took a Satisfaction-oriented n-Ach course and had an opportunity to apply what they learned in a mathematics course restructured to emphasize n-Ach; (2) students who took a Satisfaction n-Ach course but were in a normal mathematics class; (3) students in a Mastery-oriented n-Ach course who could practice in a math class restructured to emphasize n-Ach; and (4) students in a Mastery-oriented n-Ach course taking a normal mathematics course. For purely administrative reasons within the school, both restructured mathematics classes were in algebra, while the normal classes were studying "Basic Math." This difference is reflected in several background characteristics of the samples described in Table 8.1 below. Since analysis of the training yields is done separately for boys and girls, the data below are presented for boys and girls separately.

The most important differences in this table are for the boys. Those who were in the restructured algebra classes have significantly higher IQ (t = 2.73, p <.02) and come from higher SES backgrounds (t = 2.52, p <.02). As Parsons (1959) points out, IQ and SES are the two principal bases for orienting students towards college or vocational training. Further, the choice of the type of math to take in 9th grade is one of the first and best indicators of this manpower allocation. This appears to be the case here, since 12 of 14 boys in the algebra class (86 percent) went to an academic high school in 10th grade, whereas only 4 of 16 boys in the basic math class (25 percent) went to the academic high school (χ^2 = 11.75, p <.001). The others went to the vocational-technical high school in the community.* This initial difference between the boys in the achievement-oriented algebra class and the normal basic math class will have to be taken into consideration later when analyzing and interpreting the effects of additional classroom practice in increasing the n-Ach course yields. Fortunately, this systematic difference does not occur for the girls. There are

---

*Records were not available for two of the boys in the restructured algebra group and three of the boys in the basic math group.

Table 8.1

*Background Characteristics of Samples
in the Final Attempt to Maximize the Yields of
n-Ach Training*

	MALES				FEMALES			
	Restructured Math Class		Normal Math Class		Restructured Math Class		Normal Math Class	
BACKGROUND VARIABLES	*Mastery* $n = 8$[1]	*Satisfaction* $n = 8$	*Mastery* $n = 10$	*Satisfaction* $n = 9$	*Mastery* $n = 13$	*Satisfaction* $n = 11$	*Mastery* $n = 10$	*Satisfaction* $n = 13$
Age in years and months at time of n-Ach course	14 yrs. 10 mo.[2]	14 yrs. 7 mo.	15 yrs. 2 mo.	15 yrs. 4 mo.	14 yrs. 8 mo.	14 yrs. 6 mo.	14 yrs. 9 mo.	15 yrs. 0 mo.

IQ[3]	111.8 (n = 6)[5]	105.3 (n = 7)	96.1 (n = 9)	91.2	107.8 (n = 12)	106.5	106.9	95.9 (n = 11)
SES[4]	4.2	4.4 (n = 7)	5.1 (n = 7)	5.6 (n = 5)	4.8 (n = 12)	5.0	3.9 (n = 7)	4.8 (n = 10)
v-Achievement	-0.25	3.14 (n = 7)	3.30	3.00 (n = 7)	5.17 (n = 12)	0.78 (n = 9)	3.00 (n = 9)	2.90 (n = 10)

1. These sample sizes are slightly smaller than the actual number in each group, since we dropped from the subsequent analysis all students who missed more than 50 percent of the training sessions, i.e., 6 or more of the 10 sessions. There were no more than 3 from any one group.

2. The scores reported in each cell are group means.

3. This IQ is the score from the California Test of Mental Maturity administered in October, 1967, several months prior to the course.

4. Socioeconomic Status is based on ranking of fathers' occupation, using Hall, J. and Jones, D.C., Social Grading of Occupations, *British Journal of Sociology*, 1950 (1). A number of fathers were deceased (ranking of 0). This reduced the sample size in several instances.

5. When the statistic is based on incomplete data, the actual sample size is given.

no significant differences between the girls in the algebra classes and the basic math classes for any of these background variables, nor for the percentages attending the academic high school in 10th grade.

When the population is broken down according to what type of n-Ach course they received, there are no significant differences for the two groups of males on any of the background variables. For the girls, however, the Mastery group had significantly higher IQ scores ($t = 2.15$, $p < .05$) and significantly higher v-Ach scores ($t = 2.30$, $p < .02$). Of these two differences, perhaps v-Ach is potentially more important, given the predictive value for boys regarding the reported usefulness of the n-Ach course. At a minimum here, and for the boys in the two types of mathematics classes, it will be important to control for these differences statistically in analyzing the results of the training.

Treatment. The essential characteristic of the Mastery-oriented n-Ach course was the requirement that students demonstrate they surpass a minimum level of knowledge or skill at each stage of the course before proceeding to the next stage. The structure of the Mastery n-Ach course was adopted from the "Math Game" (Chapter 7). However, instead of contracting for a percent of correct answers in a chapter, the Mastery n-Ach course had four contracts, covering (1) the experience of n-Ach, (2) how n-Ach is conceptualized, (3) how n-Ach relates to the person's life, and (4) ways to practice this motive. These contracts correspond to the middle four steps in the six-step learning sequence described previously. In each contract there were ways to earn or lose mastery points. Each student had to earn at least 25 points per contract and 100 points overall to pass the course.

The first part of each contract contained a short introduction explaining the general ideas of the unit and specifying a learning goal. It also described two minimum requirements a student had to meet to fulfill the contract and to show that he had "mastered" the material. One requirement was to pass the contract test, worth 10 points (each contract gave a sample test item). The other requirement was to earn 15 points by doing one of the many listed bonus activities. The second part of the contract described two sets of bonus activities. Each activity was worth 15 points. The division between the two sets was somewhat arbitrary. Basically, the first set of activities was more stringently tied to the contract criteria. The second group was more open, creative, and "for fun." If the student did only one activity, he was asked to choose from among the first group. The third part of the contract was a list of resources that could be used in preparing to pass the contract test and do the bonus activities.

Other point-getting methods were built into the contracts. For example, a team of students could work together to complete a goal or project and earn extra points. On the other hand, students were penalized points if they failed to meet the contract deadline—each day late incurred a two-point penalty. Students could revise their contracts to change the deadline or to add or drop bonus activities, but the revision cost five points, and only one revision was allowed. If a student did not complete the bonus activities he signed for, he not only lost those potential points, but also was penalized two points for each incomplete.

A typical contract included about a week's worth of activities organized around the resources. These contracts are presented in full along with a longer descriptive commentary in *Teaching Achievement Motivation* (Alschuler *et al.*, 1970). The following table summarizes the essential elements of the four contracts.

Each contract was introduced to the students in small groups of 9 or 10. Later in the same day there was a large-group presentation aimed to get across the basic content and principles of the contract, and at the same time to capture interest and involvement. For example, we began the unit on action strategies with the Origami Game. We introduced the 10 thoughts using the n-Ach Math Game. After the initial presentation, there were about two days of workshops which students signed up for in advance, after hearing a brief description or watching a demonstration of what the workshop would entail. Finally, at least one day was devoted to small-group discussions, testing, and make-up for other workshops and contracts. In addition, students would use class time to work on projects and bonuses when they weren't involved in resource workshops.

The Satisfaction n-Ach' course was set up like a learning carnival, with several simultaneous options for students to learn

Table 8.2

*Mastery-Oriented n-Ach Course
Contract Scheme*

Purpose	Criteria	Resources
A. n-Ach Action Strategies (experience). To learn to recognize and use four n-Ach action strategies:	1. Identify and distinguish between:	1. Vocabulary workshops for concepts like strategy, initiative, etc.
1. Realistic goal setting	a. realistic and unrealistic (very high/very low) risk-taking	2. Ring Toss game
2. Proper use of feedback	b. concrete immediate feedback vs. general, delayed feedback	3. Darts-Dice game
3. Taking personal responsibility	c. personal responsibility and leaving things to fate, luck, etc.	4. Films
4. Researching the environment	2. Demonstrate the action strategies in a simple decision-making game	5. Case studies and discussion
		6. Guest speakers
B. n-Ach Thoughts (conceptualize). To learn the ten n-Ach thoughts and the goal-setting patterns they form. To relate these to the action strategies	1. Recognize and identify examples of achievement imagery and achievement goals, so as to be able to distinguish them from other goals, such as task affiliation, power	1. Ten Thoughts
		2. Story writing workshop
		3. Short story and side topics based on achievement theme. Visit by the author
		4. Crossword puzzle

2. Identify the various n-Ach thoughts in short written illustrations

3. Diagram the goal-setting pattern

4. Define and give illustrations of AIm and other n-Ach thoughts—NEED, HOS, FOF, ACT, WO, PO, HELP, FaF, SuF

5. Fill in blank stories

6. Case study and discussion

C. Self-Study (relate). To have the student relate n-Ach syndrome to three areas of his own life:
1. Reality demands
2. Self-image and personal goals
3. Values of groups and culture to which he belongs

Engage in dialogue with instructor (and small group) where issues of n-Ach and reality demands, self-image, and group values are specifically discussed personally by each student.

1. Group discussions organized around questions to help students consider possible relevance—the usefulness of n-Ach in their lives
2. Case studies
3. Films
4. Role plays
5. Guest speakers
6. Admiration ladder
7. Who Am I?
8. Achieving

D. Goal Setting (practice). To have the student actually apply what he has learned to a personal achievement goal.

Complete a one-week goal-setting project based on achievement goal, and deliberately employing achievement planning. Provide feedback and measurement of progress.

1. Aiming
2. Group discussion
3. Individual help from the instructors
4. Help from team members

the course material. Students were encouraged to go to the "booths" or groups that interested them most. Teachers were encouraged to adapt and improvise according to the emerging needs of the students. The teachers' goal was to keep students "turned on." The content of the Satisfaction n-Ach course consisted of the same games, exercises, and role plays as in the Mastery-oriented course. However, there were no contracts, no tests, and no points to be earned. The time used in the Mastery course to explain directions, give, and grade tests was used in the Satisfaction course for small-group informal discussions and impromptu activities. One activity in particular exemplifies the difference in tone between this course and the Mastery course. Since there were no tests requiring students to prove they had the basic concepts thoroughly in hand, the staff proposed a test situation that the students accepted enthusiastically; it turned out to be the high point of the course. They held a teach-in. Staff and students invited members of the school committee, representatives from the administration, the curriculum supervisors, newspaper reporters, and interested school personnel and taught them a two-hour mini-course in achievement motivation that subsequently was featured in an illustrated article in the local paper.

Half of the students in the Mastery course and half the students in the Satisfaction course had a mathematics class restructured to provide them with a clear opportunity to exercise their newly acquired skills in achievement planning and acting. The structure was modelled as closely as possible on the Origami Game (Alschuler, Tabor and McIntyre, 1970), which itself was the prototype for the original Math Game (Chapter 7) and the Mastery n-Ach course. The rules and contract format are presented in detail in Chapter 9. However, the main factors can be summarized quickly here. Students signed a contract for each chapter of the text (Peters and Schaaf, 1963), worth a maximum of 1000 points. In the contract, students specified their projected completion date, their total point goal, and the percentage contribution they wanted tests and problem sets to make toward their point goal. Chapter grades were determined as a joint function of the actual number of points they earned and how close it was to their goal. This encouraged students to set high but personally realistic goals. Students paced themselves, and could work alone or in groups, in school or outside of school. The teacher acted as a coach and spent most of his time talking with individual students.

The format for the normal basic math classes was quite traditional. Each day the teacher discussed the corrected homework from the previous day, presented a new concept, answered questions from the group, assigned new homework, and let students begin work as she spent the remaining time with individual students. This teacher determined the pace and quantity of homework, due dates, test values, and grades. Both here and in the restructured class, a Non-Zero-Sum scoring system was used. According to the coding system for motivational games presented in Chapter 7, the normal mathematics class was primarily power-oriented, secondarily achievement-oriented, with affiliation a poor third. In contrast, the restructured class was primarily achievement-oriented, secondarily affiliation-oriented, and least oriented towards power. Both classes and the two achievement motivation courses were conducted during the second semester of the 9th grade.

Measures. The main measures of course effectiveness were obtained through telephone interviews conducted twice, 6 to 8 months after the course and again 16 to 18 months after the course. The format of the interview and scoring procedures are described in complete detail elsewhere (Alschuler *et al.,* 1970). The interview generates data to assess the impact of the course on summer work, summer leisure, school term activities, future plans, and the overall usefulness of the course.

Two weeks after the end of the n-Ach courses, students were given a test to assess (1) their knowledge of how n-Ach is conceptualized, and (2) how satisfied they were with their n-Ach course. Knowledge was tested by asking students to (a) reproduce the 10 elements in the n-Ach planning pattern diagram, (b) define each element, and (c) give an example of each element. Each correct answer was given one point, thus yielding a range of possible scores from 0 to 30.

Satisfaction was asssessed in two ways: (a) students were asked to indicate on a 10-point scale how much they enjoyed the course: "1" (much less than any other course I've ever taken), "10" (much more than any other course I've ever taken); (b) students checked the three aspects of the n-Ach course they liked most and the three they liked least from the following list: the casual, informal setting; having many teachers around; the games, cocoa, and doughnuts; being able to choose from a number of activities; learning about yourself; learning the action strategies; learning Achievement planning; being on a team; working in small groups; doing an individual goal setting project; the discussions; knowing in advance what would happen next; not knowing what would happen next; getting up early for the n-Ach course;* having visitors in the class;† the films; the slide tape presentation; working for points; setting your own deadlines;† the contracts;† not having homework or tests;• or teaching visiting grownups about n-Ach.•

Results

1. *Immediate Post-Course Results.* Two weeks after the Mastery and Satisfaction courses were over, we assessed how well the students could conceptualize the n-Ach planning pattern and how much they enjoyed the course. These data are presented in Table 8.3.

As these data make clear, holding students responsible for mastery of the concepts during the course does not result in higher recall of the concepts two weeks after the course. Nor does catering to the shifting interests significantly improve recall. For the boys and girls in this experiment, both approaches were equally effective. However, these two types of training had marked effects on how much the boys enjoyed the courses; the boys liked the Satisfaction-oriented training far more than the

*To obtain enough time in a solid block, the daily course meeting began 40 minutes before the official opening of school and ran through the first period.

†These three items were asked only of the students in the Mastery n-Ach course.

• These two items were asked only of the students in the Satisfaction n-Ach course.

Table 8.3

Percent of Students Above the Mean on
Immediate Post-Course Yields

Yields	Boys			Girls		
	Mastery Course	Satis-faction Course	P*	Mastery Course	Satis-faction Course	P
Knowledge of n-Ach planning pattern[1]	8/17 (47%)	10/16 (63%)	ns	8/19 (42%)	13/23 (57%)	ns
Reported sat-isfaction with the course[2]	3/17 (18%)	14/16 (87%)	$\chi^2 = 13.43$ **	7/21 (33%)	12/23 (52%)	ns

* = $p < .05$; ** $p < .01$ 2 tail values based on χ^2 corrected for continuity.

1. Above the mean for the boys was 9 or more; above the mean for the girls was 17 or more.
2. Above the mean for the boys was 7 or more; above the mean for the girls was 9 or 10.

Table 8.4

The Most Frequently Endorsed Course Attributes Liked and Disliked by Students

	Boys (n = 33)		Girls (n = 42)	
	liked most	liked least	liked most	liked least
Mastery Course	Games (8)[1]	Getting up early (12)	Casual setting (14)	Working for points (13)
	Cocoa and Doughnuts (8)	Contracts (10)	Games (10)	Getting up early (11)
	Casual setting (7)	Many teachers (9)	Learning about self (9)	Discussions (9)
	Able to choose activities (6)	Small Groups (9)	Cocoa and Doughnuts (8)	Goal setting project (7)
		Working for points (9)		

Satisfaction course			
Games (12)	Getting up early (10)	Games (13)	Getting up early (18)
Cocoa and Doughnuts (8)	Goal setting problems (5)	No homework (13)	Goal setting discussions (6)
Learn about self (7)	Not knowing what was going to happen (4)	Casual setting (12)	Many teachers (6)
Small groups (7)	Discussions (4)		
	Many teachers (4)		

1. Numbers in parentheses are number of endorsements. Students were free to endorse as many aspects as they chose.

Mastery-oriented training. For the girls, again here, both courses were equally enjoyable.

It is possible to identify in greater detail what it is these groups liked and disliked most about the courses by examining the data from the checklist of course attributes.

Certain features were liked most and least regardless of sex or type of course. The students generally liked the games, casual setting, cocoa, and doughnuts, or what might be characterized as a party atmosphere. In contrast, students generally disliked getting up early, the goal setting project, and so many teachers, i.e., the features most like "school." The boys in the Mastery course disliked the contract format and working for points even more than having to get up early. These are the factors that appear to be responsible for the particularly marked dissatisfaction of these boys with the Mastery n-Ach course. These data are not sufficient to justify deleting the contract format and working for points if the Mastery-oriented training results in larger long-term gains. These special aspects of the course must be reviewed in the perspective of the long-term yields.

2. *Long-Term Yields.* To indicate the general level of n-Ach course effectiveness, Table 8.5 presents the percentages of reported usefulness one-half year and 1½ years after the course for all sub-groups combined.

In general these results are comparable to previous n-Ach courses in yielding approximately 30 percent at the +2 Usefulness level 1½ years after the course.

In subsequent analyses, the principal yield measure used is the higher of the two scores in the reported usefulness of the n-Ach course. In effect this gives students the benefit of the doubt. Some may make an early major application of the course but not be engaged in a major application a year and a half later, or vice versa. There does not seem to be any *a priori* reason for assuming that the usefulness of the course should remain constant. Since the pattern of results in the following analyses for the "maximum usefulness" scores are duplicated in virtually all cases for the other scales from each of the interviews, I will present results for the "maximum usefulness" score and note exceptions

Table 8.5

Number of Students Reporting "Major" and "Minor"
Usefulness of the n-Ach Course 6 Months and 18 Months
After the n-Ach Course

	first telephone interview (6 mo.)		second telephone interview (18 mo.)		one or both interviews	
Boys						
Major Usefulness (+2)[1]	2/30	(7%)	7/23	(30%)	8/30	(27%)
Minor or Major Usefulness (+1, +2)	10/30	(33%)	9/23	(39%)	13/30	(43%)
Girls						
Major Usefulness (+2)	6/43	(14%)	6/39	(15%)	12/43	(28%)
Major or Minor Usefulness (+1 or +2)	28/43	(65%)	19/39	(49%)	32/43	(74%)

1. These scores refer to the telephone interview scoring system. Scores on this scale range from +2 to -1.

Table 8.6

Maximum Usefulness[1] Reported by Students in the Satisfaction and Mastery n-Ach Courses with Achievement-Oriented or Normal Mathematics Classes

Math Class	Boys n-Ach course			Girls n-Ach course		
	Satisfaction	Mastery	Totals	Satisfaction	Mastery	Totals
Achievement-oriented	4/8 (50%)	4/8 (50%)	8/16 (50%)	5/10 (50%)	12/12 (100%)	17/22 (77%)
			NS			NS
Normal	1/6 (17%)	4/8 (50%)	5/14 (36%)	6/10 (60%)	9/10 (90%)	15/20 (75%)
Totals	5/14 (36%)	8/16 (50%)		11/20 (55%)	21/22 (95%)	
		NS		$\chi^2 = 10.34$ $p < .01$		

1. Data presented in the cells is the number of students with scores of +1 or +2.

to the generality of the findings for other scales only when they occur.

In spite of the dissatisfaction experienced by the boys in the Mastery course, it was as useful to them as to the boys in the Satisfaction-oriented n-Ach course. Short-term satisfaction does not appear to be a good predictor of the long-term usefulness for boys. The opportunity to practice what they learned in an Achievement-oriented mathematics class also does not appear to make much difference in the long run. There are no other significant differences between the Satisfaction and Mastery groups or between boys who had an Achievement-oriented mathematics class and those in the normal mathematics class on any of the other interview variables for the first or second interview. In short, there is no evidence that any of the experimental variations had a long-term effect on the boys.

In contrast for the girls, while there were no differences in knowledge or satisfaction immediately after the course, a significantly larger number of girls in the Mastery-oriented n-Ach course report that it was very useful to them later. Since these two groups differed significantly in pre-course IQ and v-Ach, these variables must be proven unrelated to the long-term yields in order to attribute the final differences in yields to n-Ach courses. In fact, IQ is not related to the long-term yields, but initial v-Ach is significantly related to the reported usefulness of the course (Pearson r = .589). Using a non-parametric statistic, 8 of 10 girls who were above the mean in maximum n-Ach usefulness (+2) were also above the mean in v-Ach, while only 9 of 28 girls below the mean in maximum n-Ach usefulness were above the mean in v-Ach. (χ^2 = 5.41 corrected for continuity; p = .02 two tail.) V-Ach appears to be a predictor of n-Ach course usefulness. This is consistent with the prior results for boys. Perhaps this relationship was not found previously for girls due to the much smaller sample size. In any case, we must control for this initial difference and then re-examine the resultant difference between groups in reported course usefulness. This re-analysis is presented in Table 8.7.

When initial differences in v-Ach are controlled, the resultant long-term difference in reported usefulness of the course disap-

Table 8.7

The Reported Long-Term Usefulness of Mastery and Satisfaction n-Ach Training for Girls After Controlling for Initial Differences in v-Ach

Level of initial v-Ach	Number of cases		Number of girls above (+) or below (-) median reported course usefulness for that level of v-Ach			
	Mastery	Satis-faction	Mastery		Satis-faction	
			+	-	+	-
High (+7 to +9)	7	2	5	2	0	2
Middle (+3 to +5)	9	8	2	7	2	6
Low (-9 to +1)	4	9	3	1	2	7
Totals	20	19	10	10	4	15

	-	+
Mastery	10	10
Satisfaction	15	4

$\chi^2 = 2.40$ corrected for continuity

$p < .02$ two tail

pears. This long-term yield is more a function of the pre-course level of Achievement valuing than of the n-Ach course differences studied here. In summary, there are no long-term differences in yields for boys or for girls attributable to either of the two major treatment variables.

Before attempting to put these results in perspective, we should dwell briefly on a positive finding. The girls in this experiment reported a significantly higher percent of "maximum usefulness" than the boys. Thirty-two of 42 girls reported a maximum usefulness of +1 or +2 compared to only 13 of 30 boys (χ^2 = 10:34; p <.01, two tailed*). This is a higher percentage for girls than for any of the groups of boys in any of the previous experiments. Thus, it challenges the earlier conclusion that the n-Ach training is more effective for boys than for girls. Because there are so many other differences between this group of girls and previous groups (e.g., school, age, course style, summed usefulness ratings, and v-Ach level), it is difficult to determine the reason for this higher percentage of long-term usefulness. However, these results, for whatever reason, do justify somewhat more optimistic expectations about the usefulness of n-Ach training for girls.

It is difficult, time consuming, expensive, and sometimes ultimately unrewarding, as in this experiment, to collect, code, collate, and analyze long-term course yields. There is the further difficulty in sequential research, such as this, that variations in experimental courses must be chosen prior to obtaining the long-term results of the previous experimental courses. For both of these reasons, it would be advantageous to identify short-term yields that were effective predictors of the long-term yields. This would save time and energy that might otherwise be wasted on several years of data collection, and allow immediate adjustments to be made from one course to the next. In addition to these advantages, the nature of the short-term predictors might provide clues as to how learning in the course is transformed into useful applications. Is it, for instance, retained conceptualizations that subsequently are used? Or, perhaps, is it memory of the "Achievement turn-on" that is later sought in new achievement-

*These data are presented in Table 8.6.

oriented situations? It would be extremely useful if either of our immediate post-course measures (recall of the n-Ach planning pattern or satisfaction with the course) predicted reported usefulness. However, increased efficiency is not to be won so easily, since neither of these two measures in fact correlates significantly with the reported usefulness of n-Ach training for the boys or for the girls.

Discussion

From the perspective of these results the original hypothesis now has the character of unsubstantiated myth, even though widely believed by psychological educators. First, Mastery-oriented training is just as potent in the long run as Satisfaction-oriented training. In the short run, for girls, it is equally satisfying and results in as much conceptual learning. Only for the boys is it less satisfying. In other respects for boys as well, Mastery-oriented training is equally productive. The implication is that a wide range of teaching styles probably are viable, provided the important components of the course are actively taught. In spite of the extreme rhetoric of advocates for both styles, we have no evidence that favors one approach over the other as far as the long-range gains from achievement motivation training are concerned.

Second, short-term levels of conceptual knowledge and satisfaction are not good predictors of long-term course usefulness. Since these are the two principal types of measures that nearly all psychological educators currently use to evaluate their success, this finding suggests that much ongoing practice may be ill advised and misleading, especially if changes in training are made specifically to maximize immediate levels of knowledge or satisfaction. These indices have the virtues of being convenient, hallowed by the sheer history of their continued use, and—on the face of it—look like they would be important predictors of long-term gain. In this research they are not. There are as many dissatisfied and relatively unknowledgeable course graduates who ultimately make great use of the course as there are bright and shining "A" students who apply what they learned in a major project. Most teachers gain tremendous personal satisfaction when students leave their courses knowledgeable and happy. It is possible that this mutually pleasurable and assumed successful state distracts teachers from organizing their courses towards short-term learning goals that actually *do* lead to long-term gains. Unfortunately, this possibility must remain a moot question. In the area of psychological education, we do not know what end-of-course yields should be the goals in an overall strategy for obtaining maximum long-term usefulness. It is tempting to generalize to more traditional forms of education from these results, since what evidence there is (and that is very little) is consistent with these findings (e.g., McClelland *et al.,* 1958).

Third, practice doesn't always help. That is too broadly stated, of course, but it is clear that the elaborate semester-long restructuring of the mathematics classes to mimic the structure of the Mastery course and many of the n-Ach course games did not contribute to the long-term gains. One way of putting this into perspective is to compare it as an input to teaching the Achievement Planning pattern. When this short conceptual input is subtracted from the n-Ach course, as it was in two of the previous experiments, the long-term yields decreased. In contrast, lengthy practice in the math class neither contributes to nor detracts from the long-term yields from the n-Ach course. Clearly, it is the nature of the input that matters, not the length or extent of the input. And just as clearly, this kind of practice did not help. But we must also be a bit suspicious about the nature of the restructured math classes. What kind of practice was it? What was it like in the restructured mathematics classes? The boys disliked the contracts and the working for points in the Mastery n-Ach course. Did they also dislike these features in the restructured math class? This restructuring was designed to match the math game as closely as possible, but perhaps the early results with the math game were not replicated here? If so, then the restructured mathematics classes must be assessed in detail (as they are in the next chapter).

Finally, differences in methods, style, and practice are not as important determinants of long-term usefulness as pre-course levels of v-Ach. This conclusion is a specific, small extension of Coleman's (1966a) finding from his nationwide study of education that certain attitudinal variables were more important determinants of gain than teacher training, physical facilities, and equipment combined. These results continue to fly in the face of ingrained optimism that, fortuitously, it is precisely those aspects of education we can control that are the most important determinants of gain. Data continue to refute this. A closer look at this particular extension of Coleman's general conclusion may be helpful. According to deCharms *et al.* (1955), "a consciously high desire for achievement (v-Ach) tends to be associated with conformity, a high valuation of expert authority, and a low valuation of unsuccessful people." These are the students in an n-Ach course who see the training as valuable in helping them avoid being unsuccessful; they believe the instructor, and conform to the planning patterns and action strategies taught to facilitate success. If any of these individual attributes were absent, the course would be markedly less effective—regardless of teacher style, amount of practice, etc. If the student doesn't value what is being taught, believe in the instructor, or use the processes he learned, then obviously the long-term yields will be less. This does not belittle the efforts of teachers, nor reduce the need for teachers to seek the most effective pedagogy available. It merely reasserts the obvious necessity of reciprocity between student needs and what teachers teach, if meaningful, long-term learning is to occur.

9.
The Algebra Game*

Several of the questions raised in the last two chapters can be answered only by a more thorough study of the effects produced by restructuring the way students learn. Can the salience of motives in students' lives be raised or lowered by restructuring the rules of the learning game? What are the initial motives and attitudes that predispose a student to benefit from specific learning structures? What happens in a classroom structure to emphasize achievement motivation? How is the classroom climate different from other, more normal classrooms? What do students like most and least about the new learning structure? Given answers to these questions, it may be possible to understand why the opportunity to practice n-Ach in a restructured algebra class did not appreciably improve the long-term yields of the n-Ach training as reported in the previous chapter. To answer these questions we need to replicate and extend the highly suggestive experiment with the restructured 5th grade mathematics class, but this time with a larger 9th grade sample, who are given a number of motive and attitude measures before, during, and after their restructured algebra class.

Procedures
Treatment: Algebra Game and Normal Algebra
The Algebra Game, like the Math Game and the Mastery-oriented n-Ach course, was modeled after the Origami Game (Alschuler, Tabor and McIntyre, 1970), which was designed to

*This experiment was made possible through the generous efforts of Scott Newell, Tom Regan, and James McIntyre.

stimulate an intense, prototypic experience of achievement motivation. Each of these games or learning structures has a Non-Zero-Sum scoring system, shifts much of the decision-making from the teacher to the students, and makes the obstacles to success as objective, external, and non-interpersonal as possible. Theoretically, these structures emphasize achievement motivation more than affiliation or power motivation. Minor modifications in the original Math Game rules had to be made to accommodate a different textbook and age group of students. However, the format and structure was made as similar as possible to the Math Game and the Mastery-oriented n-Ach course.

In the Algebra Game, as in its several predecessors, each round involved completing a contract. Each chapter in the algebra text* constituted the material covered by a contract. Each contract potentially was worth 1,000 points, which were earned by submitting correct answers to problem sets and by completing a chapter test. Each student could choose the relative weight given to working problem sets and taking the chapter test in accumulating contract points. For instance, one student who preferred to reduce his risk could elect to have 80 percent of his points come from problem sets and only 20 percent from the test. Within the problem sets, students had the additional option of doing the harder problems, worth two points, or more of the easier problems, worth one point each. Others who got bored with problem sets could choose a minimum of 20 percent and rely on results from the chapter test, worth 80 percent of the score. The allowable range was 20 percent to 80 percent, i.e., all students had to work some problems and take the test. Students also could lose points through incorrect answers and by missing the self-chosen contract deadline—50 points the first day and 20 points each day thereafter.

A novel feature of the Algebra Game compared to normal algebra was the "bid-made" matrix for determining grades (Table 9.1). The structure of this matrix encouraged each student to set the highest, personally realistic goal he could set. It was not wise

*Peters and Schaaf, *Algebra: A Modern Approach I*, Princeton, D. Van Nostrand, Inc., 1963.

Figure 9.1

Bid-Made Matrix Method of Determining Letter Grades in the Algebra Game

POINTS MADE

POINTS BID	599 or less	600-650	651-700	701-750	751-800	801-850	851-900	901-950	951+
951+	D-	D-	D	D+	C-	C	C+	B+	A+
901-950	D-	D	D+	C-	C	C+	B	A	A
851-900	D-	D+	C-	C	C+	B-	A-	A-	A-
801-850	D-	D+	C-	C+	B-	B+	B+	B+	B+
751-800	D	D+	C	C+	B	B	B	B	B
701-750	D	D+	C	B-	B-	B-	B-	B-	B-
651-700	D	C-	C+	C+	C+	C+	C+	C+	C+
600-650	D	C	C	C	C	C	C	C	C
599 or less	D	D	D	D	D	D	D	D	D

to set a low point goal and then exceed it, because a student could only get a letter grade at the level bid, e.g., note the rows beyond the diagonal. If he bid 651 and made 801, he still would have received a C+. Had he bid more realistically to begin with, say perhaps 751, his letter grade for earning 801 points would have been B instead of C+ for the same work. This aspect of the matrix encouraged students to set challenging goals for themselves. However, if they set goals too high for themselves, they ran major risks of failure. If a student bid for 951 points and made 801, he could have received a C, whereas if he had bid 801 in the beginning and earned 801 or more, he would have received a letter grade of B+ instead of C. In these ways the matrix encouraged students to set challenging but realistic goals, an action strategy characteristic of people with high need for achievement.

Unquestionably, this matrix rewarded or penalized students for behavior that was not mathematics proficiency in the strictest sense. It was designed to reward n-Achievement-oriented action strategies. Whether this is good or bad depends on each teacher's own value hierarchy. In this experiment the bid-made matrix was an essential method of encouraging increased achievement motivation in the students, a desired and predicted outcome.

It is difficult to describe a typical day in the Algebra Game classroom we studied, since there was no one agenda. Students were free to work in overall groups, individually, or to seek help from the teacher when needed. At the beginning of class, usually about half of the students would begin work immediately. One fourth would dally until they were gently prodded, and the final few students would be at the teacher's desk with questions and requests. After this initial phase the teacher usually spent his time attending to the bookkeeping and test-giving functions of the Algebra Game, or working with individual students.

In contrast, a typical day in the normal algebra class began with a review of the previous night's homework, often called "story telling time," a reference to the number of excuses given for incomplete homework. Difficult problems were worked on the blackboard with the help of students solicited by expert questioning. This review flowed naturally into the lecture presentation of the new concept to be learned and practiced in the next night's homework. The final portion of the class almost always was spent beginning that night's homework.

In the normal algebra classes, grades were earned by doing well on the chapter tests and weekly quizzes. At the end of each grading period, the total scores were converted to letter grades using a normal curve. Some weight in special instances was given for extra homework, tenacity on tough problems, or good participation in class. Virtually no decisions were left up to the students regarding the tests, the homework, the grading, the pace, or the method of getting the work done. As a result, the principal differences between the Algebra Game and the normal algebra class lay in the relative emphases on n-Achievement and n-Power. The Zero-Sum scoring system and the teacher's control of decision-making in the normal algebra class emphasized power motivation, whereas, in comparison, the Algebra Game rules emphasized n-Achievement over n-Power through its Non-Zero-Sum scoring and greater number and type of decisions made by students. Both types of classes neither encouraged nor discouraged n-Affiliation through the formal rule structure.*

Measures

We attempted to assess what was happening in the classroom in three ways: (1) through unstructured interviews and observations, (2) through a two-part algebra questionnaire, and (3) through a standardized measure of classroom climate. The interviews and observations were not intended to be systematic

---

*It should be noted at this point that our original intention was to include a third group in this study, namely, the Algebra Game classes that also received n-Ach training. However, these two groups were not included in the analysis or write-up for three reasons. First, the groups were badly (i.e., statistically significant) mismatched on a number of important background variables, like previous mathematics achievement, v-Achievement, and debilitating anxiety. Second, because the sample sizes of the Mastery and Satisfaction n-Ach-Algebra Game groups were relatively small, the problem of taking these several initial differences into account through covariance analysis was both extremely complex and unreliable. Third, research (reported in Chapter 4) led us to believe that the results of n-Ach training would not be manifest so soon or in such a narrow way in any case. Thus, these data and the additional questions posed when the experiment began are not included in this report.

data collection procedures, but instead to provide a clinical feel for what was happening and to spot any unpredicted potentially important factors that could influence the outcome.

The first part of our algebra questionnaire asked students to rank their preference for mathematics among other subjects for the first semester and for the second semester when the Math Game began. Students also were asked to rate on a five-point scale how much they liked math second semester compared to first semester (1 "much less" to 5 "much more"). The last question of this part asked students to rate how much they learned second semester compared to first semester from 1 (much less second semester) to 5 (much more). In the second part of the algebra questionnaire we asked students to check as many of the following characteristics as they would like to see incorporated into their other classes: setting your own deadlines, choosing the value of tests and homework, signing contracts, not many class lectures, go at your own speed, work in or outside of class, a point system for completed work, being able to work with others, setting your own goals for grades.

Our standardized measure of classroom climate was the Learning Environment Inventory developed by Walberg and Anderson (1969a). This instrument contains 14 scales, each with 7 items. The scale names with an illustrative item are as follows:

> INTIMACY—members of the class are personal friends,
>
> FRICTION—certain students are considered uncooperative,
>
> CLIQUENESS—certain students work only with their close friends,
>
> APATHY—members of the class don't care what the class does,
>
> FAVORITISM—only the good students are given special projects,
>
> FORMALITY—students are asked to follow a complicated set of rules,
>
> SATISFACTION—students are well satisfied with the work of the class,

SPEED—the class has difficulty keeping up with its assigned
work,

DIFFICULTY—students are constantly challenged,

GOAL DIRECTION—the objectives of this class are specific,

DEMOCRATIC—class decisions tend to be made by all the
students,

DISORGANIZATION—the class is disorganized,

DIVERSITY—the class divides its efforts among several
purposes, and

ENVIRONMENT—the books and equipment students need
or want are usually available to them in the classroom.

In order to ascertain whether certain motives or attitudes
predispose a student to doing well in the Algebra Game, and to
assess these possible yields, a variety of measures were administered during the first and last days of class; n-Achievement,
n-Affiliation, and n-Power were assessed using a four-picture
Thematic Apperception Test and scored according to the system
in Appendix I of *Motives in Fantasy, Action and Society*
(Atkinson [Ed.] , 1958). Five attitudes were assessed: (1) Realism
of vocational decision-making, (2) v-Achievement, (3) internality,
(4) debilitating test anxiety, and (5) self-esteem. The level of
algebra achievement was measured using the Cooperative Mathematics Tests for Algebra, Form A before the Algebra Game began,
and Form B at the end of the course. The numbers presented in
subsequent tables for this test are standardized scores based on
national norms. Finally, the impact of the Algebra Game on
subsequent mathematics proficiency was assessed by obtaining the
total grade point average in math for the year following the
Algebra Game.

The measures of motivation were included to validate the
hypotheses regarding the impact of structure, namely that
achievement motivation would be significantly higher after the
course in the Algebra Game class, while power motivation would
be higher in the normal algebra class. We did not make a
prediction about affiliation motivation nor about effects on the
attitude measures. These were included for exploration purposes
because of their theoretical relevance.

Sample Characteristics

This research was conducted in Broadmeadows Junior High School in Massachusetts, a predominantly lower-middle class, white suburb of Boston. This is the same school in which the previous experiment was conducted, and one of the algebra teachers in this experiment taught the Algebra Game to the 9th graders who took the Mastery- and Satisfaction-oriented n-Achievement courses. Due to these commonalities, the results here should shed light on the apparent lack of contribution of the Algebra Games to the n-Achievement training.

In order to obtain somewhat larger sample sizes for the experiment, two algebra classes in each treatment condition were combined. The teacher variable was held constant, since each of the two teachers taught one normal algebra class and one restructured Algebra Game class. In Table 9.1 the two groups are compared on a number of pre-course variables. As always, data are presented and analyzed separately for boys and for girls.

The samples are well matched for boys and for girls, with two exceptions. For both sexes the restructured classes performed substantially better in mathematics two years prior to the course and also at the start of the second semester when this experiment began. This initial difference will have to be controlled statistically when examining the mathematics learning gains after the course. Similarly, the restructured groups were higher on n-Affiliation at the outset. This difference also must be controlled when examining subsequent changes in n-Affiliation. The conjunction of these two initial differences does not immediately suggest some more basic pattern of underlying differences between the two groups.

Results

Our informal observations of the restructured classrooms and interviews with students suggested that two factors might be important in understanding the other results; neither factor had we attended to sufficiently before the experiment began. First, the teachers, along with "some Harvard psychologists," had created the game rules, not the students. Second, the grading system required midterm grades. To maintain some equity among the various 9th grade classes and to conform to the regulations, students were required to complete a minimum of two chapter contracts per half semester. Combined, these two features had the effect of decreasing the control students had over the rules that governed their mathematics lives and effectively obviated the self-pacing option, particularly for the slower students.

Although decision-making on quantity variables was available, the grading system of the city made the time dimension a sham. Grades of necessity were submitted to the office for the permanent record cards twice during the semester, thus making it mandatory that a student finish one chapter per month in order to receive a passing grade. This meant that the same time schedule was adhered to (as a minimum standard) in the Algebra Game classes as in the traditional classes. In practice, this time schedule took away not just one factor in the choice matrix, but rendered most of it inoperable for most people. The message now read to the student: "Nothing has really changed except that you now have to do it without lectures and demonstrations by the teacher." Although we paid lip service to individual pacing, the actuality was very close to lock-step.

According to the algebra questionnaire, restructuring the algebra class did not significantly increase how much students liked learning mathematics, nor how hard they worked. The girls in the restructured mathematics class, however, believed they learned much less.

It is possible to identify what students liked most and least about the restructured class by looking at the aspects of learning they most and least wanted in their other classes. (See Table 9.2.) These results are difficult to interpret, since it is not clear that all of these features were in fact part of the Algebra Game, e.g., "Go at your own speed." However, the data can be read as indicators of generally desirable and undesirable features. The three top-ranked items (being able to work with others, go at your own speed, work in or outside of class) suggest that students want several types of freedom for how they learn that do not often exist in normal classrooms. At the same time they do not appear to want the responsibility of deciding the learning goals for themselves, i.e., signing contracts, setting own deadlines, few lectures, setting their own grade goals.

Table 9.1

Mean Scores on Pre-Course Variables for Boys and Girls in the Normal and Restructured Mathematics Classes

Variables	BOYS			GIRLS		
	Normal (n = 22)	Restructured (n = 22)	t, p	Normal (n = 21)	Restructured (n = 23)	t, p
Background Characteristics						
Age (as of course, February 1968)	14 yr. 10 mo. SD = 6.9 mo.[1]	14 yr. 9 mo. 4.8 mo.	ns	14 yr. 7 mo. 5.4 mo.	14 yr. 8 mo. 6.0 mo.	ns
IQ[2]	106.43 12.31 (n = 21)[3]	109.00 10.48 (n = 21)	ns	106.76 12.56	105.64 10.99 (n = 22)	ns
California Mathematics Achievement Test[4] (October, 1966)	41.95 22.19 (n = 19)	55.43 25.56 (n = 21)	t = 1.789 $p < .10$	51.81 20.57	64.41 17.21 (n = 22)	t = 2.09 $p < .05$
Motivation Scores						
n-Achievement	0.46 1.99	0.77 2.07	ns	0.95 2.50	1.50 3.46 (n = 22)	ns
n-Affilia-	1.59	2.91 1.71	t = 2.03 $p < .05$	2.05 1.77	3.64 3.26	t = 2.00 $p \sim .05$

	2.70	2.06		2.87	2.62 / 2.72 (n = 22)	ns

Attitudes

	Group 1	Group 2		Group 3	Group 4	
Realism of vocational risk taking	19.44 / 18.86 (n = 18)	19.94 / 21.34 (n = 18)	ns	8.21 / 25.69	-0.25 / 35.56 (n = 20)	ns
v-Achievement	4.53 / 3.52 (n = 19)	4.00 / 3.48 (n = 19)	ns	2.90 / 3.09 (n = 19)	2.55 / 3.36 (n = 22)	ns
Internality	2.53 / 3.95 (n = 19)	3.53 / 3.20 (n = 19)	ns	4.63 / 4.48 (n = 19)	4.36 / 2.46 (n = 22)	ns
Debilitating Test Anxiety	2.11 / 3.56 (n = 19)	1.11 / 4.35 (n = 19)	ns	0.42 / 4.66 (n = 19)	1.73 / 6.17 (n = 22)	ns
Self-Esteem	0.53 / 3.75 (n = 19)	0.84 / 2.69 (n = 19)	ns	1.58 / 1.84 (n = 19)	1.52 / 2.60 (n = 21)	ns
Cooperative Mathematics Test (algebra) February, 1968; Form A	138.77 / 5.15	145.41 / 8.61	t = 3.10 p < .01	142.43 / 6.45	146.13 / 6.44	t = 1.91 p < .10

1. In this table the number beneath the mean scores in each case is the standard deviation.
2. California Test of Mental Maturity, given in October, 1966, slightly more than two years prior to the course.
3. When data were missing for individuals the effective sample size is given in the parentheses.
4. These scores are percentile ranks based on national norms obtained in 1963.

Table 9.2

Number and Percent of Students Who Wanted Aspects of the Algebra Game Incorporated in Their Other Classes

Algebra Game Characteristics	Boys (n = 21)		Girls (n =20)		Overall Ranking
Being able to work with others	19/21	91%	19/20	95%	1
Go at your own speed	20/21	95	17/20	85	2
Work in or out of class	19/21	91	17/20	85	3
Choosing value of tests and homework	15/21	71	16/20	80	4
A point system for completed work	15/21	71	15/20	75	5
Setting your own goals for grades	13/21	62	16/20	80	6
Not many class lectures	11/21	52	11/20	55	7
Setting own deadlines	13/21	62	8/20	40	8
Signing contracts	10/21	48	5/20	25	9

Table 9.3

Comparison of Normal and Restructured Algebra Classes on 14 Dimensions of Classroom Climate Measured by the Learning Environment Inventory

Dimensions of Climate		Normal (n = 39)	Restructured (n = 43)	P
Intimacy	mean	1.92	2.09	**
	SD	0.46	0.45	
Friction	mean	1.38	1.48	
	SD	0.51	0.37	
Cliqueness	mean	1.62	1.83	
	SD	0.39	0.32	
Satisfaction	mean	1.47	1.34	
	SD	0.47	0.34	
Speed	mean	1.25	1.58	***
	SD	0.38	0.45	
Difficulty	mean	1.39	1.63	*
	SD	0.55	0.44	
Apathy	mean	1.34	1.40	
	SD	0.50	0.50	
Favoritism	mean	1.03	1.07	
	SD	0.60	0.45	
Formality	mean	1.70	1.82	
	SD	0.38	0.38	
Goal Direction	mean	1.77	1.44	*
	SD	0.33	0.92	
Democratic	mean	1.55	1.46	
	SD	0.33	0.40	
Disorganization	mean	1.08	1.39	**
	SD	0.41	0.41	
Diversity	mean	1.70	1.78	
	SD	0.38	0.32	
Environment	mean	1.63	1.63	
	SD	0.54	0.35	

*p $<$ .05 two tails,

**p $<$ .01 two tails,

***p $<$ .001 two tails.

Results from the Learning Environment Inventory augment these findings and clarify the picture of how students felt in the Algebra Game compared to normal algebra. (See Table 9.3.) Students in the Algebra Game felt it was faster, more disorganized, more difficult, and less goal-oriented. It was seen as more intimate.

All of these data combined suggest that students in the Algebra Game felt more pressured and controlled than students in the normal algebra class. While students were given freedom, in theory at least, to set their own goals, the school-wide requirements for grading periods effectively washed out that option. Many of the available tactics for learning were appreciated. However, students did not want to have so much responsibility for setting their own learning goals. The fact that teachers were no longer setting the goals made the class seem less goal directed and more disorganized. The combination of making more options available, reducing teacher control, and requiring the same pace as in other classes did not produce a leap in the general level of student joy, energy for mathematics, and satisfaction, but instead, a sense that the Algebra Game was faster and more difficult. It is clear that the students in the experimentally restructured math classes did not experience the same sense of liberation for learning, or general enthusiasm, felt by the boys and girls in McIntyre's 5th grade math class.

Beyond these student perceptions it is possible to assess changes in motivation, attitudes, and amount of mathematics the students learned. However, of all these measured outcomes there were only two significant changes. We found that the Algebra Game significantly decreased the girls' n-Affiliation in comparison to the girls in the normal algebra class. There was a trend in the same direction for boys. The principal impact of the algebra course on the boys' motivation was in significantly *increasing* their concerns about power.

It is important to go beyond an analysis of the simple treatment effects to an examination of the possible interaction of treatments with personality type. For instance, perhaps students with initially high n-Achievement might perform best in a restructured class, whereas students low on n-Achievement might do significantly better in a normal algebra class. The yield measure chosen for this interaction analysis was gain in Cooperative Algebra test score, because it is a highly reliable measure of a clearly intended yield and also because, in this sample, gains on the test are not significantly correlated with initial differences in algebra achievement. Unfortunately, none of the initial attitudes does predict algebra gains for boys. Seventeen of 22 boys in the restructured algebra class were either below the median IQ and below the median algebra gain or above the median IQ and above the median algebra gain, compared to only 7 of 20 boys in the normal algebra class (χ^2 = 7.65, p <.01, two tailed). In other words, the higher the IQ, the more a boy gains in algebra in the restructured class. The reverse is true in the normal class; the higher the IQ, the less the boy gains in algebra score. When boys in the Algebra Game, above and below the median IQ, are compared in terms of how much they like mathematics second semester compared to first semester, high IQ boys like math significantly more (Mann-Whitney test, Z = 2.39, p <.02, two tailed). This difference does not occur between the high and low IQ boys in the normal classroom since there was no change in the way they learned in the second semester. Intelligence level among the boys is the only factor that appears to affect the level of productivity and satisfaction in the Algebra Game.

Discussion

This research presents evidence that restructuring the way a student learns does influence his motivation. If a brief instructional set can temporarily influence motivation, as was the case in the original research with the n-Achievement scoring system, it simply stands to reason that a semester-long change in the instructional process (a massive change in comparison), should influence students' motives. The problem, of course, is that the theory is not sufficient to the task of specifying what structural changes influence what motives, i.e., there were a number of predictive errors.

The fact stands out that, at best, the theory of how structure influences motivation is not wrong, but insufficient for the prediction task. There are several other factors besides the structure of the Algebra Game that produced the measured changes. First, there are certain student characteristics that made a difference. Girls responded differently from boys. High IQ boys responded differently from low IQ boys. Second, there were some school rules, procedures, and norms that influenced the results. Students had to complete two chapters per half semester, thus introducing a fixed minimal pace that was a maximum pace for many students. The sheer contrast between first and second semester algebra and the contrast with the normal procedures in the rest of the school may have caused some confusion and a sense of disorganization about such issues as what you get grades for, the role of the learner, and what a teacher is supposed to be. Third, the leadership styles of the teachers probably made a difference, just as the morale and performance of teams are determined in part by the role of the coach even though the game rules are fixed. Fourth, the subject matter itself, although it was not an experimental variable in this experiment, probably helps determine the process of learning. All of these factors, and perhaps several others, combine interactively to produce the motivational climate in the classroom, the motives aroused, the classroom behavior, and ultimate results. These results can be portrayed most succinctly in tabular form (see Table 9.4).

In general the more sources of variance that can be controlled, the more an innovator can predict the outcome for students. That much is axiomatic. Theoretically, the sources of variance extend back beyond the classroom to the school norms, procedures, rules, policies, and back still further to the community of which the school is a part. Nevertheless, it is impractical and unreasonable to make the working assumption that influencing children's motivation in a classroom requires prior change in the larger community, although this may be true to some degree. The practical question is how many and how much of the social systems surrounding the classroom must be controlled to obtain a desired level of student change. A workable solution lies somewhere between the highly focused attempt to change one element like the classroom structure, and the rather broad focus on changing the several meta-systems surrounding the classroom.

Table 9.4

*Motivation and Climate Model of Classroom Behavior
(adapted from Litwin and Stringer, 1968, p. 41)**

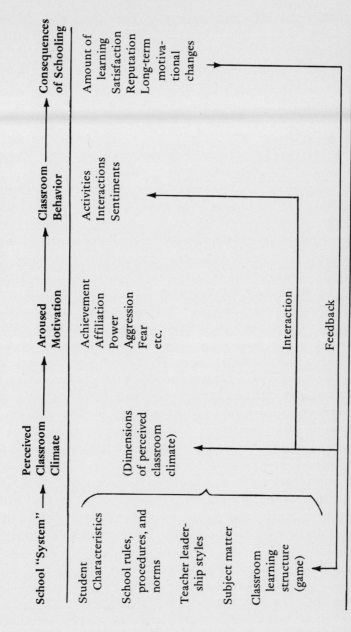

*If something like this model operates in actuality, it is easier to understand how slippage occurred between the restructuring and the intended motivational outcomes. It is obvious that to control the aroused motivation in the classroom, more of the "School system" variables must be controlled.

10.

Towards a Self-Renewing School[*]

There is an apocryphal story of an educational reformer who began as a classroom teacher, tried unsuccessfully to get administrative support for his innovations, and decided he needed to be in control of the school. When he became principal, the increased authority allowed him to inaugurate more sweeping changes, which in turn caused broader-based community resistance. Nevertheless, his energy and ideas were respected, especially from a distance, and he was invited to become superintendent of a system ripe for change. But there too he was defeated in his visionary reforms, this time by state mandated curriculum requirements and laws that officially defined his "open campus" high schools as illegal, school-enforced truancy. Impatient for the freedom to create his own rules, the man started a private consulting firm that actively lobbies for new laws permitting communities to redesign their school systems. The logic of this well-intentioned educational reformer is as consistent as his history of escalated failures.

This man's story is equally exciting and depressing because both the promise and the risk are clear in dealing with the several layers of meta-systems surrounding the learning process. At each level there is more power over the systems that cradle the

*I wish to express my admiration for the work of the entire faculty at Jamestown Community College. In addition I extend my appreciation to the participants in the Bergamo Workshop for their time and honesty. A special note of thanks is due to Roger Wingett, Dean of Students, and Duane Faulkner, who helped make the possible, real. While this chapter reports on community college-level activities, I believe that the contents are applicable to high schools as well—the major focus of this work.

182

classroom and less direct influence over the learning that occurs in the classroom. Only a calculus of power could identify the precise distance from the classroom where the combination of system leverage and influence on specific acts of teaching and learning is maximized.

Our research effort began humbly enough, designed to try out and assess some methods of increasing adolescents' achievement motivation. We decided to be as practical as possible as early as possible in order to avoid the frequent failure of researchers who are either personally unable or professionally unwilling to translate their laboratory successes into institutionalized procedures. We chose to do our research in classrooms. As part of the entry quid pro quo with our "laboratory" schools, we agreed to provide resources (personnel, money, time) to train some of their teachers as research collaborators. Everyone agreed that this was an advantageous arrangement, since it would create an indigenous corps of teachers to carry on the motivation training after the inevitable departure of the researchers. To our mystification, when we left, motivation training ceased in spite of the enthusiastic teachers, in spite of proven results, and promises of support. The complexities of counter-balancing pressures in the system of schooling mocked our good intentions. It appears now as if this knotty, recalcitrant, and frustrating system contains a deep wisdom, and supra-individual rationality that if given a voice would say, "I will guard my children against ill-conceived reforms by being exceptionally difficult to change. I will yield to you, but only if you back your proposed innovations with the persistent energy that comes from firm convictions in their value. If the reforms command that much dedication, I will allow them . . . but slowly."

Out of respect for the powerful, institutionalized conservatism that we witnessed but do not fully understand, we stated the obvious—a rather refreshing act for those of us long rewarded for complexifying reality. Getting motivation training set up in schools would require more direct efforts than the fallout effects of our action research. At the same time, we were reluctant to engage in that potentially endless quixotic escalation of the apocryphal reformer. Thus we settled on a compromise, fortunately, in retrospect, a good one: We would work only on the next layer of the system beyond the classroom that exerts itself most frequently and forcefully on the teaching-learning processes—the school in which motivation training was to be instituted. This chapter is a case study reporting the *successful* process of introducing achievement motivation training and generally facilitating other educational innovations in Jamestown (N.Y.) Community College. Our attempts to puzzle out the reasons for success there are far from definitive, since the causes remain almost as elusive as the reasons for our earlier failures. Only one conclusion is clear: solving the puzzle of school reform will require a genius cryptographer, and probably several of them.

Jamestown Community College sits at the bottom of a gentle hill on the edge of a quiet town in western New York State. The buildings in the center of Jamestown are taller than one expects for a rural community, but their color, darkened with age, portrays the town's history. The rich, rolling farm land within eyesight of the commercial section epitomizes the integration of rural and urban ways of life in Jamestown. There is a tiny "inner city" with noticeable but minor racial problems. The financial crisis that is choking educational innovation across the country is cause for careful spending in Jamestown, but there have been no layoffs, nor angry revolts of teachers or taxpayers. These tidal waves of change elsewhere ripple into Jamestown. Thus it remains a good place to raise a family, rural enough for fresh air and clear water, yet close enough to Buffalo for cultural life, small enough to walk outside at night safely and big enough to have a college and a diverse array of human relationships.

"The College" is the oldest community college in the State. Perhaps because of this achievement, it never attempted anything else sufficiently controversial to create echoes heard in the State Education Department. Nor has there been strong external pressure for change such as found elsewhere—the cry for community control, a funding crisis, the shifting borders of a segregated minority. For its 20 years, Jamestown Community College simply did its job of preparing students for vocations or for transfer to a four-year college. The only clearly visible event that foreshadowed the workshop introducing psychological education in January,

1970, was the enthusiastic participation of about 15 faculty members in a series of "self-run" encounter group meetings facilitated by "Encounter tapes," a commercially available set of audio-taped suggestions for how a group can develop more openness, trust, authenticity, and generally enhanced human relationships. It was a judiciously small testing of the readiness for change, since there are always faculty members who believe "psychological education" is insidiously deceptive jargon for brain washing.

The objectives of the workshop are as simply stated as they are hard to attain. First, we wanted to introduce motivation training to the college in such a way that, one year to two years later, it would still be a course offering for students. Second, we wanted to introduce workshop participants to enough of the other available courses, techniques, and orientations in psychological education to facilitate their efforts to innovate. In our rhetoric we talked about developing a "self-renewing" system, where an established climate of change encourages all members to modify or create new instructional bridges between the needs of students and the demands of life after school. But even while the words were in our mouths, we knew there would be a gap between the ideal of a self-renewing school and the results of the workshop. The only question was the size of that gap.

The workshop ended on Friday.* Registration for the second semester courses began the following Monday. The 24 faculty members and three students from the workshop were still glowing from the invigorating affection they had won the previous week by learning together, but more important, by facing up to and knocking down a number of long-standing interpersonal barriers, misunderstandings, and distrusts that typically are an integral part

---

*The content and strategy of the five-day workshop will not be described here since it is presented in two other places: Chapter 2, An Achievement Motivation Workshop for Teachers, in *Teaching Achievement Motivation*, Alschuler *et al.*, Education Ventures, Inc., Middletown, Connecticut, 1970; and Humanistic Education, in the May, 1970, issue of *Educational Technology* Magazine. I am indebted to Hal Skorpen, Ed Maurer, and Bailey Jackson, who helped conduct the workshop, and to Dan Callahan for helping to interview the participants 18 months later.

of every school's covert operating procedures. These kinks in the system and personal irritations drain energy. This is so much the norm in most institutions that when some of the problems are resolved, even temporarily, there is a natural strong counter-reaction of delightful surprise and exuberant expression of affection. In the eyes of the rest of the faculty, who did not go through the fear, pain, tears, and eventual re-recognition of previous adversaries, the dramatic changes were not understandable. For them registration was a shock. As usual it was held in the grim gym, because it was large enough to hold all the tables with all the forms to be signed. In contrast to the usual heavy, steady mumble of many simultaneous voices and the dehumanizing routines, the workshop faculty made it into a reunion. "Creedence Clearwater" and "Country Joe and the Fish" played loudly over the PA as they had been heard during the workshop. Members greeted each other with hugs rather than the typical standing side-by-side with mutual emission of words. Their warmth even spread to students who were ushered from desk to desk in the style of a happy airline stewardess. The blooming determination of workshop participants to maintain and spread their good feelings was matched by the suspicions of the others and the rock-hard norms against public display of affection in school, however innocent and mild.

Institutionalizing this momentum immediately became a two-fold problem. First, the motivation course and other specific innovations had to be instituted. Second, the climate of friendly cooperative support had to be spread through the institution from the new "in" group to the uninitiated "out" group. The record is clear, if not completely successful in both areas. In three semesters since the workshop, 207 of the 1350 day students took a five-day achievement motivation course, approved by the faculty for three credits. The eight separate motivation courses were taught by five members of the Dean of Students' counselling staff, one of whom was reassigned from the psychology department to concentrate full time on this area. Another member of the counselling staff was assigned half time and a number of faculty were given release time to work in this area. The five motivation trainers also have conducted four workshops for 122 faculty and students in the other colleges. Within Jamestown Community College itself there have been 115 additional participations (one person in one workshop is one "participation") by a majority of the 65 faculty members in nine other workshops sponsored by the Program in Humanistic Education on such topics as "public knowledge and private concerns," "growth-oriented groups," "value clarification," "synectics," and "advanced training in psychological education." This does not include a number of in-house seminars and mini-workshops for Jamestown faculty, conducted by members who wanted to share and spread what they learned from the outside workshops. Using a very crude statistic, in three semesters there were 444 extensive "participations" by faculty and students following the original workshop experience of 24 faculty members and three students. Thus, the rough "spread" ratio is 16:1.

There also have been new policies and projects that affect the whole school. One of the early decisions by the Academic Standards Committee was to adopt a "no flunk out" policy in which students who were dropped for academic reasons could return to school if they took an achievement motivation course. Gentle coercion or not, this policy kept the back door open and has helped a number of students.* By public decision the faculty also chose to give up its minutely legislated prerequisites for graduation. Now, within the required 48 credit hours in liberal arts and sciences, students are almost completely free to choose what kind of courses to take and how many of them. Further, all faculty committees have been opened to students, a clear public declaration of trust in the good judgment of their young partners in the educational process. Various members of the faculty subsequently sought and obtained $277,000 in special grants for projects ranging from an "Institutional Grant for Science," "Multi-media learning center for career students," "Law enforcement education program," "Education Opportunity Program," to "Greater Sensitivity [sic] for the New Technologies in Medically Oriented Careers" and a planning grant to find ways of incorporating drama into philosophy, anthropology, psychology, etc. During

---

*The following year some students were dropped for academic reasons without recourse to the motivation course. Thus there now is a partial "no drop out" policy.

the equivalent period of 18 months prior to the motivation workshop, no outside grants had been obtained. Several other projects were conducted that did not require special funding. Three of the workshop participants created a multi-media, experience-based English course. Four teachers synthesized what they learned in several advanced workshops and presented to the faculty their own "Process Teaching Workshop." In the fall of 1970, the Dean's staff organized a special small-group experience-and-discussion orientation program for new students. During the summer of 1971 a group from the faculty planned a "Developmental Studies Program" that used motivation training, among other procedures, to provide special help for the "problem" students who now are entering college under New York's open-enrollment plan. Over half of the original workshop participants have been key members in lobbying for policy changes, obtaining grants, or planning and conducting these and other special projects that have had at least an indirect effect on everyone at Jamestown Community College.

The greatest variety of applications and the most direct effects on students have occurred in teachers' classes. Nineteen of the 21 teachers interviewed 18 months after the workshop* had tried out two or more procedures learned in the workshop. These included: the use of music, milling, touching, name games, and other warm-up, get-acquainted exercises the first day of class; as much as 50 percent of class time now spent on examining the relevance of the subject matter to the individual lives of the students; negotiation with the students to decide collaboratively the method of course evaluation and the course content; changes in the teacher's role from director to facilitator of student-chosen projects; group tests; individualized student-chosen pacing; the use of achievement motivation learning sequences to help plan the course; use of video-tape replays for feedback on group processes; creation of mini-free university in class (a kind of carnival with different learning booths); role playing, fantasy trips, sensory awakening techniques, "value whips," and other techniques to

*Of the 24 faculty members at the workshop, one was on sabbatical and two chose not to be interviewed. Thus the figure reported here is 21.

experientially get into poetry and literature; more personal anecdotal illustrations in class; restructured scoring system (see Chapter 7); learning contracts; more systematic use of attention-getting techniques; more time spent talking with individual students outside class; student-made exams; use of permanent sub-groups in class for fun and work. What characterizes most of these changes is a greater inclusion of students' needs in the conduct of teaching. Whether through explicit negotiation or techniques that tap students' concerns beyond their thoughts, nearly all of the teachers have taken steps to make broader human contact with their students.

This is not always a quick process instantly rewarded by the affection of students who finally attain their long held secret goal of recognition as a fully human being in the learning process. From the first gush of registration day some students stiffened at what they experienced. The logic of their feelings made "is" into "ought." "Schooling is not like this, and this is not the way it is *supposed* to be." The immediate reaction was some general confusion over what the new relationship rules were to be in class. Some wanted the security of anonymous distance and structured instruction. They had learned well that learning is content, not process; abstract, not personal; receptive, not proactive engagement; and authoritative, not, in some primal and ultimate senses, uncertain. For these students, their teachers' attempts to humanize learning was weird, and something, at best, to endure until things got back to "normal." A number of teachers in turn were deeply discouraged (literally, they lost their courage) when their bold steps toward students produced a student retreat in equal measure.

A factual listing of the number and variety of innovations is persuasive. However, pure statistics, for all their accuracy, miss an important historical dimension of reality, and they lie by omission. Some pain accompanied each success like a shadow. The experience during the workshop, of what learning among peers could be like, revolutionized their expectations and made the continuing reality of their classrooms and their unchanged students a daily reminder of an unattained goal. One teacher reported:

I really value the workshop and what happened to me. There was an awakening of a sense of love that I wanted to permeate my teaching. I seized on techniques, but when many of them didn't work, it was a real low in my life. By comparison, I wasn't sure I had anything important to say. Teaching was painful. Even now I'm considering leaving teaching.

Or, again, from another teacher:

I felt disorganized and depressed for a while last spring. Some students wondered what was bothering me. I wasn't less effective as a teacher, but I was just examining all aspects of my relationships. First I recognized my attempts to manipulate and control students, especially in individual conferences. So I tried to be less directive and allowed students to take more initiative. We still get there, but it's more relaxed. Now I just feel more comfortable. It's easier to accept them where they are without lecturing or moralizing to them. It's easier to really listen to different points of view. But for a while last year I couldn't concentrate on a lot of new techniques because I was hung up on myself.

And, yet again:

For two months after the workshop I was depressed. In the school, by comparison there was less meaning, loss of contact with others, and less intimacy. There was an emptiness and a real identity crisis for me. I raised a lot of questions about teaching, relationships, and trust. It didn't impair my teaching, though. Now I have warmer relationships with the kids, my own and the students, but it took me a while.

One professor admits with bittersweet pride to being a "teacher of literature," accustomed to the pleasures of his discipline and dedicated to stimulating this same appreciation in his students. Gentleness and good intentions shine through his formal bearing and measured, absolutely correct grammar.

> The workshop convinced me I had to get closer to my students. I wish I could do easily some of the things I see others doing. I'm saddened at my inability, but I can't do these things. I have adopted the attitude of knowing my strengths, developing my weaknesses but stopping when it threatens my strengths.
>
> At first we worked in small groups to minimize lecturing and maximize class discussion. It seemed to fail, so I abandoned it. I just can't open up in class. However, I can open up in my office. I seek out students and their previous teachers to find out what interests them most. I encourage them to see me after class in my office where I can hook up the course with their ultimate interests. That way they can satisfy my expectations at the same time they satisfy themselves. Last year perhaps I saw three students each week in my office, mostly about the mechanics of expression. This year I see an average of 15 students each week in my office and we talk about their interests. I find that I enjoy this contact very much.

Other teachers, like this budding Mr. Chips, have persisted in spite of initial difficulties to the point where changes are more satisfying to students and to themselves. None of the teachers interviewed said this had occurred immediately without disappointments, nor had been as successful as they ultimately hoped.

Among the most poignant observations are those from the faculty who did not attend the workshop. Their reactions are mixed and tend to be extreme:

> For years there has been a polarization of the faculty based on cliques. People from both cliques went to the workshop and came back with the urge to unite. The most pleasant unity in eight years is now present.

People who didn't go felt left out. It divided the faculty into two groups. The major problem is the communication gap between those who went and those who didn't. Explanations were tried, but they didn't help. Sometimes they made it worse.

People came back with enthusiasm and there's a much friendlier atmosphere.

I was disappointed with the people who came back from the workshop. Their religous fervor was contrived and unreal. It was brainwashing. There is suspicion about the faculty who went and came back the "workshop warriors."

I'm new here. The faculty seems to have fewer tensions than other places. I never felt like I was in an "out" group. It stirred up a lot of talk about teaching and students.

It hurt some people.

It helped some people. My daughter went through an n-Ach course and it had a good effect on her.

The counselors are not doing their job now. (They are teaching motivation courses instead.)

Even among those who attended, there is some division in their overall evaluations, although the majority is positive.

Not all the results are beneficial. There is more tension. Some of it's from letting more feelings be known and being unsure of reactions. I have the feeling that students are becoming less responsible. They are going off on the emotional side. It interferes with their classwork. Hard work is good for the soul.

There were numerous changes in personal lives reported by participants that will not be described here out of respect for their privacy. The majority of comments were basically positive. At the same time, however, there was enough emotional pain to command continued reflection on the responsibilities of workshop trainers and the risks inherent in any change they facilitate.

Second Thoughts on the Year Before

In the interviews with participants, I was surprised at how much progress they had made. But there was something curious about their reports that was both obvious and hidden; I knew there was something they weren't telling me but I didn't know what it was. My puzzlement crystallized when I instinctively disagreed with a statement made by one of the workshop participants: "The workshop shook this place. All the things that have happened were started and made possible there." That just could not be true. The "start" had been made prior to the workshop and perhaps the "possibilities" too were embedded in the College—needing only to be awakened. I asked them about the effects of the workshop and they told me *all* of the changes that had occurred at the college as if the workshop had been THE cause of all the changes rather than one of a number of forces for change. My own words began to echo in my ears (earlier in this book): It is egocentric to assume that, fortuitously, precisely those aspects of education we control produce most of the gains. The mass of accumulating data gently instills humility in change-agents. The most important determinants of change are not the quantity, quality, or delivery of the educational input, but characteristics of the learners, e.g., belief that one can control one's destiny (Coleman, 1966a); value of achievement (Alschuler, previous chapters); motivation; and intelligence (Luborsky *et al.,* 1971). Perhaps at Jamestown Community College there were institutional equivalents of these personality characteristics, a conviction that changes are possible, important, desired, and wise. Given such an institutional commitment, the variety of sustained changes triggered by the workshop would seem more understandable. Certainly this reading of the existing state of the college makes more sense than assuming it was an inert system brought to life by the workshop.

A quick re-examination of the reported changes provides immediate support for this notion. The participants' pre-workshop commitment to change resulted in their seeking and financing the short training program, as well as their successful recruitment of about 30 volunteers from the faculty. Subsequently they continued their commitment to teacher training through a series of additional workshops. At most, their original commitments were deepened, but certainly not created by the workshop. Of the $277,000 in new grants, several were the direct results of contacts or ideas from the workshop, but others were stimulated by the new college president, selected later that spring, who set a goal to obtain $100,000 in grants for the next academic year. The multi-media English course was conceived and dedicated independently and only was facilitated by techniques, procedures, and orientations learned in the workshop. From this perspective the workshop had the effect of emphasizing and greatly stimulating an already existing function of the system—the concern with developing fully human beings. It was as if the workshop taught new uses for a neglected but functioning bodily organ, like eyes or ears. As they saw and heard more, the existing organization was strained, was reorganized in part, and in general experienced the excitement and pain of organic growth. But the functioning organ was there to begin with, along with others that contributed to the sustained development of education at Jamestown Community College. Conversely, the workshop was something more than an inert tool used by the Jamestown faculty, and a good deal less than Prince Charming awakening the college with a five-day kiss.

To understand how Jamestown Community College was able to make such good use of the workshop, we must have a clear picture of its state of readiness and commitment to change. This understanding, in turn, requires a brief detour into the theory of social systems as developed by Parsons.

Every social system has two functional imperatives, one oriented externally (task performance) and the other oriented internally (system maintenance). For each functional imperative there are distinct goals and means of attaining those goals. This can be presented in tabular form.

Table 10.1

Functional Imperatives of Social Systems
(Adapted from Black, 1961, p. 331)

	Means	Goals
Task Performance	Adaptation (technology)	Goal Attainment
System Maintenance	Pattern Maintenance (norms, tension management, conflict reduction, etc.)	Integration (system survival)

Every social system must *both* attain its goals and survive. If a system consistently fails to attain its goals, it will not survive. Conversely, if it lacks sufficient coordination of its members, it disintegrates, the system doesn't survive, and it cannot attain its goals. Both integration and goal attainment are necessary.

Typically, the introduction of new technology to foster goal attainment upsets norms that maintain integration and system survival. For instance, individualized instruction through learning contracts results in children doing many different things at the same time. The appearance of disorder and the real noise challenge the deeply ingrained survival norm of overtly controlling students' behavior in class. Also, the introduction of new norms usually upsets the task performance in a school, e.g., both busing to achieve school integration and the move towards decentralized community control are current headline examples of temporarily disruptive changes in school norms. Achievement motivation training is new technology designed to accomplish goals that in practice are secondary in schools—the development of basic social values (independence, acceptance of personal responsibility) and the psychological aspects of the entrepreneurial role. This threatens other aspects of a school's functioning by competing for time, money, and personnel from a finite pool of resources. In addition, motivation training threatens a number of established norms: the taboo on public exploration and education of students' feelings, and the degree of allowable openness, authenticity, and intimacy in teacher-student relationships. As a result, achievement motivation training is doubly difficult to introduce in schools. Yet, at Jamestown Community College, achievement motivation training was instituted—and there appear to be supporting norms. How did this happen? What was it about the goals, technology, norms, and integrative functions that made this innovation possible?

To find answers to these questions we must go one step deeper into Parsons' theory as applied by Miles (1967) to school systems. For each of the four cells in Table 10.1, Miles describes certain genotypic properties of school systems and their resulting endemic problems.

Goal Attainment

Educational goals usually are vaguely stated, multiple in nature, conflicting, emotionally loaded, and difficult to measure. For these reasons it is nearly impossible to use outcome measures as levers for introducing change. In their absence, decisions often are made on the basis of moral or ideological grounds that stimulate value conflict. It is not surprising that there are frequent retreats to the one justification that touches everyone, . . . money: "See how much we care! Look at how much we spent!" or, "See how frugal we have been this year."

Technology

The teachers perform out of sight of other adults and are judged on once-removed criteria, e.g., average class grades on standardized tests. Teachers get little feedback on the effectiveness of particular procedures. Awareness and direct use of relevant knowledge about the teaching process is low, and diffusion of new practices is difficult, in part because there are virtually no internal R&D functions in schools such as those in industry. Various constituencies are in regular conflict over who is most expert, and the quality of teachers is uneven. All of this causes administrators to be overloaded.

Pattern Maintenance

Most teachers are not linked to a common fate in the sense that they must rely on each other to accomplish a single common goal as is the case for players in an athletic team. Teachers have a low degree of interdependence. Nor do most schools spend much money to help teachers learn, grow, develop, or innovate.

Integration

Although public schools are essentially non-competitive with other schools in the area, they are nonetheless highly vulnerable to criticism at any point, almost at any time, by nearly every one of the area's constituencies. The board of education or board of trustees is often the epitome of these conflicting groups, and good decisions are difficult to get. In this context frequent survival mechanisms are passivity and defensiveness. While this may increase the ease of pure system survival, these reactions do not make for great leaps forward in improved technology and higher goal attainment.

Now, having reviewed Miles' explication of Parsons' model, we can begin to answer how Jamestown Community College was able to institutionalize motivation training and a new norm supporting innovation. In brief, through a peculiar sequence of events, most of these typical system problems did not exist. The absence of severe problems was an opportunity exploited by Dean Roger Wingett. To be sure, there were, and are, several other prime movers at Jamestown who have contributed to the increasingly healthy climate there. Dean Wingett does not stand out by being undeniably charismatic, but by being first, most consistent, most firm, and most competent in orchestrating the available talents. Therefore, his history, while not always central to developments, always touches the action and provides a unifying thread in understanding the college's evolution.

Dean Wingett left a middle-sized New York university after 10 years of advancement from Director of Resident Halls to Dean of Men and acting Dean of Students. He correctly predicted a stormy, politicized work climate, obtained his current dean's post, and walked directly into an analogous situation at Jamestown. Faculty trust of the President was at such a low ebb that they resorted to the state labor relations law in negotiating salaries. Dean Wingett was hired by the President and in this sense was the President's man. Thus the Dean was the prime candidate for Red Herring of the year. Even the innocuous decision to improve parking regulations was struck down by the faculty as usurping their prerogatives. Effective functioning required the Dean to act collaboratively, and be trustworthy and open in a climate where the first and last question always was, "Which side are you on?" It was Dean Wingett's considerable accomplishment to remain his own man and earn general respect. Innovation at this time, however, was a distinct luxury. During the spring of the Dean's second year there occurred a prolonged, bitter hassle over the firing of a faculty member, which divided the institution and unified the faculty in opposition to the President. In August the President announced his resignation with thirty days' notice. A former chairman of the board of trustees, a retired banker, was named acting President and school began in a quiet hiatus blessed by all.

For the Dean, the politic thing to do would have been to coast, building relationship capital with faculty members until the new President was chosen and his style, direction, and stance were known. Dean Wingett did not choose this course, and in so not-doing touched a variety of strengths hidden in this unusual situation. Neither diagnostic super-brilliance nor dumb luck activated the Dean, but instead, deep unactualized convictions.

> At that point we were an institution that talked about creating an educational climate that was satisfying to students. "Education" was passing us by. We needed to examine what we were doing and what we were giving to students. The student body is always changing. We must try to understand these students and relate to their needs. For me, we *have* to be changing our educational models continuously. I am committed to changing and it wasn't going on here (Dean Wingett, personal communication).

The Dean began in the absence of institutional precedents without visible support or opposition from the faculty. During the previous turbulent spring one of the Dean's staff members, Robert Oddy, tried to create a constructively still backwater. With Dean Wingett's public endorsement, Oddy collected a group of volunteer faculty members, students, and administrators to meet weekly and be guided by a series of audio encounter tapes. It was a mild success, leaving the participants pleasantly engaged and sufficiently unsatisfied to want more. The following fall the Dean searched for a way to continue this interest, contracted the Program in Humanistic Education at the State University at Albany, requested and obtained supplemental funds for the workshop from the acting president, recruited about two-thirds of the 65 faculty through individual conversations, and set up interviews between faculty volunteers and workshop staff members to explore needs, goals, and possibilities. This is the lonely grit of change agentry.

Consider this situation compared to the genotypic problems of most schools. There were no emotionally loaded debates over vague, confusing, multiple, and conflicting goals. There was relative calm, continuing goals of preparing students for vocations or transfer to four-year colleges, and Dean Wingett's clear, yet open, commitment to examine "what we were doing and what we were giving to students." By going personally to all faculty members and getting a majority of volunteers, Dean Wingett honored their strong tradition of faculty decision-making. They reciprocated by accepting, albeit conditionally, his goal statement. Voila! *Goal clarity* and *maintenance* of decision-making patterns.

Dean Wingett sees himself as a "change agent," and head of the college R&D function. He did not present himself to faculty as an expert on all that's new in education. Therefore, he *avoided conflicts* over who is most expert. He only sought to provide exposure to *new practices and technology* in an adult-peer learning context. His continued focus on faculty group projects before and after the workshop reduced role visibility, increased interdependence, reduced feelings of isolation, depression, and non-confirmation by peers, and stressed the *norms* of professional development and innovation.

In contrast to the style of the ex-president and the frequent defensive, passive mode of chief school administrators, the acting president also disclaimed expertise in educational matters and therefore supported *every* recommendation made by the Dean of the College and the Dean of Students for their special areas. The acting president applied his own banker's acumen to untangling the college's financial snarl. His stance and work facilitated internal *integration* amid general calm. In the absence of preempting external threats, the President's backing of the two Deans and others fostered adaptations in practice that contributed to the system's survival as a relevant, effective institution of learning.

In this context, what the workshop did was to increase existing interest, to partially satisfy aroused curiosity about new technology, and to continue converting faculty solidarity formed in opposition to the ex-president into a consolidated group proposing innovations. The workshop intensified and quickened the system's self-renewal that began inauspiciously in the stillness after the storm. After the workshop, Dean Wingett, now joined by others, continued to do what he had done before—lobbied for faculty decisions through personal contacts, set up more workshop activities for other faculty, promoted new group projects, sought additional funding, and maintained his commitment to change. "I don't know what precisely we'll be doing a year from now, but I hope we have made improvements and are doing things differently." The new president validated the faculty's vigor by publicly declaring himself in favor of innovation, and increased the momentum by energetically leading the search for more outside seed money to make real his pledge. And so, it continues. Such is the nature of self-renewal in schools.

Psychological Education and Organizational Development in Schools

It is a bitter paradox of the Alice-in-Wonderland world of public education that it is devoted almost exclusively to fostering growth in children, yet remaining itself highly resistant to change. New curricula, dedicated teachers with good ideas, hot-shot administrators who take on schooling because it is a dragon worthy of their finest efforts—each makes a dent. But the problem is bigger than individuals. It is in the system of schooling, the very fixedness of roles, role relationships, procedures, policies, norms, goals, the coercive hierarchy of requirements, and the raised guillotine of standardized testing. It is the system that must be changed before, after, above, and beneath all else. This is the mission of organization development (OD) in schools: to foster self-renewing systems.* That it can be done is illustrated by changes at Jamestown Community College.

We started with a circumscribed problem: how do we introduce motivation training into schools so that when we leave, it stays? The solution demanded that we work with the system. Dean Wingett needed outside experts to facilitate the institutional changes he and other faculty members desired. Together we went through what Schmuck and Miles (1971) describe as the typical sequence of events in the initiation and development of an OD program:

1. Middle or top management of an organization becomes interested in OD and feels that the organization has problems which can be met through training.
2. Management invites an outside OD consultant to visit the organization.
3. After the outsider's entry, legitimation, and contact with a variety of roles and groups, the organization works out a contract with the outsider specifying the nature of the projected relationship, its goals and procedures.

*It is beyond the scope of this book to describe the range of system problems, foci for solutions, and alternative modes of intervention that comprise the field of OD. There are several basic references for the reader who wishes to explore this new field in greater depth: *Organizational Development in Schools*, Schmuck and Miles (Eds.), National Press, Palo Alto, California, 1971; The Development of Innovative Climates in Educational Organizations, M.B. Miles, EPRC research note, Stanford Research Institute, Palo Alto, California, 1969; *Change in School Systems*, G. Watson (Ed.), Washington, D.C., NTL, 1967; *Concepts for Social Change*, G. Watson (Ed.), Washington, D.C., NTL, 1967; *The Planning of Change*, W. Bennis, K.D. Benne and R. Chin, Holt, Rinehart and Winston, Inc., New York, 1969 (2nd edition).

4. The outsider, working with insiders, collects data about the organization.

5. These data form the basis of a joint diagnosis of the points of difficulty in the organization.

6. A first "intervention," usually some form of intensive meeting involving several key roles.

7. The intervention is evaluated via new data collection. Often future success of the effort depends on the degree to which key figures have been freed up to be more open, concerned, and creative about organizational improvement.

8. Next steps in intervention are planned following this, and so on.

9. The OD function itself becomes institutionalized within the organization. An OD department is formed and it takes central responsibility for continuing the OD process.

10. The internal specialists become increasingly professionalized, responsible for their own continuing professional development and growth.

Results of the diagnostic interviews set up by Dean Wingett were fed back to workshop participants in the latter part of the five-day training program. This led to intense work on issues that resulted in freeing up a number of key decision-makers.* The momentum now is maintained in large part through Dean Wingett's staff, who act like an internal OD team. They have obtained advanced

---

*One result of the workshop was the subsequent decision by the deans and faculty as a whole to sponsor an Educational Opportunity Program, funds for which were provided by a member of the State Education Department who had participated in the workshop as a guest. Late the following summer, during the pre-registration, special orientation program, one of the janitors discovered about 15 Black students asleep in the lounge at 7:30 a.m., quite against the rules. In a sequence of events reminiscent of Henny Penny, he brought a buddy to confirm the reality of what he saw. They then ushered in the supervisor, who went to the Dean of the faculty, who came, saw, and conquered the situation by joining the whole group for coffee and doughnuts. Dean Schlifke had been to the workshop and was "more open, concerned, and creative about organizational improvement."

training themselves, teach what they know, or find outside experts, and coordinate internal resources. Psychological education now is installed at Jamestown Community College. This required active collaboration with members of the college in an OD effort.

The successful practice of Organizational Development also is dependent on psychological education. The roles, rules, role-relationships, procedures, and norms of systems have a meta-individual permanency. They tend to continue regardless of who specifically occupies the role, plays by the rules, etc. Though these stable system properties can be legitimately abstracted in thought and spoken about as if they had tangible thingness, in fact they have reality only so long as they are given life by the role occupants, the rule-follower, etc. This is merely a fancy way of saying that the approach to organization development always is through individuals, clarifying or changing the goals individuals share, improving stable patterns of communication among role inhabitants, altering their shared expectations, helping the leading person lead differently, improving the efficiency of problem-solving done by groups of individuals, and facing and resolving conflicts between people, collaboratively redefining roles. Not surprisingly, most of the OD methods (training, process consultation, confrontation, data feedback, problem-solving) are at most extensions of psychological education techniques developed originally for promoting self-renewing people.

Perhaps now it is more accurate to say there is a common pool of techniques from which OD specialists and psychological educators draw. Using these techniques, the organizational health of educational systems can be increased through individuals. Using these techniques, the psychological health of students can be improved in schools. Only the focus is different. OD aims to increase the health-giving properties of schools available to all who pass through. Psychological education attempts to increase the health the individuals carry with them through every institution.

11.
The Future of
Psychological Education

The aim of the research reported in this book was to find generic solutions to problems in the field of psychological education by studying the education of one human motive in great detail. The potential value of this strategy lies in the richness of the research analog. What can we now say about the field as a whole? How many findings can be legitimately generalized? In what ways can the methods of maintaining increased achievement motivation be used effectively in maintaining the effects of other psychological education courses? Conversely, what perspectives can we gain about achievement motivation training by seeing it as one aspect of psychological education?

This task assumes that there is a well-defined field to which this research can be related. Unfortunately, this is not true. During the six years of this research the field has become an ever larger collection of techniques, courses, "centers," people, projects, and goals without a higher order structure to guide the developmental efforts. Therefore, specifying the contributions of this research to the field or, vice versa, viewing the research from the vantage point of the entire field requires the prior delineation of the field. Completing this larger task could result in a basic textbook in itself, and by comparison would make this book seem small. Certainly, this final chapter can do no more than sketch the structure that needs to be established with far greater precision and detail. Nevertheless, even an outline of the field will serve the purpose of this chapter by helping to identify what has been accomplished and what remaining problems in psychological education require solutions.

The chapter is divided into three sections. The first section describes the four major goals of psychological education. The second section outlines the existing strategies and tactics used to attain these goals. Together these sections provide details of the definition of psychological education—the use of educational methods to promote psychological growth. Discussion of the research on achievement motivation training is embedded in this presentation, as it illuminates important issues. The first two sections define the structure of the field and what currently exists. The last section identifies the unsolved problems in curriculum development, teacher training, and research.

The Goals of Psychological Education

There is general agreement at the platitudinous level that education should help individuals exercise their inalienable right to pursue a full life. Thus one might expect psychological education to be heartily welcomed in all quarters as a vehicle for undeniable good. However there are diverse answers to the question of what specifically constitutes the good life. Closely reasoned analysis of education and human values (Rich, 1968) is the quietest voice among many that include impassioned advocacy of education for ecstasy (Leonard, 1968) and the screaming Right who see in psychological education the long, sinister arm of international Communism (Allen, 1968). Within the diverse array of proposals and rebuttals concerning the development of human potential, there are four basic goals, with associated rationales legitimizing them. Since most existing goals are derivations and variations, it is more useful to discuss and exemplify the four basic categories than to present a compulsively complete catalog of all specific course goals.

The first broad goal of psychological education is to promote the existing aims of education, especially the often neglected psycho-social goals. Acting in the service of this aim requires an adaptation in the traditional role of educational psychologists. In contrast to removing blocks to learning among the noticeably deviant and difficult students, psychological educators attempt to teach positive attitudes, motives, and values that facilitate learning among all students. Some of these training programs are inspired by research, as for instance, "origin" training developed by deCharms and associates (deCharms, 1969; Shea and Jackson, 1970). The Coleman report (1966a) found that students' attitudes toward fate (whether they saw themselves as origins of what happened to them or as pawns of fate) accounted for a significant amount of variance in how much these students learned in school. DeCharms has shown that training students to act like origins and helping teachers create "origin" climates in the classroom increases learning as measured by widely used standardized tests (McClelland and Alschuler, 1971). Other psychological educators make a direct appeal to the stated aims of education, and justify their training programs on the basis of apparent relevance rather than research findings, e.g., improving memory (Roth, 1952; Lorrayne, 1957; Furst, 1960), and increasing creativity (Massialas and Zevin, 1967; Crawford, 1968; Gordon, 1961; Gowan, Demos and Torrance, 1967; Torrance, 1970; Parnes, 1967; de Mille, 1967). A similar type of justification was made for achievement motivation training: it encourages commitments to basic social values such as independence, acceptance of personal responsibility, mastering the environment according to standards of excellence, and entrepreneurial role responsibility. These are among the generally acknowledged aims of public education as an agent for socializing the young into the predominant cultural norms (Parsons, 1959; Dreeben, 1968).

Brown (1971) also accepts the value of what is taught in school after he has restated its most hallowed aim of educating the whole man. According to Brown this means integrating the cognitive and affective components of learning at an experiential level. Wholeness is not just a clear, complete concept of heroism, for example, or even also an intellectual understanding of fear. It requires the experiential understanding of the students' own courage and fear. Thus Brown advocates teaching such standard fare as *The Red Badge of Courage*, but learning it through writing themes and doing theater improvisation to make sense of it intellectually and physically. When learning touches students' feelings in this way it is personally relevant, and, according to Brown, students will even learn more as measured by tests of academic knowledge. On one standardized test for 9th graders assessing knowledge of the American Constitution, the specially taught classes obtained 210 A's and 153 grades of B, C, D, or F, in contrast to traditional classes with comparable students in which there were only 39 A's and 326 grades of B, C, D, or F ($\chi^2 = 178.3$, p $\ll .0001$).

The second basic goal of psychological education is to teach students effective and pleasurable processes to reach the goals they choose. To attain the widest variety of consciously chosen goals, students need a large, flexible repertoire of process skills. This increases students' options and in this sense increases their freedom. Achievement motivation is one such process skill, involving moderate risk taking, careful planning, using feedback to improve performance, and striving for excellence. Choosing the specific goals for which the achievement motivation process may be useful is the prerogative of students. Achievement motivation trainers do not claim that this is the only or best motivational process, but simply that it is a potentially helpful and enjoyable tool for one's psychological kit. In other courses, students are taught how to clarify their values, not what values to clarify (Raths, Harmin and Simon, 1966) or how to relax and attend, not when (Ivey, 1971).

The most elaborate rationale and set of "process" courses has been developed by Newberg and Borton (Newberg and Borton, 1968; Newberg, 1969; Borton, 1970). Based on a cybernetic model of information processing, both their "Urban Affairs" and "Communications" courses teach students new ways to get personally relevant data, make sense of the data, act on the basis of the information to attain goals, and evaluate the discrepancy between intended and actual outcomes. The discrepancy then becomes new data to be analyzed, acted on, etc. Specifically, the processes they teach are: how to get immersed through sensing, being quiet, and gaming; how to get reoriented through focusing, mirroring, and sorting; how to analyze through symbolization, simulation, and ritualization; how to contemplate alternatives through dreaming and meditating; how to consciously act by experimenting, multi-role playing, choosing, developing style, and forgetting the skill. Newberg and Borton believe these psychological skills are just as basic to effective information processing as learning to read, write, and calculate.

Some psychological educators start and finish more explicitly with student choices, a strategy that violates long-standing school norms—in which teachers determine the curriculum. The first step in Weinstein and Fantini's (1970) curriculum is to identify the high-priority student concerns through a series of ingenious diagnostic activities. Usually, student interests are variants of concerns, with identity, connectedness (relationships with others), and power. Weinstein then teaches students to act like scientists about their concerns through a series of "experimental" procedures, i.e., confronting (experiencing variations in the concerns), inventorying their unique responses *vis-a-vis* other people, finding the patterns in their responses, identifying the consequences of those patterns, trying out alternative patterns, evaluating the new patterns, and finally, choosing to change or stay with the existing patterns. These curricula reflect mainstream values in modern Western civilization—to be humanely scientific and to be effective information processors. The new twist is the application of these guiding ideals to the world of internal personal experience.

At one level the explicit policy of these process curricula— never to choose goals for students—does not need to be consciously enforced because existing student choices permit and limit what is learnable. Conducive student values, goals, interests, and attention appear to be necessary conditions for learning in the first place. If students are not interested, do not attend or pay attention, *they don't learn.* We found in achievement motivation training, for instance, that getting attention was a relative matter—the setting, style, tone, content, and expectations had to be, and could only be, moderately different from existing student norms if we wanted to get and maintain attention. We had to take our cues from the norms of student experience. We also found that if students did not value achievement goals in life, they did not benefit as much from the course. Their level of existing interest thus served a gate-keeping function. Related research by McClelland and Winter (1969), Luborsky *et al.* (1971), and Coleman (1966a) also suggests that *initial attitudes, interest, and motivation determine more of the variance in how much is learned than any educational input or combination of inputs controlled by teachers.* Students are not passive vessels eternally ready to contain any educational content. That is obvious. What is less immediate but equally true is that implicit student choices make teaching either meaningful or irrelevant. It appears that students' psychological make-up may be their best guardian of healthy, relevant growth, and best guard against psychological imperialism.

A third goal of psychological education is to teach positive mental health. Helping students act like scientists with their personal data or become better information processors are two proposed attributes of positive mental health. Many other, less cybernetic-sounding traits have been suggested with accompanying rationales that range in truth value from carnival barkerism to the imprimatur of Sigmund Freud. One group of practitioners claims that the royal road to mental health is the body. You should stop betraying your body (Lowen, 1967), relax (Jacobson, 1962), awaken and relax your senses (Gunther, 1968, 1970), find inner beauty and outer youth (Enelow, 1969), breathe properly (Proskauer, 1968), control your brain waves (Tart, 1969), have peak experiences in the nude (Bindrim, 1968) and ultimately achieve the *sine qua non* of mental health, a quivering, vibrating, pulsating, mind-boggling orgasm (Reich, 1942; Lowen, 1965). At minimum the collection of activities invented by these innovators are useful additions to the growing repertoire of psychological education techniques. Beyond that, such reputable establishment physicians as Karl Menninger are cautiously approving: "Does it benefit anyone? Does it further physical and mental health? Does it bring joy and peaceful preoccupation along with its physical benefits? Her [Gertrude Enelow's] students have no doubt of it. And their commitment impressed me. I watched for a long time and liked what I saw" (from the foreword to *Inner Beauty and Outer Youth*).

At the other end of the continuum, there are those who describe positive mental health as the psychological equivalent of spiritual fulfillment: Individuation (Jung, 1959a), Psychosynthesis (Assagioli, 1965), Self-Actualization (Maslow, 1968 b, d, g). These concepts of positive mental health tend to be supported by more sophisticated, less turgid rationales, but are not any more closely linked to the results of empirical research. In between the body and the spirit there is a large group of practitioners with theories and followers who espouse healthy interpersonal communication: how to fight fair with those you love (Bach and Wyden, 1970), how to communicate effectively with your children (Gordon, 1970), with your family as a whole (Satir, 1967; Watzlawick, Beavin and Jackson, 1967), and how to develop your family's strengths and potential (Otto, 1968). What characterizes all of these programs is their preoccupation with the previously neglected positive end of the mental illness-health continuum.

These mini-theories and action programs are a small portion of the vast array of alternative goals available in the field of mental health. The diversity itself within this small sample, however, raises the fundamental question, "What is mental health?" After an exhaustive review of the extant theories, Jahoda (1958) concluded that no completely acceptable, all-inclusive definition exists. There are nonetheless a finite number of concepts, and considerable overlap among them. Allport (1961) describes this overlap most succinctly:

> In particular we find six criteria that sum up the area of agreement. The mature personality will (1) have a widely extended sense of self; (2) be able to relate warmly to others in both intimate and non-intimate contacts; (3) possess a fundamental emotional security and accept himself; (4) perceive, think, and act with zest in accordance with outer reality; (5) be capable of self-objectification through insight and sense of humor; (6) live in harmony with a unifying philosophy of life.

Even this identification of the consensus that exists is not completely satisfying because it avoids the question of values.

> By this label (of "mental health") one asserts that these psychological attributes are "good." And, inevitably, the question is raised: Good for what? Good in terms of middle-class ethics? Good for democracy? For the continuation of the social status quo? For the individual's happiness? For mankind? For survival? For the development of the species? For art and creativity? For

the encouragement of genius or of mediocrity and conformity? The list could be continued (Jahoda, 1958).

These same questions can be asked of the programs designed to promote learning in school and student-chosen goals. Ultimately, for what and for whom are these programs good? Answers should be explicit so that educators, students, and parents can make knowledgeable choices after open discussion.

The fourth major goal of psychological education is to promote normal development. It is natural to ask why it is necessary to help pass through a normal sequence of stages that most people manage to traverse on their own. While this is true by definition, each stage is more or less problematic and some people falter at each stage, remaining psychologically stunted in particular ways. The earlier in life these difficulties occur, the more long lasting and widespread are the effects, and the more difficult they are to correct later (Bloom, 1965). For instance, one of the most important skills learned during the first two years of life is the control of attention. From awareness of "booming, buzzing confusion" the child learns to selectively attend to aspects of his environment—a face, a noise, something that moves. In the early months, selective attention is determined mostly by the environment; whatever changes rapidly gets attention. However, as the child develops ritual patterns of action and response (grasping, sucking, hitting, shaking), attention to objects is determined more by the number of action-hypotheses the child can test out on an object. Progressively, attention comes under the control of the child and is determined more by internal factors than external ones. The richness and variety of stimulation in the environment, especially the mother, plays a central role in determining the rate at which the control of attention is internalized. Thus it is not surprising that institutionalized infants have major developmental deficits and a general retardation of learning in comparison to their more fortunate age mates in homes with mothers.*

Given the fact that attention is a prerequisite for learning

---

*I am indebted to Irene Alschuler for a helpful review of the literature on the growth of attention in children and existing remedial programs.

(even Pavlov's dogs did not condition if they weren't paying attention, i.e., had bored, flopped-down ears), these deficits have profound importance for all later learning (Kagan, 1967). As most elementary teachers know from their experience, many learning problems result from inability to voluntarily control and sustain attention: "The child is distractable, his attention span is too short." According to developmental research and theory, the most effective time to intervene with psychological education programs aimed at facilitating the development of attention is during the critical period in its growth—or roughly 0 to 3 years of age. In fact, many of the government-sponsored enrichment programs in day care centers, Head Start, and Parent-Child Centers are designed to prevent such deficits. That they are "remedial" for children of age 4 indicates that they already are somewhat late and ineffective (Jensen, 1969). As a result, curricula are being developed for training mothers in specific behaviors that should increase internalized attention during the first year of life and selected attention to speech (thus language development) in the second year. The implications for formal education (not how much students are given, but how much they get out of what they are given) should be profound. A number of other programs have been created to train mothers of infants to facilitate their psychological development (Gordon, 1969; Hunt, 1971; also, there are relevant school-sponsored programs at Boston University, Peabody College, University of Florida, Los Angeles, and Oakland, California). These programs are too recent for long-term scientific evaluation. However, early results are encouraging. Infant education itself is in its infancy.

Another critical period in the psychological development of children begins at about the age of 5 to 7, when they come to understand certain fundamental attributes of the world in a new way. Piaget refers to this as the period of "concrete operations" because cognitive processes emerge from the magical thinking of the previous period, can operate on concrete objects, but are not yet able to reason about reasoning, or operate on cognitive operations without external referents (the period of formal operations). During the period of concrete operations, children learn that certain aspects of physical reality (number, class membership, length, mass) remain the same despite apparent changes. Children are able to make new logical inferences using such processes as the inclusion of lower-order classes in higher-order classes, transitive seriation, logical multiplication of classes, and quantity. As a result, children also develop new understandings of time, space, causality, and morality. Because these cognitive abilities underlie and make possible so much of what is supposed to be learned in the primary grades, a number of training programs have been created to facilitate this stage of psychological development (Smedslund, 1961; Sigel, Roeper and Hooper, 1966; Wallach, Wall and Anderson, 1967; Wohlwill and Lowe, 1962; Gruen, 1965; Beilen, Kagan and Rabinowitz, 1966).

One extension and elaboration of Piaget's theory is the work of Lawrence Kohlberg (1963, 1964, 1968), who has described the developments in reasoning about moral problems made possible by the growth of cognitive operations (Kohlberg, 1963, 1964, 1968, 1969). Prior to concrete operational reasoning, children's thinking is egocentric and magical. A child judges good as what helps him, what he wants or likes. Their opposites are bad. There are no concepts of mutual obligation or rules to obey independent of the child's desires. When children reach the stage of concrete operations they become less egocentric and appreciate certain stable, concrete aspects of moral rules. As children develop formal operational thinking they progressively appreciate non-immediate aspects of the world, more abstract possibilities, obligations and reasoning. Moral decisions come to be based on what is "conventional." Ultimately, the development of moral reasoning may evolve to autonomous considerations of universal ethical principles. This sequence of developments in moral reasoning is hierarchical in that each stage includes the previous stage in a higher synthesis. It is an invariant, logical, and psychological sequence, although this complex aspect is less apparent in this brief synopsis.

Because cognitive development allows but does not guarantee moral development (Kohlberg, LaCross and Ricks, 1970) it is appropriate to create training programs specifically for this aspect of development. Longitudinal research conducted by Kohlberg (1969) identified a critical period in moral development between the ages of 9 and 12. The degree of development during this period determined more variance in the final level attained by individuals than development during any other age period. The potential impact of widespread moral education for this age group is great because the data show clearly that virtually no one with a high level of moral reasoning in early adolescence was subsequently involved in serious anti-social violations of the law as adults. It is natural, therefore, to find Kohlberg now deeply involved with moral education in schools and prisons (Kohlberg, 1966b, 1970c; Kohlberg and Turiel, 1971a, 1971b; Blatt and Kolberg, 1971).

A number of other developmental theories provide ordered sequences of goals for psychological education courses (Drews, 1970; Erikson, 1950, 1959; Harvey, Hunt and Schroeder, 1961; Loevinger *et al.*, 1970; Peck and Havighurst, 1960; Sullivan, Grant, and Grant, 1957; Van den Daele, 1968; Werner, 1961).*

One of the most intriguing theories is being elaborated by a philosopher who claims that the evolution of self-awareness through history is recapitulated in the course of each individual's life (Skorpen, 1970a, b). During the mythic period of "immediate self-hood," human beings did not know themselves apart from nature, gods or the community. The advance in self-awareness made during the Greek period of "socially defined self-hood" was the exploration of Man's uniqueness in contrast with nature, in his striving for excellence in word and deed. During the Renaissance period of "society-emerging self-hood," individuals discover their differences from "Men" in general through their special abilities. Singularity has its special prerogatives, as is most markedly illustrated by Renaissance artists. The word for "self" does not even appear in the lexicon until the Enlightenment period of "self-creating self-hood" when men discover differences *vis-a-vis* other individual men. There is an emphasis on becoming independently and rationally self-developing within the social system. Finally, the current Existential period of "self-transcending self-hood" emphasizes the autonomous and principled creation of

*For a useful summary table that illustrates the similarities between these developmental theories see Kohlberg, 1971, Table 4.

a new inner self as opposed to the rationally developed external social self. This summary is so brief that it is a caricature. It is enough, nonetheless, to suggest how the history of man's evolving self-hood can be used as a mirror for understanding psychological development. In the course of normal development, each person passes through an egocentric stage in infancy when he does not differentiate himself from the world around him, then learns to act on the world around him to make things happen, then develops special talents, his unique identity in the world, and his inner life. There are enough striking parallels between cognitive, ego, and moral development on the one hand, and Skorpen's interpretation of the historical roots of self-hood on the other hand, to suggest that it may indeed be one of those rare, grand unifying theories currently in the making. This reciprocity between history and psychology is the core notion of a new psychological education and humanities course, an experiential recapitulation of personal and world history.*

These four basic goals indicate the great diversity of existing objectives, and suggest how many more await a translation into curricula. Hallowed though some of these sources may be, they nevertheless do not fully answer the questions of legitimacy and limits. In general these sources are widely accepted but there is always (and in a sense, always *only*) the individual student with particular parents and a specific fallible teacher. Difficult, ulti-mately practical questions remain: How does a teacher choose from among the available goals and courses? Are the goals and courses good? For what? From whose point of view? Should psychological education teach what is normal in a partially sick society? Should this training be an instrument of social reform? Who should decide? Is there a close correspondence between the goals, what is taught, and what is actually learned? How do you assess these goals and outcomes? These are problems of ethics, implementation, and research.

Implementation of Psychological Education

Psychological educators are a practical breed, more interested

---

*This curriculum is being developed at the Center for Humanistic Education at the State University of New York at Albany.

in what "works" than in academic "truth" for its own sake. Since the practitioners have seized the initiative from academicians, the criteria available and important to teachers, not researchers, have guided the development (and elimination) of procedures to educate the psyche. Practical criteria tend to be lodged in the here-and-now—what turns kids on, what gets attention, what keeps students working on their own, what is manageable within the limits of 45-minute classes and the tolerance of neighboring teachers; and, finally, *what is so visibly successful that statistical confirmation is irrelevant.* But surviving the test of classroom viability is not enough, as teachers are coming to realize. Enthusiasm of students is at best a day-to-day objective, and may not be related to the long-term usefulness of what is taught. Effectiveness is a moot question for teachers who see the classroom all too closely and the long-term consequences all too rarely. Academicians, of course, have the opposite myopia: What seems obviously necessary for long-term growth may be totally impractical in schools. Fortunately, a convergence is occurring that matches teachers' "know-how" with academicians' "know-what." Educators and psychologists have created an enormous repertoire of procedures, exercises, techniques, games, and role plays that *work*, at least in the most immediate context of the group (Otto, 1970a; Lewis and Streitfeld, 1970; Brown, 1971; Human Relations Project, 1969; Schutz, 1967; Miles, 1959; Nylen, Mitchell and Stout, undated; Malamud and Machover, 1965; Perls, Hefferline and Goodman, 1965; Lyons, 1971; Zuckerman and Horn, 1970). The complementary bodies of expertise of teachers and researchers also have met in devising effective organizations of these procedures into tactics and strategies for reaching the goals of psychological education.

Tactics

Psychological education procedures have been organized into three tactics. "Congruent courses" teach a psychological characteristic solely and directly. "Confluent courses" attempt to integrate academic and psychological subject matter at an experiential level. "Contextual approaches" alter the social environment to stimulate desired psychological states. These three tactics are not mutually exclusive. In fact, all three are important in implementing a maximally effective strategy for promoting psychological growth.

1. *Congruent courses.* There are numerous courses, like achievement motivation training, that attempt to teach a well-defined, limited aspect of psychological growth. Research presented in this book provided empirical evidence that supported the value of a six-step learning sequence for maximizing the effectiveness of congruent courses. Other psychological educators have arrived at similar sequences through practical experience and common sense. For illustrative purposes, several of these sequences are presented in Table 11.1.

In spite of the rich array of procedures for implementing each step of these sequences and the evolving consensus about this sequence itself, many congruent courses as currently practiced are partial at best. This is most notably true in the short courses offered for adults in "growth centers" around the country. The "here-and-now" ethic and frequent anti-intellectual stance mitigate against the process of clearly conceptualizing, relating the experience to one's "there-and-then life," choosing, practicing, and internalizing. These activities take time and often are less exciting. To omit them, however, inevitably reduces the long-term yields of these courses (Campbell and Dunnette, 1968; McClelland and Winter, 1969; Houts and Serber, 1972).

There are two relatively distinct types of congruent courses. The large majority of congruent courses attempt to expose students to alternative patterns, processes, motives, or goals without trying to facilitate advancement in the hierarchy of developmental stages. This type of course increases *lateral* freedom by helping people explore and enrich their repertoire of options for action, response, and enjoyment. The second type of course increases *vertical* freedom by teaching higher-order capacities in developmental hierarchies. This is not simply an academic distinction, because the procedures and experiential portions of lateral and vertical courses are somewhat different. Vertical courses almost always use methods that focus on conflicts between developmental stages. For instance, in fostering moral development, Blatt and Kohlberg (1971) chose moral dilemmas to be argued by two students who were at adjacent stages of moral

Table 11.1

Comparison of Tactical Sequences
in Three Types of Congruent Courses

Motivation Training (Alschuler *et al.*, 1970)	Process Teaching (Weinstein and Fantini, 1970)	Educating Student Concerns (Newberg & Borton, 1968)
Get attention through moderate novelty.	Identify high priority student concerns.	Sense discrepancy between intended and actual outcomes.
Intensely experience the thoughts, actions, and feelings comprising the motive.	Confront concerns by experiencing variations.	Get immersed through sensing and reoriented through focusing, mirroring, and sorting.
Clearly conceptualize the experience.	Inventory unique responses and find patterns.	Analyze through symbolization, simulation, and ritualization.
Relate the experience to one's life demands, self-image, and cultural values.	Identify the consequences and how it serves person.	Contemplate alternatives through dreaming and meditating.
Apply and practice the motive.	Try alternative patterns and evaluate them.	Consciously act by experimenting, role playing.
Internalize the motive by progressively withdrawing external supports.	Choose to change or stay the same.	Choose, develop style, forget the skill.

development. The most successful techniques for raising the level of cognitive development engage individuals in logical conflicts. For instance, a child counts the number of buttons on a table. The trainer spreads the buttons apart and asks, "How many are there now, more or less?" If the child says more, as pre-concrete operational children are wont to do, the trainer asks the child to count them again. The training consists of manipulating the perceptual display and exploring the contradictions until the child realizes that number remains constant in spite of irrelevant changes in arrangement (Smedslund, 1961). Recently, Rokeach (1971) demonstrated relatively long-lasting attitude and behavior change in students simply by pointing out contradictions in the hierarchy of their expressed values. In contrast to these cognitive conflict situations, lateral congruent courses more often expose students to new action and affective experiences that may be assimilated into one's repertoire with as little conflict as possible.

2. *Confluent courses.* If competition between teams in a game to build the most paper airplanes in a six-minute production period can be used to teach achievement motivation (Alschuler, Tabor and McIntyre, 1970), why can't literature be used to teach a wider range of emotional responses, social studies used to confront value dilemmas, and chemistry used to develop information-processing skills? Confluent courses exploit this obvious but neglected potential of academic courses. Ingenious practitioners working at the concrete level of daily lesson plans have invented hundreds of integrations in virtually all subject matter areas. These integrations involve making the subject matter personally relevant here-and-now through the use of imagination, touching students' feelings, and translating ideas into actions (Leeper, 1967; Brown, 1971; Kirschenbaum and Simon, 1969; Howard, 1970; Leonard, 1968; Human Relations Project, 1969). Harmin and Simon (1968) illustrate one of the easiest transitions from a low-level fact-oriented lesson to a value-clarifying lesson. At the fact level, a lesson on the Pilgrims would pile fact upon fact in chronological order by eliciting answers to the following sequence of questions: Why did the Pilgrims leave England? Why did the Pilgrims go to the Netherlands? What did they find there? What was the journey to America like? At a second level, relationships and generaliza-

tions are stressed. What are the causes and effects of prejudice and intolerance? Why do people migrate? How does one establish a community in a hostile environment? At the value-clarifying level, the story of the Pilgrims is used to stimulate questions like: Have intolerance or prejudice ever touched your life? Are there freedoms you consider so precious that you would probably leave any place in which they were denied? Would you work to preserve the freedoms you see as threatened now? The aim of such questions is to clarify whether a person has all seven criteria of true values. It must be (1) prized and cherished, (2) part of a repeated pattern, (3) chosen from among alternatives, (4) freely chosen, (5) chosen after due reflection, (6) publicly affirmed, and (7) acted upon (Raths, Harmin and Simon, 1966).

Confluent tactics such as value-clarification questions have the virtue of publicly supporting and enriching what is already being taught in school. Conversely, the subject matter is used simultaneously to facilitate psychological learning.

The intentions of confluent tactics are clear. Aside from the obvious and valuable gains in the morale of students, however, it must be asked whether confluent courses contribute to any or all of the goals of psychological education. To date, I know only one empirical study showing that confluent courses increase academic gains (Brown, 1971) and, unfortunately, not one single study showing resultant psychological gains. It is possible that confluent tactics have little or no effect beyond immediate boosts in interest. The inventions tend to be *ad hoc*, diverse, and without any long-term plan or follow-up. Confluent techniques seem to be strongest in getting attention and providing an experience base, but progressively weaker in conceptualizing, relating study to one's own there-and-then life, practicing new psychological patterns and internalizing them. This may be due to a basic loyalty of most confluent educators to the academic discipline and goals. Thus social studies, mathematics, or English retain their academic structure and sequence. This may make it difficult to retain fidelity to psychological goals which would require different emphases.

On the other hand, the creative, improvisatory, here-and-now, unsequenced character of confluent tactics may be weak in itself but virtuous in conjunction with congruent courses. The number and diversity of confluent experiences could provide students the opportunity to explore and expand the processes they learned in congruent courses, thus becoming part of the "application," "internalization" phases of the six-step learning sequence. Imagine the natural integration that would occur for a student after a training course in moral reasoning if he had a number of opportunities in academic classes to try out his newly acquired reasoning through exercises in value clarification of the kind suggested by Raths, Harmin and Simon (1966). Even if congruent courses were not available, it is still possible that students exposed long enough to a wide enough variety of confluent experiences might be healthier, better information processors, cognitively more mature, and more knowledgeable. It is a moot question because, at the moment, no school system in the country has such pervasive confluent education.

3. *Contextual methods.* Changing the stable psychological characteristics that students carry with them from situation to situation is not enough because the expectations, roles, rules, and cues in the situation also determine in part students' thoughts, actions, and feelings. Thus it is also possible to promote psychological growth by changing the demand characteristics of situations, e.g., the classroom, the school as an organization, the family context, informal peer groups, etc. The research presented in this book strongly suggests that several overlapping and interdependent systems must be coordinated if psychological education is to survive and be effective in a school, specifically, classroom climate and the school organization. The case study of what happened at Jamestown Community College is a vivid example of this proposition (Chapter 10).

Classroom climate appears to be an intervening variable that mediates between such factors as classroom structure, teachers' leadership style, physical environment, etc., on the one hand and the psychological states of students on the other. The basic tactic for creating a desired classroom climate is to measure the climate, provide teachers with these data, coach them on altering the climate, reassess the new climate, inform teachers, modify procedures, and so on, until the desired climate is obtained. McClelland and Bergthold (in McClelland and Alschuler, 1971) have developed a classroom climate survey based on the work of Litwin and Stringer (1968) on Organizational Climates in industry. Specifically, they define classroom climate as

> a set of measurable characteristics of the social environ-ment of the classroom as perceived by the students and assumed to influence their motivation and behavior.

McClelland and Bergthold's survey assesses six characteristics related to achievement, affiliation, and power motivating climates in classrooms (see Table 11.2).

Numerous other classroom climate assessment instruments exist that focus on other characteristics. In each case the tactic for altering the classroom climate is to provide teachers with regular feedback so that they can monitor the effects of the changes they introduce.

One way to alter the classroom climate is to change the rules of the learning game (Chapter 7). Variations in the scoring system, the nature of the obstacles that must be overcome to score, and how decisions are made determine in part what motivational processes are called forth (Chapter 9). Summaries of other contextual methods have been written describing how to establish classroom climates that foster creativity (Prince, 1968b, 1969; Torrance, 1970) and affiliation motivation (Schmuck and Schmuck, 1971).

Perhaps the most systematic research on this tactic has been done by deCharms and colleagues at Washington University. DeCharms developed an "origin climate" questionnaire that assesses the degree to which students feel in control of what they do in the classroom, set their own goals, find their own means of attaining those goals, feel rewarded for doing things on their own and develop self-confidence (McClelland and Alschuler, 1971). DeCharms then provided Origin-Pawn training (a variant on n-Ach training) to a group of teachers, and subsequently consulted with them on structural changes and leadership styles as they created origin climates in their classrooms. As predicted, this resulted in more "origin" attitudes in students as measured by a specially devised Thematic Apperception Test coding system. These scores

Table 11.2

Summary of Classroom Climate Questionnaire Scales

Motive	Classroom Characteristic	Definition
Achievement	Organizational Clarity	Students know results when they do well, and feel they are fairly graded.
	Responsibility	Students work at their own speed and have a chance to make decisions on their own.
Power	Morale	The students obey, do not cheat, are proud to belong to the class, etc.
	Standards	Teacher holds up high standards of work and good order.
Affiliation	Warmth	Teacher provides warmth, support, and encouragement.
	Togetherness	The students like each other and are friendly in class.

in turn predicted higher school performance. Both academic and psychological goals were maximized through the creation of origin climates.

Being able to influence the psychological processes in the classroom is not enough nor is it even possible to do effectively unless there is a conducive school organization. Installing psychological education raises issues about norms and expectations, creates some tension, involves conflicts among educators, and requires the help of change agents if the school is to survive the innovation and accomplish its goals more fully. The procedures available to help schools incorporate such innovations fall within the field of organizational development (OD). The range of OD procedures can be summarized briefly by indicating the organizational problems OD addresses, the variety of foci for solving those problems, and the alternative modes of intervention that can be used. The "OD-cube" generated by these three dimensions is presented in Table 11.3. Schmuck and Miles (1971) have made a complete presentation of the current status of OD in schools.

OD procedures have been presented as a set of tools for introducing psychological education in schools. While that is the proper perspective for our purposes here, it also neglects other relevant contributions of OD. First, the usefulness of OD is as broad as the contexts in which psychological education occurs: parent-child centers, day care centers, Headstart programs, community centers, Sunday schools, Upward Bound programs, Vista and Peace Corps training programs, Job Corps centers, adult education programs, industrial training sites, mental hospitals, halfway houses, communes, community organizations, retirement communities, and even nursing homes. Second, several million adult Americans work in schools. The goals of OD for these adults are the same as the goals of other contextual methods for students in classrooms. The methods are somewhat different because school organization is somewhat different from classroom organization and because adults have somewhat different needs than students. However, there is considerable overlap. Both schools and classrooms fundamentally are systems with tasks to accomplish and the psychological health of their members to promote. In conjunction with congruent courses for adults, OD methods can develop school

Table 11.3

A Scheme for Classifying Organizational Development Interventions (Used by Permission of the Authors, Schmuck and Miles, 1971)

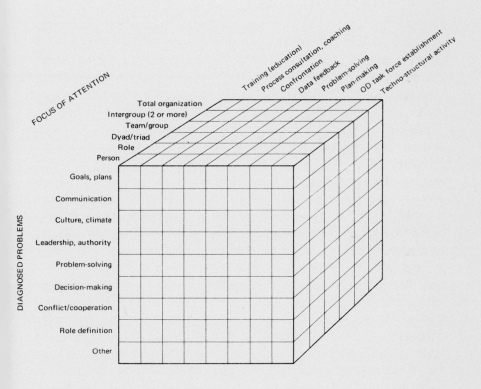

contexts that support the psychological health and growth of adult educators.

Strategy

Strategy refers to the arrangement of tactics in an overall plan to attain a desired goal. The immediate excitement of many psychological education procedures can lead teachers into an obsessive preoccupation with finding new techniques to keep students involved. Involvement is a short-term goal at best. Reaching important long-term goals requires guidelines for how to organize these techniques and coordinate congruent, confluent, and contextual approaches. There are many alternative strategies, ranging from grand plans for utopias to special relationships with Gurus. Several aspects of the strategy for increasing achievement motivation will illustrate guidelines for planning psychological education aimed at more modest and typical goals.

1. *Tactics should be arranged to promote internalization rather than mere arousal of the characteristic to be learned.*

Although necessary for learning, attention is not sufficient for internalization to take place. Interest, affective arousal, and excitement can be highly misleading. For instance, there is almost no relationship between how much students enjoyed the n-Ach course and how much they benefitted from it several years later. Similarly, knowledge as tested at the end of the course is unrelated to long-term usefulness. Thus, focusing on short-term Mastery or Satisfaction may be an irrelevant, though tempting, decoy. Similar null findings have been obtained in research on the predictive power of grades in school (McClelland *et al.*, 1958; Kirschenbaum, Simon and Napier, 1971) and treatment of emotional disturbances in children (Kohlberg, LaCross and Ricks, 1970). Rather than work for immediate gains (knowledgeable, happy students), it may be more important to make the course content an instructional bridge between the existing values and goals of students on the one hand and the opportunities and demands of reality on the other. This is one implication of the findings that students who value achievement goals in their life before the course begins make most use of the course and apply it in areas outside of school where they can exercise their entrepreneurial spirit—sports, hobbies, work. The six-step learning sequence for congruent courses is a guide line for building such instructional bridges. There needs to be as much work on relating the learning experience to ideal self-image, cultural values and the demands of reality, setting goals and providing follow-up support, as on the initial problems of getting attention, providing an intense, integrated experience and clearly conceptualizing it. The latter work typically does not result in boundless immediate enthusiasm or dramatic gains in testable knowledge, but it does appear to be important for long-term internalization.

2. *Systematic organization of eclectic procedures to attain a specific limited objective is more effective than using one set of procedures to accomplish a wide variety of goals.*

This is a complicated way of saying that helping a person to change behavior, thoughts, and feelings is very difficult. Therefore, chances of success are increased if one is modest, limited, and specific in goals and as thorough, eclectic, and diverse as possible in bringing facilitating procedures to the change task. This strategy is basic to behavior therapy and behavior modification and a major reason for the relative success of this approach. The same rationale is behind the current movement in education toward translating educational goals into well-defined behavioral objectives while at the same time increasing the number of instructional alternatives. Achievement motivation training began with the operational definitions of n-Ach used in some 20 years of research. Because there was prevailing pessimism about the possibility of significantly increasing a motive in adults or adolescents, as many relevant procedures were included in the n-Ach course as possible (McClelland and Winter, 1969). "Systematic organization of procedures" means dealing with the functional prerequisite of the course as a social "system." There need to be ways of establishing norms, handling conflicts, and reducing tensions so that the temporary system (the course) will survive until its system goals have been reached. If the system doesn't survive, then course participants will not have the opportunity to learn the new motivation process skills important to reaching their own goals (see Chapters 2 and 10 for fuller explanations of the course as a social system).

3. *The goals of psychological education are more effectively reached through holistic than through elementary approaches.*

Holistic means working with the several relevant systems of which the person is a part. In achievement motivation training this means matching the person's achievement goals with appropriate life situations (work, sports, hobbies, school) or attempting to alter the contexts to fit students' motives. This concern was the impetus for our contextual approaches to restructuring the classroom learning games. The same strategy principle was behind our work with Jamestown Community College; we needed to deal with the whole system in order to introduce motivation training in such a way that the college both accomplished its mandated tasks more effectively and enhanced its norms, expectations, and procedures for daily survival operations. Contrast this orientation with typical strategies for changing education where elements, but not the whole, are changed. Teachers' colleges provide teachers with new techniques that often are not used in schools, due to pre-empting immediate problems or lack of support and encouragement from the school. New curricula frequently are distorted or discarded by teachers who don't know how to use the curricula. Each of these elements can only be partially effective because change in schools must take place *in* schools, not in teachers' colleges, or researchers' laboratories. This means integrating these elements in working with schools as whole systems.

4. *The effectiveness of psychological education will be maximized by intervening at critical periods and levels of development.*

Researchers have identified a number of "critical periods" of development in which psychological skills (e.g., attention, moral reasoning, formal operational thinking) grow at a relatively rapid rate. Intervention at these times has relatively greater, longer-lasting consequences than the same degree of effort earlier or later. A similar case can be made for critical levels of development where interventions can have maximum impact. For example, it now appears that affective development is more caused by, than a cause of, cognitive development.

> In part this is because the development of cognitive traits is largely cumulative, sequential and irreversible, while much of the development of affective traits and experiences is not clearly sequential or irreversible. To conscious experience, moods change, anxieties disappear, loves and hates fade, the emotion of yesterday is weak and the emotion of today doesn't clearly build on the emotion of yesterday. The Trauma theory of neurosis is dead; the evidence of irreversible effects of early childhood trauma is extremely slight. Each childhood maternal deprivation, parental mistreatment, separation, incest, all seem to have much slighter effects upon adult adjustment than anyone seemed to anticipate (Kohlberg, LaCross and Ricks, 1970).

Two examples may help clarify this notion. Children of the ages 4 to 8 learn that certain properties of the external world (e.g., number, mass) remain constant in spite of changes in irrelevant attributes (e.g., arrangement, spacing). The development of this cognitive capacity in children to conserve certain attributes of the world allows the stabilization of affective gender identity: "I am and always will be a boy" (Kohlberg, 1966a). Later, when adolescents acquire formal operational thinking, they are able to meaningfully anticipate future events and imagine situations that have never existed before. Their concerns about identity then can become future-oriented: "What do I want to be?" It is only at this point that achievement motivation training which focuses on the "planning pattern" becomes effective. To summarize, those aspects of emotion that are reversible, non-sequential, and long-lived tend to have very heavy cognitive components. This does not mean that responding to short-lived emotional crises is unimportant. It means only that the most fundamental, long-range, widespread impact on affective development probably comes from training desired to facilitate growth in critical levels at critical periods in the development of capacities—with major cognitive components.

If one were to follow all of these principles of strategy as closely as possible, it would entail the selection of a basic psychological process, probably a cognitive capacity. It would be facilitated during the critical period in its development with the aim of helping students internalize, not just experience, this new capacity. A wide range of procedures would be systematically coordinated to attain this relatively limited, specific, and important goal. The introduction of this new type of psychological education would take place in schools so that curricula, teacher training, and administrative support could be coordinated within the whole system.

Prospectus for Psychological Education

The first two sections of this chapter have identified the goals espoused by psychological educators and the basic methods used to reach those goals. The purpose has been to indicate the domain, boundaries, and structure of the field. Describing what exists necessarily precedes a discussion of unexplored, undeveloped areas. This final section identifies some of the important unsolved problems in the field.

Goals and Implementation:
Curriculum Needs

The existing theories, methods, and research on promoting positive mental health, normal development, the aims of education, and useful psychological processes are diverse, extensive, and growing at an exponential rate. Still, there appear to be some major omissions. For instance, in spite of the claim that psychological education is for people from the cradle to the grave, there are no programs that deal directly with the growth crises of the aged. American culture uniquely misfits people for coming to terms with death. Cultural values that are actualized from childhood through late adulthood are diametrically opposed to those values necessary for accepting death with integrity. During the difficult disengagement process (Cummings and Henry, 1961) the aged must give up a "doing," "achieving" orientation in favor of a "self-expressive," "being" orientation. The present and the past must become more important than the future. From a life-long orientation toward mastering one's inner nature and outer environment (or at least being in harmony with nature), death represents the final conquest of consciousness by nature. In other cultures, where values are consistent with those demanded by peaceful dying, being old is the desired, respected prime of life (Alschuler, 1962). In general, the large majority of congruent, confluent, and contextual procedures have been designed for goals relevant to people under 40 and over 4. If psychological education is to constitute a full curriculum, procedures must be organized to promote relevant growth in the very old and the very young.

A full curriculum also requires more courses designed to promote vertical growth. Nearly all of the several hundred courses now in existence are designed to expand and strengthen one's repertoire of processes and responses at a given level of functioning, or what I have termed lateral growth. Training for vertical growth is particularly important because of the long-term consequences. In their comprehensive review of all the longitudinal data on childhood predictors of adult mental health, Kohlberg, LaCross and Ricks (1970) concluded as follows:

> Put bluntly, there is no research evidence available indicating that clinical analysis of the child's emotional status or dynamics leads to any more effective prognosis of adult mental health or illness than could be achieved by the man on the street who believes psychosis is hereditary and that criminality is the result of bad homes and neighborhoods in the common sense meaning of that concept . . . The findings we have reviewed support this position in suggesting that the best predictors of the absence of mental illness and maladjustment are the *presence* of various forms of competence and ego maturity rather than the absence of problems and symptoms as such. Within the general psycho-educational or ego-developmental approach just stressed, the findings suggest two "critical period" foci of mental health intervention. The first is a concern for cognitive orientation, interest, style, and attention in the years 6

to 9 (transition to concrete operational thinking and adjustment to school). The second is a special concern for peer relations and relations to adults in the years 9 to 12 when moral character development appears to become crystallized. In both of these areas, there is a continuum between the efforts of a humane education to stimulate ego development and more therapeutic efforts to achieve the same end.

Emotional problems in childhood are reversible and tend to go away. They don't predict adult maladjustment. Levels of cognitive, ego, and moral development in childhood do predict adult adjustment, because these capacities are non-reversible and cumulative. High levels of development in childhood remain and are augmented. In contrast, children between the ages of 9 to 12 who are at comparatively low levels of ego and moral development have worse peer relationships, as rated by peers, and engage in significantly more anti-social behavior. These aspects of development immaturity are the two best existing childhood predictors of all forms of adult maladjustment. The educational implications are clear. Although congruent, confluent, and contextual methods focused on enriching children's affective states may have immediate humane value, "affective education" during this period probably has few long-term consequences on mental health in adulthood. I know of no stronger way to make the case for the development of courses that promote vertical growth during critical periods in development.

This dialogue between the "seemingly" obvious and the "empirical" facts illustrates one virtue of a close association between research and curriculum development in psychological education. Such mutually enhancing relationships are rare, to the detriment of both potentially useful research and potentially significant practice. The relationship between achievement motivation research and training is a prototypic example of the many ways research and training can be mutually beneficial. From the outset, the operational definition of achievement motivation constituted our behavioral objective for training. Empirically established consequences of high and low n-Ach were measured outcomes of training. Situations that had been devised originally for research purposes were converted to training devices. For instance, the Ring Toss Game (Alschuler and Tabor, 1970b) was invented originally to *test* theoretical predictions about the effects of differing levels of n-Ach on risk-taking behavior. We used the same game to *teach* students moderate risk-taking. Similar conversions of research situations into training devices have occurred in the vertical growth training of Smedslund (1961), Blatt and Kohlberg (1971), and many types of creativity training (Parnes and Brunelle, 1967). In each of these examples, the extensive existing research also helped identify those for whom the training was most relevant, in what context the training was most useful, and how it helps students when they become adults. Finally, evaluation research, such as that reported in this book, provides feedback for knowing more precisely under what conditions the courses are most effective. This type of information resulting from the partnership of researchers and trainers is necessary if new curricula are to be introduced in schools responsibly.

Implementation and Implementers:
Teacher Training Needs

Most psychological educators have obtained their special training through the hunt-and-peck method of in-service education and short workshops. Some schools of education are beginning to provide relevant training, but the programs are checkered with glaring omissions as obvious as their exciting new courses.* The field simply has not been sufficiently well mapped to provide guide lines for what should be included in training programs. Based on the structure of the field presented in this chapter, the components of training for psychological educators are somewhat clearer.

To promote psychological growth, obviously, trainees must have detailed knowledge of ideal functioning. This would involve

---

*The two schools of education with most extensive existing graduate training programs in psychological education are at the University of Massachusetts at Amherst and the University of California at Santa Barbara.

studying the nature of mental health and mental illness, developmental psychology, the social and psychological aims of education, and useful problem-solving processes. Simple reading awareness is insufficient, because trainees need working knowledge. At minimum, extensive observation of children at various ages, and work with people across the spectrum of mental health-illness would be appropriate. Many current teachers of psychological education have never seen psychotic patients. Thus they lack perspective on what constitutes normality, mere health, and ideal functioning. One of the best ways to develop this working knowledge is to acquire skills in psychological assessment. This might involve using Piagetian tasks and lines of questioning to determine stages of intellectual development, or mastering Rorschach technology and theory to understand how health and illness are embedded in perceptual styles, or perfecting the art of diagnostic interviewing to comprehend the range of unique personal issues and their age-related commonalities. Beyond individual psychological assessment, trainees should learn to administer and interpret group tests designed to assess individual and group functioning. There are numerous other schemes for diagnosing ongoing group processes, classroom climate and structure, school climate, and organizational health. This range of assessment skills would allow psychological educators to diagnose the individual's, group's, or organization's status prior to training and also to evaluate the progress at the end of training. Most important, assessment skills make possible a more precise, objective definition of the gap between what is and what can be.

In addition to these gap-finding skills, trainees need curriculum-building skills to reduce existing gaps, i.e., the ability to coordinate procedures and tactics in implementing a strategy. Fortunately, the hundreds of specific procedures cluster into families, making it possible to learn a few essential types of procedures. Four such clusters have been identified (Alschuler, 1969a): (1) procedures designed to foster a constructive dialogue with one's imagination, (2) procedures that increase one's repertoire of action strategies and communication skills, (3) procedures which increase the range and richness of one's emotional life, and (4) procedures designed to focus awareness on the "here-and-now." These procedures constitute the common pool of moves that implement congruent, confluent, and contextual tactics.

While almost all currently practicing psychological educators are reasonably familiar with the clusters of procedures, there is a good deal of specialization in tactics, and there is some danger of losing the larger perspectives of strategy and goals. For instance, achievement motivation training is not equally relevant at all ages. Or, simply clarifying values may miss the important developmental changes in moral reasoning. Or, focusing on confluent methods may ignore contextual methods of restructuring classroom processes that at times are more effective. Or, doing organizational development exclusively for schools can blind one to the simultaneous needs of individuals for specific types of congruent training courses. For example, in spite of extensive work with school administrators, task forces, and institute directors on the creation and management of "temporary systems" (Miles, 1965), the numerical majority of temporary systems managers (the teachers) in schools have never had such training. One way to insure that these imbalances, losses of perspective, and systematic blindness *will* occur is to train psychological educators in only one type of tactic. However, merely developing ability in several tactics does not insure balanced perspective. Practice in *strategizing* is needed. This is the step after the diagnosis of the gap has been made but before tactics and moves are begun. It involves answering such questions as: what characteristics need to be internalized by these human beings, what are the relevant tactics and moves that can be organized systematically to foster that internalization, how many layers of the system must we work with in order to maximally promote this internalization, what critical periods of development are relevant, and what is the best timing for our interventions? It is easy to imagine a number of ways to practice strategizing, e.g., the Harvard Business School case study method, supervising trainees' consultations with client teachers or students, and conducting research on the effectiveness of alternate strategies for a given problem.

Adequate training in goals, diagnosis, evaluation, moves, tactics, strategies, and inventing is increasingly possible as comprehension grows of the field as a whole, and is increasingly necessary as casualties resulting from poor training multiply. The sense of urgency comes from the phenomenal growth of encounter groups and sensitivity training conducted by persons inadequately trained according to almost anyone's standards.

Implementers and Effectiveness: Research

Research is time consuming, costly, and often unproductive. These "costs" act as existential criteria for researchers; they must be deeply convinced their questions are important and potentially of wider generality than the specific operational procedures of their experiments. Of all the interesting questions in psychological education worthy of research, one problem stands above all others for this author: *the identification of short-term predictors of long-term gains.* Such knowledge would identify the transformations that constitute maturation and guide training programs in promoting long-term growth.

It is a convenient assumption for teachers to believe that students should be trained in precisely those attributes, skills, processes, motives, etc., that constitute the desired long-term end state: to be a good citizens as adults, students should be taught to be good citizens in school; to be effective information processors or self-scientists as adults, teach them these processes as adolescents; to increase entrepreneurial activity among adults, teach achievement motivation to children. The assumption behind these examples is open to question on theoretical and empirical grounds. Adults are not simply collections of childhood skills; maturation is not simply an increase in the number of such skills. Fundamental transformations take place, not quite as dramatic as the emergence of a butterfly from the cocoon of a caterpillar, but of that nature. At successive stages of growth, skills are reorganized and used in such new ways that they are transformed. For instance, after sufficient experience in thinking-in-action with concrete material, a new period emerges, beginning about ages 12 to 14, when children can think about their own thoughts and rearrange their thoughts with as much flexibility as they once did with external objects. Up to the transition to "formal operational" thinking, the best way of promoting this vertical growth may be to increase lateral growth during the period of "concrete operations" until there is sufficient experience in concrete thinking to be thought about in formal operational thinking. Similar illustrations can be derived from other developmental theories.

The assumption of isomorphism between end-of-training success and life success also is questionable on empirical grounds. We found that neither knowledge or satisfaction at the end of the n-Ach course were particularly good predictors of long-term usefulness. For over 20 years, evidence has been accumulatory that grades in school (as distinct from number of years of education) do not predict anything of much importance in adult life, e.g., marital success, career satisfaction, creative productivity, mental illness, anti-social behavior (Kirschenbaum, Simon and Napier [appendices], 1971; Kohlberg, LaCross and Ricks, 1970; Hoyt, 1965). Even more surprisingly, it is the rule rather than the exception that scores at the end of training do not predict professional success among clinical psychologists (Kelly and Fiske, 1951), psychiatrists (Holt and Luborsky, 1958), or Air Force pilots (Air Force Assessment Staff, 1946). In these instances, the professional success criteria were not sufficiently analyzed *prior* to creating end-of-training criteria (Stern, Stein and Bloom, 1956). Again, the message is that the relationship between training goals and long-term success cannot be assumed, even when they seem to be as obvious as the "necessary" skills of a fighter pilot. The same negative conclusion is true in the treatment of emotional disturbances in childhood, since it does not appear to improve adjustment as adults compared to untreated control groups (Kohlberg, LaCross and Ricks, 1970). From these general theoretical and empirical perspectives, the 25-word ads in "growth center" brochures promising "joy," "more joy," "peak experiences," "self-actualization," etc., are frontal assaults on intelligence. Those who *assume* a relationship between what they teach and specific long-term consequences run a large risk of being very wrong.

There are several potentially useful approaches to solving this problem. First, trainers can avoid the problem if they make use of existing longitudinal data, as for instance in n-Ach training. We know that the long-term consequences of high levels of adolescent n-Ach are greater degrees of entrepreneurial behavior as adults. A number of longitudinal studies exist that can be used to identify those early antecedents of desired later states and processes. Of the existing psychological education courses, only the few training programs to promote normative development are based on sound longitudinal data. The existing longitudinal studies are a relatively untapped source of curriculum ideas.

A second approach to the problem is based on the frequent finding that pre-course attitudes, motives, and values are good predictors of long-term gains (Coleman, 1966a; Luborsky *et al.*, 1971; McClelland and Winter, 1969). The general finding seems to be that reasonably high but realistic expectations for what can be gained from the training maximize the usefulness of the training. If training is seen as irrelevant, little learning occurs, no matter how dramatic the presentation. If expectations are unrealistically high, disappointment, and even casualties, are more likely to result from training (Yalom and Lieberman, 1971). The practical implication of this finding is to maximize intelligent self-selection by providing adequate information about the course prior to training. A research possibility flows from this procedure: likely predictors of who will and will not benefit from training could be obtained by identifying differences between those who select themselves into the course and those who select themselves out. These potential predictors would have to be followed by empirical confirmation in at least one long-term study. However practical this procedure and these data may be, it avoids the problem of discovering the end-of-course yields that maximize long-term gains.

A third approach to the problem is based on the paradoxical finding that expert trainers' predictions of who benefitted most from their course usually are highly inaccurate judged against long-term criteria, while inexpert, global peer ratings tend to be comparatively more accurate even when the long-term criteria are not well understood by the peers (Bolger and Coleman, undated). This is also true for the prediction of casualties from encounter groups. Yalom and Lieberman (1971) found that the single best predictor of encounter group casualties was two or more nominations by peers in a group of about 10 to 15. Seventy-seven percent of those nominated as having been hurt did sustain prolonged serious decompensation.* One way of understanding the predictive accuracy of peers is to realize that they are insiders. Experts are outsiders by virtue of their special expertise, leadership role, or age separation. Researchers, like teachers, must invoke a web of theoretical propositions or temporarily de-maturize themselves to see what is obvious through the eyes of peers. The implication is obvious: use and/or analyze peer ratings. What is it that allows peers to make relatively accurate predictions of long-term gains? What individual changes during a course are relatively hidden from the experts and are so obvious to peers that they don't even need to know the long-term outcome criteria to be accurate in their predictions? The accuracy of peer ratings is mysterious indeed, but a fascinating, potentially productive route to understanding the short-term predictors of long-term gains.

It almost goes without saying that useful short-term predictors can be validated only against good long-term measures of mental health, useful processes, the psychosocial aims of education, or stages in normative development. There are far fewer of these measures than for the academic results of education. Creation of these ultimate criterion measures is underway, but the task is difficult. Such measures must respond adequately to profound ethical issues of what is good, as well as to the practical problems of psychometric soundness and ease of administration. However, it is in such continuing activities that the efforts of researchers, curriculum builders, and teachers meet to define and implement a truly humanizing education.

---

*The existence of this finding now makes it professionally irresponsible not to obtain such data routinely at the end of group training to identify potential casualties to be supported and followed.

APPENDIX

APPENDIX
What Is the Effect of Achievement Motivation Training in the Schools?*

David C. McClelland

A number of attempts have been made to develop achievement motivation in school children and to observe the effect of such training on their behavior in and out of school. What conclusions can be drawn from these studies? Previous work with adults has demonstrated that brief intensive training courses in achievement motivation for businessmen increase their entrepreneurial activity for some years after the training (McClelland and Winter, 1969). If achievement motivation can be developed in adults, why not try to develop it in children? The question seemed eminently worth trying to answer if only because teachers so often complain that many children are "unmotivated." If psychologists have invented a technique for increasing motivation, it might well be applied to school children in such a way as to make them want to work harder and learn more. Though such an argument seems simple and straightforward, it glosses over a theoretical difficulty. The achievement motivation measure (n-Achievement Score) used in previous studies—based on content analysis of fantasy—has never been shown to be consistently related to academic performance, to grades in school, or to scores on tests of academic talent. Why, then, should increasing achievement motivation improve

*Much of the research reported in this volume was conducted under a grant from the U.S. Office of Education. In our final report, David McClelland summarized our findings and those of companion researchers in St. Louis, San Francisco, and Philadelphia. His summary complements the final chapter of this book. McClelland's summary stays closer to the empirical results and is less speculative. Thus it can serve as a concise report for those readers who want a brief overview of our findings.

school performance? Despite this obvious problem, the studies were undertaken because achievement motivation training *might* work, and because it ought certainly to help children to think more seriously about their work habits and career planning, even if it does not directly affect their grades. Furthermore, it might well improve grades a little for those most likely to drop out of school by helping them to see the importance of at least minimal school success for attaining longer-range vocational goals. Finally, direct attempts to increase motivation in school children have been so few and far between that it seemed likely much might be learned just from making the attempt.

By now dozens of achievement motivation courses have been given for hundreds of pupils in Boston, St. Louis, and California. A full description of how they were carried out has been published by Alschuler, Tabor and McIntyre (1970). In general they involved teaching children directly how to think, talk, and act like a person with high n-Achievement and then to examine carefully the extent to which they wanted to plan their lives in the immediate future according to this model. Extensive materials have been published for teaching achievement motivation. Many teachers have been instructed in how to use the material. Pupils who have been trained have been followed up one and two years later to see whether their in-school or out-of-school performance has changed in any way as compared to control groups of students who have not been trained in achievement motivation.

Most of these studies have been conducted under the aegis of two independent though allied groups of researchers. Beginning in 1965, the Office of Education granted funds to Harvard University, to be used under the general direction of Professor McClelland, to explore the effects of achievement motivation in the schools. In the first year of this project, Professor Richard deCharms visited Harvard University and participated fully in the early planning of the research. When he returned to Washington University in St. Louis, he started his own project, eventually received separate funding for it, and is reporting his work separately. However, his findings are very much a part of the total enterprise and many of the most important ones will therefore be summarized here. The projects at Harvard University and Washington University started out with quite similar training ideologies, and then pursued different but complementary research strategies. Manohar S. Nadkarni, who had conducted achievement motivation training courses for businessmen in India, trained those who later gave motivation courses both at Harvard and in St. Louis. The Harvard group then decided to continue the tradition of giving short intensive courses for school children to be offered by trained project staff. They followed this strategy because in the early days the main thrust of the project was in the direction of trying to find out how best to introduce achievement motivation into schools so as to maximize its impact. Thus, it was desirable to try out many different types of short courses. Furthermore, the Harvard group focused especially on the effects of motivation training outside school, since it was considered likely on theoretical grounds that increasing achievement motivation would have slight effects on academic performance.

The St. Louis group under Professor deCharms, on the other hand, concentrated primarily on studying the effects of achievement motivation training* on school work. Partly for this reason, they trained the teachers themselves to introduce achievement motivation training into the classrooms in whatever way they found most convenient. Thus, so far as most of the pupils in the St. Louis experiments were concerned, they experienced achievement motivation training inputs throughout an entire school year more or less as a part of other things that they were studying. In contrast, in the Harvard studies, the pupils were exposed to brief intensive courses given by outsiders which were separate and distinct from the rest of what was going on in class and usually concentrated into something like 20 to 40 hours of work spread out over 3 to 10 days, or at most 3 to 4 weeks. These contrasting strategies tended to increase the variety of information obtained about the effects of achievement motivation training on junior high and high school pupils.

The Effects on School Performance

No very convincing evidence is provided by the Harvard

*Later this developed into a form which he has labelled "origin training" to distinguish it from what is described in Alschuler *et al.* (1970).

studies which show that achievement motivation training improves grades or test scores. In the first study of potential dropouts from Arlington High School (see Chapter 3), the boys who stuck out residential training in a rural setting did show a slight improvement in grades (from D+ to C- on the average) but it was not large and selection was confounded with treatment. Perhaps those who stuck it out were made of sterner stuff and did better for that reason rather than because of the training. In later studies at Arlington High School (Chapters 5 and 6), grades did improve more in the 10th grade for the boys who received the complete motivation training course as contrasted with controls, but the girls did not show an improvement and even for the boys the gain had disappeared by the 11th grade. In short, the findings from these studies so far as academic performance is concerned are inconsistent, small, and not impressive (McClelland and Alschuler, 1971).

On the other hand, the St. Louis group has reported quite dramatically different results. Consider the findings reported by Ryals (1969), for example, as summarized briefly in Table A.1.

He had arranged for achievement motivation courses to be given for 8th graders on four different weekends, either on the school grounds ("campus") or in a camp in the mountains. He corrected test scores and grades for differences before the testing, and found that while there were no effects of training on grade point average or social studies test scores, training did seem to improve science and math performance quite significantly in the year after the training. Furthermore, the gains on the average were larger for pupils coming from a high school containing a high proportion of minority groups (blacks, Chicanos) than for students coming from a middle-class, white high school. The chief difference between these brief training courses and those sponsored by the Harvard group was that the students were taught by their own teachers who had received achievement motivation training from Nadkarni.

Training by teachers from the schools concerned is even more effective when it is spread out over the entire year, as illustrated by the findings summarized in Figure A.1. These charts present average scores on parts of the Iowa Test of Basic Skills, which is standardized by grade level so that any average class should score,

Table A.1

Effects of Achievement Motivation Training on Residualized Gain Scores*
(San Mateo County, 8th and 10th Grades Combined)

Training Group	All Students						Students Attending 3 or 4 Weekends			
	N	GPA**	N	Social Studies Test	N	Science Test	N	Science Test	N	Math Grades
Campus	68	48.6	55	49.2	56	50.1	42	50.8	45	52.3
Camp	68	50.9	49	49.0	49	50.5	44	51.3	47	59.6
Control	75	51.7	49	49.3	49	46.9	49	46.9	69	47.0
Significance of Training Effect		ns		ns		$p < .05$		$p < .01$		$p < .05$

*Actual score obtained one year after training subtracted from predicted score based on pretesting plus 50. Thus, scores over 50 represent greater than predicted gains.

**Grade point average, English, social studies, and math grades combined.

Figure A.1

Mean Grade Placement on Iowa Test of Basic Skills for Students Trained and Untrained in Achievement Motivation Self-Contained Classrooms

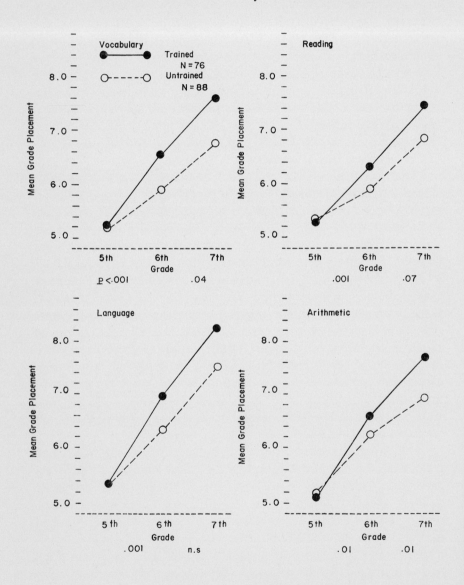

for example, 7.0 at the beginning of the 7th grade. The children involved here are all from ghetto schools in a largely black area of the city of St. Louis. Those who did not receive achievement motivation training from their teachers in general fall more and more behind expected grade levels on various test scores as they get older. However, they ended up with scores which are at or a little above grade norms for the test, as Figure A.1 makes clear. Results such as these which have been reported by the deCharms project leave little doubt that achievement motivation training can have fairly dramatic effects on school performance if it is properly understood by teachers and integrated throughout the year with their regular classroom work.

Effects on Non-School Activities

As noted earlier, the Harvard group, under the leadership of Alfred Alschuler, focused primarily on trying to discover whether intensive achievement motivation courses changed the way teenagers spent their time, and worked, planned, and thought about the future. Here the findings are quite consistent across different courses. Nearly all groups receiving full achievement motivation training reported 8 to 18 months later in a telephone interview that they were spending their time in more achievement-related ways. For example, when the trained potential dropouts from Arlington High School were asked, "What are the most important things you do or think about?" 100 percent of them mentioned doing well in school or in their work as it related to a future career. In contrast, only 4 out of 15, or 27 percent, of the controls mentioned school or work as "most important." They spoke about the fun they were having with their girlfriends or in various recreational activities.

Or, to cite another instance, some 11-year-old boys who were trained in the summer were queried extensively about what they had been doing, in a telephone interview a year later. Their answers were classified under 11 different types of activities, ranging from working vs. not working, to extent of travel they had undertaken to explore their surroundings, types of games played, or TV shows watched (Achievement-oriented or not), etc. Each boy was given a +1 if he was above the median for the group in the extent to which he displayed an achievement orientation in each of these activities. These scores were summed to get a total achievement activity index. Some 77 percent of those who received achievement training were above the median on this index as contrasted with only 11 percent of those who had a comparable motivation course dealing with establishing more friendly relationships with others. At the high school level, for 16-year-olds, the result was similar. Significantly more of the better-trained boys in Arlington High School reported that they were more involved in achievement-related ways in 20 different types of activities outside of school. However, the same result was not obtained for girls. No matter how much training they had received, or of what type, they reported about the same amount of participation in achievement-related activities. It may well be that achievement motivation training is more relevant to boys. They are required normally to be more work- and career-oriented and to take initiative towards solving such problems. Girls, on the other hand, may adopt a more reactive style, holding off on career planning until they have settled the question of marriage. Or the usual achievement motivation training course may simply be less effective for girls.

It is potentially very important to find that achievement motivation training helps boys at least adopt a more pro-active approach to setting work and career goals. However, is it possible that they have just learned to talk a better game? After all, the motivation courses have taught them a certain language, or way of talking about achievement and career goals, that they might be more likely to use in answering questions in a telephone interview, particularly from someone associated with the courses. Control boys not exposed to the training or the trainers might be less apt to give such answers. The coding system devised by Alschuler and his associates to obtain the achievement activities index does depend to some extent on the reasons why students say they are doing various things. (See Alschuler *et al.,* 1970, page 173.) That is, they get a higher score if they say they work in the summer to save up money for buying a car (a long-term goal) rather than to spend money for dates and clothes (affiliation goals). On the other hand, it is not reasonable to dismiss the results as being entirely due to a desire on the part of the student to talk in ways that will please the investigator. The interview was very specific in the sense of asking what they did last summer, how often they did it, how much they earned, what they were doing right now, etc. Obviously, if a person had been doing nothing special, it was not possible for him to get a score for achievement-related activity. Furthermore, if he was able to state further plans connected with the activity, he obviously must have thought about them in advance of being asked, which means that the plans undoubtedly had some influence in directing his activities. Finally, and most convincingly, in different experiments there were important differences in whether the boys or the girls showed significant increases in achievement-related activities 10 to 20 months after the training. By and large in studies at Arlington High School, the boys reported more achievement-related activities later, whereas in experiments in Quincy, the girls reported more activities later. If the results are due to response bias in answering the interviewer, why should the boys in one set of experiments be biased favorably, and the girls in another set? The conclusion seems inescapable that the achievement motivation training courses had demonstrable long-term effects on achievement-related activities outside of school, although these effects varied considerably, depending on the type of training experienced.

Variations in Training Effectiveness
    What factors influenced the effectiveness of achievement motivation training? The Harvard group concentrated on trying to find out what factor or combination of factors would maximize the impact of achievement motivation training on school children. Many variables were found to be important.
    Age and maturity. How early can n-Ach training be introduced into the schools? The question received attention because n-Ach training had started with adults and obviously it had to be revised considerably if it was going to be used with young children. Furthermore, many observers of the school system have noted that if motivation training is to do any good, it has to be introduced fairly early before children get set in a learning "track" which prevents them from switching to a track requiring a higher

level of accomplishment. The Harvard group showed that effective achievement motivation training could be given to 11-year-olds, although in general the "action" inputs (games, etc.) proved more useful than the "thought" exercises, which required a level of abstraction that was too high for at least some of the children. The St. Louis group also showed that effective achievement motivation training could be integrated into the regular curriculum for 6th graders. Some efforts have been made by Kowatrakul and Stivers (1969) to give some kind of achievement motivation training for kindergarten-age children, largely using games, but the effects were not impressive and for the moment it seems safer to conclude that achievement motivation training, at least in its present form, is best suited to the junior high school years and above. Ryals (1969) found that the effectiveness of training did not seem to be a function of moral maturity as measured by the Kohlberg instrument among 8th and 10th graders, although the program, in general, was more effective for the 8th graders.

Sex. A number of the studies show important sex differences in the impact of various types of training. The traditional training as designed for adult businessmen was oriented almost entirely towards male preoccupations and life style. The first studies in the schools employed only male subjects. Later, when girls were included in the courses, it turned out that the effects of the usual type of training were greater on boys than on girls, at least so far as achievement activities outside the school were concerned. The deCharms group has not reported sex differences in improved academic achievement as a result of achievement motivation training. On the other hand, the courses given at the Broadmeadows Junior High School generally were found more effective in producing long-range changes in girls' achievement activities outside school. These courses differed from the earlier ones in that some of them stressed learning the motivation materials to mastery and also restructuring math classes so that they required use of the strategies taught in the achievement motivation courses. The boys generally liked restructuring and insisting on mastery less than the girls, and the boys did not later report that they were involved in as many activities as the girls. The results may be due to initial differences between the girls in the treatment conditions, but it is at least suggestive that structuring achievement motivation training may help girls to benefit more from it, whereas boys tend to benefit more if it is given in its traditional form in which they are freer to take it or leave it.

Subject matter. What evidence there is suggests that achievement motivation training improves performance more in those subject matters which require more concrete action. Kagan and Moss (1962) reported that the n-Achievement score in boys is highly correlated with "constructional activities"—which require concrete, explicit actions that give immediate feedback as to whether they are done correctly or not. The data reported in Table A.1 from the Ryals study (1969) confirm the fact that achievement motivation training improves performance in math and science more than in social studies. Mehta and Kanade (1969) have reported that trained high school boys in India score significantly higher two years after training than matched classmate controls on higher secondary examinations in physics, chemistry, and mathematics. These findings make good theoretical sense because many studies have shown that people with strong achievement motivation are interested in concrete feedback on how well they are doing and tend to set goals in concrete enough terms so they can measure more or less precisely whether they are moving closer to those goals or not. In fact, much n-Ach training involves teaching participants to plan their progress in these concrete terms. Some subject matters like literature and social studies do not readily permit this degree of specificity in measuring progress.

Several of the Harvard studies contrasted the effectiveness of more or less complete courses with those which emphasized or left out one or another aspect of the training. A complete course involved teaching achievement motivation in thought and action, self-study, goal setting and planning, and some morale building or group solidarity inputs. In general, courses which involved all of these characteristics were more successful than those which involved less than the total package. However, age made a big difference here. With younger children, aged about 11, teaching the achievement action strategies seemed more effective than just teaching achievement thinking. With older children, aged around 16, on the other hand, leaving the achievement action strategies out and stressing achievement thinking and planning seemed to subtract little from the effectiveness of the training.

The way the courses were taught was also systematically varied. Usually the participants went through the various exercises, performing very differently on particular ones, learning as much as possible from mistakes and from observing how others performed. The objective was to maintain the interest of the students as much as possible and no attempt was made to make them go back over what they had experienced until they had learned it to some standard of perfection. These were called "satisfaction" courses. Other courses followed the programmed learning model in the sense that students were required to master the material to a criterion before being allowed to go on to another exercise. It seemed possible that requiring a higher level of mastery of the achievement motivation exercises might improve their effectiveness in the long run. This did not prove to be the case, at least for the boys, who generally disliked the mastery courses more and did not learn more. On the other hand, the reverse tended to be true for the girls: those who experienced the mastery courses reported significantly more achievement-related activities one to two years later than the girls who had had the traditional "satisfaction" courses. These preliminary results suggest that there is a sex by treatment interaction and that one style of teaching is better for boys in general and the other for girls. Such a finding is of no particular use to the classroom teacher who must somehow find an approach which is appealing and effective for both sexes.

Classroom structure. A persistent problem throughout the research was how the motivation training should be related to traditional classroom instruction. I have already noted that the St. Louis group under Professor deCharms put the regular teacher in charge of the motivation training; he usually integrated it with other classroom work over a considerable period of time. This approach seems to be clearly more effective than "segregated" motivation instruction by outsiders so far as improving academic performance is concerned. However, since the deCharms group did not obtain any long-term follow-up measures outside the school, it is not possible to say whether it is equally effective in producing work- and career-related changes.

The Harvard group, having concentrated on training the children separately from the regular classroom, began to worry about whether teachers would not do things that would discourage the new strategies of goal setting and learning taught in the motivation courses. So some math teachers were persuaded to restructure their regular course work in a way which would be consistent with the approach taught in the motivation courses. For instance, a contract system was introduced in which the pupils had to choose how many problems of a given difficulty they wanted to solve by a given date. They made the choice working from a table on which it was shown what grades would be awarded for doing various numbers of problems as a function of their difficulty, whether or not the person handed the exercise in on time, without mistakes, etc. Thus, the pupils had a chance to set moderate goals for themselves as they had been taught to do in the achievement motivation course, whereas in the traditional math class the teacher assigns the same number of problems to be done by all students regardless of their ability or reaction to the restructured classroom.

The restructured classroom by itself had no effect on math performance or achievement motivation, and many of the students, especially those with lower IQ's, disliked this way of learning. This last finding was also confirmed by other studies undertaken for the project. It had seemed possible from the beginning that the right kind of classroom climate might encourage the development of achievement motivation without formally introducing instruction in motivational concepts at all.

Thus, it was with some hope that the staff of the Harvard project evaluated the motivational impact of educational innovations in the Duluth, Minnesota and Newton, Massachusetts school systems. In both cases, the instruction had been drastically shifted from the traditional classroom structure in the direction of giving children more autonomy in deciding what they wished to do, when, and how they went about getting the information necessary to complete their work. This emphasis on self-reliance and self-direction, we thought, might increase achieve-

ment motivation, but in fact, it did not in either case (Alschuler
and Ham, 1971; Alschuler and Zelnicker, 1971). In the Duluth
study it appears that the achievement motivation of the girls was
actually lowered by the increased stress on self-reliance. Since
none of these classroom restructurings seemed to be increasing
achievement motivation indirectly, the inference is inescapable for
the present that some kind of direct instruction in achievement
motivation is essential if long-range effects in pupil behavior are to
be obtained.

Helping the Teacher

    The research findings so far reported are of interest to the
educator in demonstrating that achievement motivation training
can have some very important effects both inside and outside the
classroom and in showing how it can be made more or less
effective for younger or older boys and girls in different kinds of
settings. However, the goals of the research were also to be useful
to the average classroom teacher. So the project's staff tried hard
to find ways to make the information that was being accumulated
available in some generally useable form. Too often research
information never gets converted into teacher practice. Several
steps were taken to disseminate information about achievement
motivation training in the schools. The most important was the
publication of *Teaching Achievement Motivation* by Alschuler,
Tabor and McIntyre (1970), a manual which explains in detail the
techniques of motivation training used in the Harvard experiments
and to a considerable extent the St. Louis experiments.

    As we trained the teachers and worked with them more
directly, it became clear that many of them wanted to restructure
their classrooms along lines which would be more consistent with
what they had learned themselves in the achievement motivation
course. Some of them wondered if achievement motivation
training in itself was really necessary if they reorganized what they
usually did in ways that would encourage the students to develop
their achievement motivation. As noted above, our experience
with simply restructuring classrooms had not been altogether
favorable. It was obviously important to get at how pupils
perceived the attempts at restructuring. A teacher might decide to

give more individual responsibilities to encourage achievement motivation, but if the students perceived this change as introducing great confusion as to what they were supposed to do, the teacher would not have gained much. So the project turned its attention to designing a classroom climate questionnaire which would give the teacher feedback from her pupils as to how her behavior was perceived.

The questionnaires were patterned after similar ones designed by Litwin and Stringer (1968), who had been studying the effects of organizational climate on motivation in simulated business settings. Staff and workers (all business school students) were recruited to work in an elaborate two-week-long production game organized in three quite different ways. In one "company," British Radar, "the President placed emphasis on the maintenance of a formal structure. Members of the organization were assigned their roles, their spheres of operation were tightly designed, and they were held responsible for the strict performance of their duties." The questionnaire given to everyone in this company at the end of the two-week period clearly showed that they perceived their organization as authoritarian and knew that they were expected to toe the line and be highly disciplined. They also scored higher in a fantasy measure of power motivation (n-Power). By analogy it seemed obvious that some teachers run their classrooms in a very similar way. So the Litwin and Stringer items applying to business procedure were rephrased to apply to classroom procedure to make up two questionnaire scales measuring emphasis on discipline and pressure for high performance. Presumably classroom climates scoring high on these dimensions would produce effects like those in the comparable business situation.

In another of Litwin and Stringer's "companies," Balance Radar, "a loose informal structure was endorsed by the President . . . he stressed friendly, cooperative behavior, group loyalty, team work . . ." The climate questionnaire showed that the members of this organization perceived it as a warm, friendly group, and their affiliation motivation scores (n-Affiliation) were elevated. Similar items were included in a classroom climate survey to get at the extent to which the pupils perceived the teacher and the other members of the class as warm and friendly.

Finally, in still another simulation, Blazer Radar, "high productivity was valued by the President . . . Each participant was encouraged to set his own goals and to take personal responsibility for results . . . Competitive feedback was given frequently so that progress towards the goals could be easily evaluated. Rewards for excellent performance were given in the form of recognition and approval . . . " Questionnaire results correctly reflected the fact that the participants in this simulation felt that they had been given more responsibility and more feedback on how well they were doing. Their achievement motivation scores were also higher, and in the end this business organization outproduced the other two. It was therefore reasoned that a teacher who could produce a climate that was perceived in this way by her pupils might be encouraging achievement motivation and better performance. So the Litwin and Stringer items were rephrased for the classroom climate survey which measured the dimensions of responsibility and feedback.

Factor analysis of the classroom climate survey showed that psychometrically it needed further development. The scales designed to measure the different dimensions of climate did not come out as clearly as one could wish for and some of the scales were ill defined, with relatively few items consistently measuring them. Furthermore, no evidence has yet been gathered showing that the same results were obtained in the classroom as had been obtained in the simulated business situation—showing, for instance, that teachers who are perceived as stressing responsibility and feedback produce higher achievement motivation and better performance in their pupils. The chief value of the classroom climate survey so far has been its use as a teaching device. To dramatize the three types of classroom climates, multimedia film-slide-sound shows were produced in collaboration with Education Ventures, Inc. and Intermedia Systems Corporation. One each illustrated power-, affiliation-, and achievement-oriented classrooms. The slides, films, and tapes were taken during actual classes and teachers observing the shows found it easy to believe what they saw and to identify with the various problems the teacher was facing. As they tried to think through the ways in which they wanted to create different climates in their classrooms, they found the behavior of the teachers observed of great importance in guiding them as to what to do. Further, climate surveys had been filled out by the pupils in each of the three classrooms, and the teachers in the workshops therefore had an opportunity to compare their own perceptions of the teachers' styles with how they were perceived by the pupils in those classrooms. Finally, the teachers left the workshops with copies of the climate survey so that they had a device for not only assessing how they were currently perceived, but also how they might be perceived at some future date after having made structural changes. With this additional assessment device, it would be unlikely that any of them would find himself in the situation we uncovered in the restructured math class in Broadmeadows Junior High. As noted earlier, the teacher had restructured the classroom to give more responsibility to the students and to give them feedback tied closely to their performance, but it had been done in such a way as to make the students feel that the class was disorganized and they were getting little help. So the restructuring did not improve performance because it had changed the classroom climate in undesirable ways.

The St. Louis group, under Professor deCharms, had also concerned itself with classroom climate, but developed a different questionnaire for pupils to fill out which focused exclusively on the extent to which the teacher had fostered an "origin" climate. By an origin climate, he meant one in which pupils felt that they were in control of what they did in the classroom, that they could set their own goals, find their own means of obtaining them, feel rewarded for doing things on their own, and develop self-confidence. In other words, they felt like origins in the classroom rather than pawns. In comparison with the Harvard Climate Survey, the St. Louis instrument stresses the achievement-oriented dimension as contrasted with the power dimension and leaves out the affiliation dimension. DeCharms and associates also developed an origin score for TAT stories, the components of which were very similar to those just described for the origin questionnaire. The results of their studies are summarized in Figure A.2. As previously noted (Figure A.1), they found that n-Ach training for teachers converted into n-Ach training for pupils leads to gains in school learning from one grade to the next. But they also found that teachers who had been trained in achievement motivation tended to operate classrooms which were perceived by the pupils as encouraging more origin behavior. That is, the pupils felt more like origins in classrooms operated by n-Ach trained teachers. Furthermore, the deCharms group found that classrooms with high origin climate scores tended to contain pupils who gained more in school learning, whether or not the teachers in those classrooms had been trained in n-Ach. In other words, some teachers naturally create origin climates without special training and without introducing achievement motivation training for their pupils.

These teachers also produce greater gains in school learning. Thus it can be argued that what n-Ach training does is help teachers to create the kind of climate (which some teachers create spontaneously) which fosters school learning. The presumed mechanism by which this takes place is that origin climates foster origin thinking, as reflected in higher origin TAT scores of pupils in these classes. Origin TAT scores are in turn associated with better school performance, with IQ partialed out, although the St. Louis group has not yet shown that origin TAT scores predict *gains* in school learning.

Figure A.2 raises the further interesting question as to just how n-Ach training for teachers produces origin climates and gains in school learning. A recent research report by Kounin (1970) suggests which classroom management techniques may be involved (broken lines in Figure A.2). In studying carefully video tapes of classrooms in which students were really involved or not involved in their work, he was able to identify characteristic behaviors on the teacher's part which were highly correlated with whether her students were involved in their work and free from deviant behavior in the classroom. For the sake of analytic clarity, these characteristic teacher behaviors can be grouped under three main headings:

(1) *Getting attention.* Here he found that such teacher behaviors as challenge arousal, zest, and variety in learning situations were very important for getting work involvement.

Figure A.2

*Obtained (→) and Expected (- - →) Effects
of Motivation Training for Teachers on Classroom Climates
and Gains in School Performance
(deCharms' studies)*

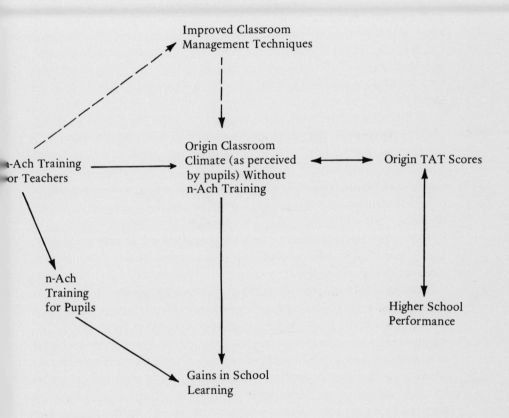

(2) *Insuring participation.* The central variable here seemed to be whether the teacher was able to keep all of the children on their toes most of the time by such techniques as group alerting (so that they would not know who was going to be called on next), variety in learning, requiring child responsibility for recitation, and the like.

(3) *Making individuals feel accountable.* Here is Kounin's most important teacher variable, which he called "withitness," or the ability of the teacher to communicate "that she knows what is going on regarding the children's behavior." She can attend to "two issues simultaneously when two different issues are present." What this means from the child's point of view is that he knows that he is going to be correctly identified with whatever he does, and held accountable either positively or negatively for it. Kounin discovered that a lot of teachers misidentify who does what in a classroom. They are clearly not "withit," and students are apparently discouraged from participating responsibly in the classroom if they feel that the teacher does not know what is going on.

These three dimensions of teacher behavior are, of course, well designed to foster learning. If a child is to learn, he must first pay attention, then make a response (participate himself), and get correct feedback as to whether he has done it right or not. Now let us turn back and take a look at achievement motivation training in the light of this analysis. What it involves both for the teachers and for the pupils is an improved technique for insuring that these three processes are heightened in the average classroom. The motivation training materials and methods are novel and varied, so that they insure *attention.* They are tailored to individuals and require *participation* by everyone in the classroom in playing a game or filling out a form, and they give very precise *feedback* on an individual basis as to whether the person has done the exercise well or not (e.g., learned the scoring system for n-Ach, or obtained a high score on the Origami Game). In using the materials, the teacher is automatically applying many of the techniques which

Kounin found to be associated with better work involvement in the classroom. She is also doing things which ought to make pupils feel more like origins in the sense that they are making decisions in connection with the various exercises as to what they want to do next. One could predict with some confidence that video tapes of teachers trained in n-Ach would show them scoring higher on Kounin's variables than those not trained in n-Ach. Hence the broken lines in Figure A.1.

But notice that nothing so far has been said directly about increasing achievement motivation in pupils. If the analysis just given is correct, one should get improved learning in the classroom without its being necessary to assume that achievement motivation has been increased. This seems paradoxical because the initial purpose of the research was to try to increase achievement motivation in school children so that they would perform better. Is it possible that achievement motivation training improves school performance without increasing achievement motivation? Even deCharms in his analysis (see Figure A.2) talks about increasing origin feelings, not increasing achievement motivation. It seems entirely possible that achievement motivation training is effective in the classroom without affecting much the level of achievement motivation in the students. What it does for the teachers is to improve their classroom management techniques, we have argued, and these in turn improve school learning by getting more attention, participation, and accountability from the students. The effect of the achievement motivation training on the pupils may be somewhat similar. It teaches them to manage their lives better, just as it taught the teachers how to manage their classrooms better. That is, the pupils learn to pay *attention* more to the goals they are setting in life, to *participate* more often in acts achieving those goals, and to collect *feedback* (through planning manuals, etc.) on whether or not they are moving toward those goals. Thus, motivation training techniques are simply encouraging them to plan their lives better, and the long-term effects picked up by the Harvard group of researchers may simply reflect that, rather than an increase in achievement motivation itself.

Such an interpretation has the added virtue of resolving a theoretical problem that plagued the research from the beginning.

How could achievement motivation training improve school performance if level of n-Ach is so clearly not related to school performance? The resolution of this paradox is now clear. Achievement motivation training may work, not by increasing n-Ach, but by improving classroom and life management techniques. Are we then deceiving children in telling them we are giving them courses to increase their achievement motivation, when we are unsure as to whether in fact that is what we are doing? Not really. The contradiction is largely semantic in nature. "N-Achievement," as a term used technically by psychologists, may not be increased by the courses, but certainly achievement thinking, achievement planning, and achievement consciousness are all raised by the courses, and, so far as the layman is concerned, these concepts are synonymous with being more motivated to achieve.

A final word of caution is in order. While we have constructed an explanation of the impact of achievement motivation training which does not require an increase in n-Achievement levels, we cannot be certain that such an increase does not occur. The problem is difficult to solve directly because the main measure of achievement motivation from the TAT cannot be used to measure n-Achievement levels after the individuals have been instructed in how to write TAT's with high n-Achievement content. Other measures, such as increases in achievement-related activities out of school, could of course change as a result of other changes in the individuals, such as a better style of life management. So it is hard to know, technically speaking, whether n-Achievement levels have actually been changed by the courses. We cannot rule out the possibility, but at this stage of the game, we think it is more parsimonious and more theoretically sound to conclude that achievement motivation training courses improve school learning by improving classroom and life management skills rather than by changing n-Achievement levels directly.

BIBLIOGRAPHY

BIBLIOGRAPHY

PSYCHOLOGICAL EDUCATION, HUMANISTIC EDUCATION, AFFECTIVE EDUCATION, THE EUPSYCHIAN NETWORK, CURRICULUM OF CONCERNS, THE HUMAN POTENTIAL MOVEMENT, PERSONOLOGICAL EDUCATION, SYNOETICS, PERSONAL LEARNING, INTRINSIC EDUCATION, CONFLUENT EDUCATION, ETC.*

This bibliography serves the standard purpose of providing a complete notation for each reference cited in the text. The bibliography is also designed to provide a relatively complete list of books, articles, and journals in the field of psychological education. The variety of names under which this bibliography could be listed gives some indication of the difficulty we have had in putting limits on its contents. In order to make a useable bibliography, we have restricted ourselves to those entries which have:

1. As their goals, education to increase such poorly defined but nonetheless important qualities as sensitivity, creativity, joy, and motivation.
2. As their methods (in addition to "regular school" methods), an emphasis upon non-verbal learning, the use of fantasy, direct attention to the student's own emotions, "here-and-now" confrontation, and group encounters.
3. As their basic content vehicle, the person himself.

We have not included those books which describe attempts to achieve these goals by relying on the traditional approaches of the "discipline" areas such as English or science, nor those books which discuss methods used primarily to alleviate psychopathology.

*An earlier version of this bibliography appeared in the New York State Education Department's *Educational Opportunities Forum,* Fall, 1969.

The bibliography begins with our answer to the frequently asked question, "What are the first books I should read?" We have listed and annotated seven works which discuss the goals of humanistic education, which give detailed examples of methods employed, and which discuss research evidence. The remaining items in the bibliography are initialled to indicate emphasis on (B) Background and theory, (M) Methods and techniques, and (R) Research.

To Begin With . . .

Jones, R.M. *Fantasy and feeling in education.* N.Y.: New York University Press, 1968.

> Discusses the relationships of the humanistic education emphasis on fantasy and feeling to such major curriculum innovations as the Educational Development Center's "Man—a course of study." Criticizes Jerome Bruner's theory of instruction, and attempts to make distinctions between psychotherapy and education.

McClelland, D.C. and Winter, D.G. *Motivating economic achievement.* N.Y.: Free Press, 1969.

> This book reports the research results of achievement motivation training for groups of businessmen in several countries. The findings constitute the best evidence to date for the efficacy of humanistic education procedures and the limitations of these approaches.

Miles, M. *Learning to work in groups.* N.Y.: Bureau of Publications, Teachers College, Columbia University, 1959.

> A comprehensive "how-to-do-it" manual for planning and conducting humanistic education group meetings.

Otto, H. and Mann, J. (Eds.) *Ways of growth.* N.Y.: Grossman Publishers, Inc., 1968.

> This is a collection of articles by 19 innovators who have developed specific means and methods designed to actualize human potential. It is an easily readable overview of the field.

Parnes, S.J. and Harding, H.F. *A sourcebook for creative thinking.* N.Y.: Charles Scribner and Sons, 1962.

> Twenty-nine articles by researchers, theoreticians, and practitioners provide a thorough introduction to all

aspects of the development of the creative processes.

Perls, F.S., Hefferline, R.F. and Goodman, P. *Gestalt therapy: excitement and growth in the human personality.* N.Y.: Dell (paperback), 1965.

> This book contains a section of exercises for the reader to do to experience and grow in ways described in the second half of the book, devoted to theory. These methods and ideas may consider many approaches as variations on its themes.

Spolin, V. *Improvisation for the theater.* Evanston, Illinois: Northwestern University Press, 1963.

> Although Spolin's book grew from her work with novice actors, the ideas and procedures have been transformed for most types of groups, from students in elementary school to businessmen in T-groups. Familiarity with these methods will facilitate the use of non-verbal methods, games, role-plays, psychodrama, and sociodrama.

BOOKS AND ARTICLES

Air Force Assessment Staff. "Psychological research on pilot training in the Air Force." *American Psychologist,* January 1946, 1, 1, 7-17. (R)

Alexander, F.M. *The use of the self.* Manchester, England: Re-Educational Publications, Ltd., 70 Derby Road, Fallowfield, Manchester 14, 1932. (B)

Allen, G. "Hate therapy." *American Opinion,* January 1968, 73-86. (M)

Allen, M.S. *Morphological creativity.* Englewood Cliffs, N.J.: Prentice-Hall, 1962. (B, M)

Allensmith, W. and Goethals, G.W. *The role of schools in mental health.* New York: Basic Books, 1962. (B)

Allport, G. "The mature personality." Chapter 12 in *Pattern and growth in personality.* New York: Holt, Rinehart and Winston, 1961. (B)

Alpert, R. and Haber, R.N. "Anxiety in academic achievement situations." *Journal of Abnormal and Social Psychology,* 1960, 61, 207-215. (R)

Alschuler, A.S. "The problem of the aged; a cross-cultural study of values." Unpublished manuscript, available from the author, 1962. (B)

Alschuler, A.S. "Psychological education." *Journal of Humanistic Psychology,* Spring 1969a. (B, M)

Alschuler, A.S. (Ed.). "Humanistic/psychological education." *Educational Opportunities Forum,* Vol. 1, No. 4, Fall 1969b. (B, M)

Alschuler, A.S. "Humanistic education." *Educational Technology Magazine,* May 1970. (Also Chapter 23, *Curriculum design in a changing society.* Burns, R.W. and Brooks, G.W. [Eds.]. Englewood Cliffs, N.J.: Educational Technology Publications, 1970.) (B, M)

Alschuler, A.S. and Ham, P. "The effects of individualized instruction in Duluth, Minnesota," in McClelland and Alschuler. *The achievement motivation development project.* Final report to USOE project No. 7-1231, Bureau of Research, April 1971. (B, M, R)

Alschuler, A.S. and Tabor, D. *The origami game.* Middletown, Conn.: Education Ventures, 1970a. (M)

Alschuler, A.S. and Tabor, D. *The ring toss game.* Middletown, Conn.: Education Ventures, 1970b. (M)

Alschuler, A.S. and Tabor, D. *The darts-dice game.* Middletown, Conn.: Education Ventures, 1970c. (M)

Alschuler, A.S. and Tabor, D. *Who am I?* Middletown, Conn.: Education Ventures, 1970d. (M)

Alschuler, A.S. and Tabor, D. *Ten thoughts.* Middletown, Conn.: Education Ventures, 1970e. (M)

Alschuler, A.S. and Tabor, D. *Aiming.* Middletown, Conn.: Education Ventures, 1970f. (M)

Alschuler, A.S., Tabor, D. and McIntyre, J. *Teaching achievement motivation: theory and practice in psychological education.* Middletown, Conn.: Education Ventures, 1970. (B, M)

Alschuler, A.S. and Zelnicker, D. "The effects of individualized instruction in Meadowbrook Junior High School," in McClelland and Alschuler. *The achievement motivation development project.* Final report to USOE project No. 7-1231, Bureau of Research, April 1971. (B, M, R)

Anderson, Gary J. and Walberg, Herbert J. "Classroom climate and group learning." *International Journal of the Educational Sciences,* October 1969. (R)

Anderson, R.C. "Can first graders learn an advanced problem-solving skill?" *Journal of Educational Psychology,* 1965, 56,

6, 283-294. (R)

Andreas, B. *Psychological science and the educational enterprise.* New York: John Wiley and Sons, 1968. (B)

Andrews, John. "Achievement motivation and life style among Harvard freshmen." Unpublished doctoral dissertation, Harvard University Department of Social Relations, 1965. (R)

Aronson, E. "The need for achievement as measured by graphic expression." In Atkinson, J.W. (Ed.). *Motives in fantasy, action and society.* Princeton, N.J.: D. Van Nostrand, 1958. (R)

Ashton-Warner, S. *Teacher.* New York: Simon and Schuster, 1963. (M)

Assagioli, R. *Psychosynthesis.* New York: Hobbs, Dorman, 1965. (B, M)

Atkinson, J.W. (Ed.). *Motives in fantasy, action and society.* Princeton, N.J.: D. Van Nostrand, 1958. (B, R)

Atkinson, J.W., et al. "The achievement motive, goal-setting, and probability of preference." *Journal of Abnormal and Social Psychology*, 1960, 60, 27-36. (R)

Atkinson, J.W. and Feather, N. (Eds.). *A theory of achievement motivation.* New York: John Wiley and Sons, 1966. (B)

Atkinson, J.W. and Litwin, G.H. "Achievement motive and test anxiety conceived as motive to approach success and motive to avoid failure." *Journal of Abnormal and Social Psychology,* 1960, 60, 52-63. (R)

Atkinson, J.W. and McClelland, D.C. "The projective expression of needs. II. The effect of different intensities of hunger drive on thematic apperception." *Journal of Experimental Psychology,* 1948, 38, 643-658. (R)

Atkinson, J.W. and Reitman, W.R. "Performance as a function of motive strength and expectancy of goal attainment." *Journal of Abnormal and Social Psychology,* 1956, 53, 361-366. (R)

Bach, G.R. and Wyden, P. *The intimate enemy: how to fight fair in love and marriage.* New York: Avon Books, 1970. (M)

Badouin, C. and Lestchinsky. *The inner discipline.* London: George Allen and Unwin Ltd., Ruskin House, 40 Museum Street, London, WC 1, 1924. (B, M)

Baker, Bruce. "Symptom treatment and symptom substitution in enuresis." *Journal of Abnormal Psychology,* February 1969, Vol. 74, No. 1, 42-49. (R)

Bandura, A. and Walters, R.H. *Social learning and personality development.* New York: Holt, Rinehart and Winston, 1963.

(B, R)

Barth, R. and Rathbone, C. "Internal education, a bibliography." *The Center Forum,* July 1969, Vol. 3, No. 7. (B, M, R)

Batchelder, R.L. and Hardy, J.M. *Using sensitivity training and the laboratory method: an organizational case study in the development of human resources.* New York: Association Press, 1968. (M, R)

Beilen, H. "Learning and operational convergence in logical thought development." *Journal of Experimental Child Psychology,* 1965, 2, 317-339. (M, R)

Beilen, H., Kagan, J. and Rabinowitz, R. "Effects of verbal and perceptual training on water level representation." *Child Development,* 1966, 37, 2, 317-328. (M, R)

Belka, M. *Being and becoming.* (Group Guidance Series. 4 vols.: *Encounter, Identity, Involvement, Commitment.*) Milwaukee: Bruce Publishing, 1966. (B, M)

Bennis, W. "Goals and metagoals of laboratory training." In Bennis, W., *et al. Interpersonal dynamics: essays and readings on human interaction.* Homewood, Ill.: Dorsey Press, 1968. (B)

Bennis, W., Benne, K. and Chin, R. *The planning of change.* New York: Holt, Rinehart and Winston, 1969. (B, M)

Bennis, W., *et al. Interpersonal dynamics: essays and readings on human interaction.* Homewood, Ill.: Dorsey Press, 1968. (B)

Benoit, H. *The supreme doctrine.* New York: Viking Press, 1955. (B)

Bensen, O. "Simulation of international relations and diplomacy." In Borko, H. (Ed.). *Computer applications in the behavioral sciences.* New York: Prentice-Hall, 1962. (M)

Bergin, A. "Some implications of psychotherapy research for therapeutic practice." *Journal of Abnormal Psychology,* 1966, 71, 235-246. (M, R)

Berman, L. *New priorities for the curriculum.* New York: Merrill Press, 1969. (B)

Berne, E. *Games people play.* New York: Grove Press, 1964. (B, M)

Berzon, B. "Self-directed small group programs: a new resource in rehabilitation." La Jolla, Calif.: Western Behavioral Sciences Institute, January 1968. (B, M)

Berzon, B., Reisel, J. and Davis, D. "Peer: planned experiences for effective relating: an audio tape program for self-directed small groups." La Jolla, Calif.: Western Behavioral Sciences

Institute, 1968. (M)

Berzon, B. and Solomon, L.N. (Eds.). *The encounter group: issues and applications.* San Francisco: Jossey-Bass, 1970. (M, R)

Berzon, B., Solomon, L. and Davis, D. "The self-directed therapeutic group: three studies." *Journal of Counseling Psychology,* Winter 1966, 13, 5. (R)

Bessell, H. "The content is the medium: the confidence is the message." *Psychology Today,* January 1968, 32-35+. (B)

Bessell, H. and Palomares, U. *Methods in human development.* San Diego, Calif.: Human Development Training Institute, 1967. (B, M)

Bindrim, P. "Facilitating peak experiences." In Otto, H. and Mann, J. (Eds.). *Ways of growth.* New York: Grossman Publishers, 1968. (M)

"Bionics." *Journal of Creative Behavior,* Winter 1967, 52-57. (B, M)

Birnbaum, M. "Sense and nonsense about sensitivity training." *Saturday Review,* November 17, 1969. (B)

Birney, R.C. "The reliability of the achievement motive." *Journal of Abnormal and Social Psychology,* 1959, 58, 266-267. (R)

Black, A. *The young citizen; the story of the Encampment for Citizenship.* New York: Frederick Ungar Publishing, 1962. (M)

Black, M. (Ed.). *The social theories of Talcott Parsons.* Englewood Cliffs, N.J.: Prentice-Hall, 1961. (B)

Blank, L., Gottsegen, G. and Gottsegen, M. *Encounter confrontation in self and interpersonal awareness.* New York: Macmillan, 1971. (B, M)

Blatner, H. *Practical aspects of psychodrama.* Author, 1203 Greenacre Avenue, Los Angeles, California 90046. (M)

Blatt, M. and Kohlberg, L. "The effects of classroom discussion programs upon the moral levels of pre-adolescents." In Kohlberg, L. and Turiel, E. (Eds.). *Moral development and moral education.* Cambridge, Mass.: Harvard University Press, 1971. (B, M, R)

Bloom, B.S. *Stability and change in human characteristics.* New York: John Wiley and Sons, 1965. (B)

Bloom, B.S. (Ed.). *Taxonomy of educational objectives, handbook I: cognitive domain.* New York: David McKay, 1956. Krathwohl, D.R., Bloom, B. and Masia, B. *Taxonomy of educational objectives, handbook II: affective domain.* New York: David McKay, 1964. (B)

Bloomfield, L.P. and Padleford, N.J. "Three experiments in political gaming." *The American Political Science Review,* 1959, LIII, 1105-1115. (M, R)

Bois, J.S. *The art of awareness.* Dubuque, Iowa: William C. Brown, 1966. (B, M)

Bolger, J. and Coleman, J. "The review of research with peer ratings in training." Divison of Research, Peace Corps, Note No. 8. (B)

Boocock, S.S. "Effects of election campaign game in four high school classes." Department of Social Relations, The Johns Hopkins University, Baltimore, Maryland, 1963. (Mimeograph.) (M, R)

Boocock, S.S. "An experimental study of the learning effects of two games with simulated environments." *American Behavioral Science,* October 1966, 8-17. (M, R)

Boocock, S.S. and Schild, E.O. *Simulation games in learning.* Beverly Hills, Calif.: Sage Publications, 1968. (B, M, R)

Borton, T. "Reaching the culturally deprived." *Saturday Review,* February 19, 1966, 77-78+. (B, M)

Borton, T. "Reach, touch, and teach." *Saturday Review,* January 18, 1969. (M)

Borton, T. *Reach, touch and teach: student concerns and process education.* New York: McGraw-Hill, 1970. (B, M)

Boy, A. and Pine, G. *Expanding the self: personal growth for teachers.* Dubuque, Iowa: William C. Brown, 1971. (M)

Bradford, L.P., Gibb, J. and Benne, K. (Eds.). *T-group theory and laboratory method: innovation in re-education.* New York: John Wiley and Sons, 1964. (B, M, R)

Brenman, M. and Merton, G. *Hypnotherapy.* New York: John Wiley and Sons, 1944. (B, M, R)

Brooks, C. and Trout, I. Holt Impact Series: *I've got a name, At your own risk, Cities, Larger than life.* New York: Holt, Rinehart and Winston, 1968. (M)

Brown, G. "Awareness training and creativity based on Gestalt therapy." Mimeographed paper available from the author at School of Education, University of California, Santa Barbara. (B)

Brown, G. "An experiment in the teaching of creativity." *School Review,* 1964, 72, 4, 437-450. (M, R)

Brown, G. *Now: the human dimension.* Esalen monograph No. 1 available from the author and Esalen Institute, Big Sur, California, 1968a. (B, M)

Brown, G. "A plague on both your houses." Available from Esalen Institute, Big Sur, California, 1968b. (B)

Brown, G. *Human teaching for human learning.* New York: Viking Press, 1971. (M)

Brown, G. and Gaynor, D. "Athletic action as creativity." *Journal of Creative Behavior,* 1967, 11, 2, 155-162. (B)

Brown, N.O. *Hermes, the thief.* Madison, Wisconsin: University of Wisconsin Press, 1942. (B)

Brown, Roger. *Social psychology.* New York: Free Press, 1965. (B, R)

Bruner, J. *The process of education.* New York: Vintage Books, 1963. (B)

Buchanan, P.C. "Evaluating the effectiveness of laboratory training in industry." In *Explorations in human relations training and research, No. 1.* National Training Laboratories, National Education Association, Washington, D.C., 1965. (R)

Bugental, J. *The search for authenticity.* New York: Holt, Rinehart and Winston, 1965. (B)

Bugental, J. *The challenge of humanistic psychology.* New York: McGraw-Hill, 1967. (B, M, R)

Bugental, J. and Haigh, G. "Psychology and retreats: frontier for experimentation." Chapter 11 in *Call to adventure,* Magee, R. (Ed.). New York: Abingdon Press, 1967. (M)

Bugental J. and Tannenbaum, R. "Sensitivity training and being motivation." *Journal of Humanistic Psychology,* Spring 1963. (B)

Buhler, C. *Intentionality and self-realization.* San Francisco: Jossey-Bass, 1968a. (B)

Buhler, C. *Psychology for contemporary living.* New York: Hawthorne Books, 1968b. (B)

Buhler, C. "Basic theoretical concepts of humanistic psychology." *American Psychologist,* April 1971, 378-386. (B)

Buhler, C. and Massarik, F. (Eds.). *The course of human life: a study of goals in the humanistic perspective.* New York: Springer, 1968. (B)

Burgess, L. "Personality factors of over- and underachievers in engineering." *Journal of Educational Psychology,* 1957, 47, 89-99. (R)

Burgess, L. *Fragments.* Newton, Mass.: Educational Development Center, 1970. (M)

Burnstein, E., Moulton, R. and Liberty, P. "Prestige vs. excellence as determinants of role attractiveness." *American Socio-*

logical Review, 1963, 28, 212-219. (R)

Burris, R. "The effect of counseling on achievement motivation." Unpublished doctoral dissertation, Indiana University, 1958. (R)

Burton, A. (Ed.). *Encounter, the theory and practice of encounter groups.* San Francisco: Jossey-Bass, 1969. (B)

Butler, J.M. and Haigh, G. "Changes in the relation between self-concepts and ideal concepts consequent upon client-centered counseling." In Rogers, C. and Dymond, R. (Eds.). *Psychotherapy and personality change.* Chicago: University of Chicago Press, 1954. (R)

Campbell, J. and Dunnette, M. "Effectiveness of t-group experience in managerial training and development." *Psychological Bulletin,* August 1968, 73-104. (R)

Carkhuff, R.R. *Helping and human relations, a primer for lay and professional helpers.* Vol. 1, *Selection and training,* Vol. 2, *Practice and research.* New York: Holt, Rinehart and Winston, 1969. (B, M, R)

Carkhuff, R.R. and Banks, G. "The effects of human relations training on relations between races and generations." *Journal of Counseling Psychology,* 1969. (M, R)

Carkhuff, R.R. and Bierman, R. "The effects of human relations training on parents of emotionally disturbed children." *Journal of Counseling Psychology,* 1969. (M, R)

Carkhuff, R. and Truax, C. "Lay mental health counseling." *Journal of Counseling Psychology,* 1965, 29, 426-431. (B)

Carnegie, D. *How to win friends and influence people.* New York: Simon and Schuster, 1937. (M)

Cartwright and Zander. *Group dynamics: research and theory.* Elmsford, New York: Row, Peterson, 1960. (B)

Chambers, B. *How to hypnotize.* New York: Stravon Publishers, 1957. (M)

Cherryholmes, C.H. "Developments in simulation of international relations for high school teaching." Unpublished masters thesis, Kansas State Teachers College, 1963. (R)

Cherryholmes, C.H. "Some current research on effectiveness of educational simulations: implications for alternative strategies." *American Behavioral Science,* October 1966, 4-7. (R)

Child, I.L., Storm, T. and Vernoff, J. "Achievement themes in folk tales related to socialization practice." In Atkinson, J.W. (Ed.). *Motives in fantasy, action and society.* Princeton, New Jersey: D. Van Nostrand, 1958. (R)

Childs, K.E. "Prediction of encounter group outcomes as a function of selected personality variables." Thesis Committee on Human Development, University of Chicago, 1971. (R)

Churchman, C.W. "Humanizing education." *The Center Magazine,* November 1968, 10-33. (B)

Clark, C. *The conditions of economic progress.* 3rd edition. London: Macmillan, 1957. (B, R)

Coleman, J.S. "Academic achievement and the structure of competition." *Harvard Educational Review,* 1959, Vol. 29, No. 4. (R)

Coleman, J.S. *Equality of educational opportunity.* United States Office of Education, OE 38001, 1966a. (R)

Coleman, J.S. "Introduction: in defense of games." *American Behavioral Science,* October 1966b. 3-4. (B)

Craig, R.L. and Bittel, L.R. *Training and development handbook.* New York: McGraw-Hill, 1967. (M)

Crandall, V.C., Katkovsky, W. and Crandall, V.J. "Children's beliefs in their own control of reinforcements in intellectual-academic achievement situations." *Child Development,* 1965, 36, 91-109. (R)

Crawford, R.P. *Direct creativity, with attribute listing.* Wells, Vermont: Frazer Publishing, 1968. (M)

Crockett, H.R., Jr. "The achievement motive and differential occupational mobility in the United States." *American Sociological Review,* 1962, 27, 191-204. (R)

Cummings, E. and Henry, W.E. *Growing old.* New York: Basic Books, 1961. (B, R)

Cummings, S.N. and Carney, J.J. *Communication for education.* Scranton, Pa.: Intext Educational Publishers, 1971. (M)

deCharms, R. *Personal causation.* New York: Academic Press, 1968. (B, R)

deCharms, R. "Origins, pawns and educational practice." In Lesser, G. (Ed.). *Psychology and the educational process.* Evanston, Ill.: Scott Foresman, 1969. (B, R)

deCharms, R. *Motivation in the schools.* Unpublished manuscript. (M, R)

deCharms, R., Morrison, H.W., Reitman, W.R. and McClelland, D. "Behavioral correlates of directly and indirectly measured achievement motivation." Chapter 38 in McClelland, D. (Ed.). *Studies in motivation.* New York: Appleton-Century-Crofts, 1955. (R)

deCharms, R. and Rosenbaum, M.E. "Self-esteem and overt

expressions of aggression." In Washburne, N.F. (Ed.) *Decisions, values and groups. Vol. II.* London, Pergamon Press, 1962. (R)

DeLara, L.E. "Cigar box to personality box." *Mental Health,* October 1968, 52, 4, 577-581. (M)

Delza, S. *Body and mind in harmony.* New York: David McKay, 1961. (M)

deMille, R. *Put your mother on the ceiling.* New York: Walker, 1967. (M)

Dennison, G. *The lives of children: the story of First Street School.* New York: Random House, 1969. (M)

Dorn, R.C. Murdoch, P. and Scarborough, A.T. *Manual for self-development workshops.* Greensboro, N.C.: Center for Creative Leadership, 1970. (M)

Dreeben, R. "The contribution of schooling to the learning of norms." *Harvard Education Review,* Spring 1967, Vol. 37, No. 2. (B)

Dreeben, R. *On what is learned in school.* Reading, Mass.: Addison-Wesley, 1968. (B)

Drews, E.M. "Self-actualization: a new focus for education." In the Association for Supervision and Curriculum Development 1966 yearbook, *Learning and mental health in the school.* Washington, D.C.: National Education Association, 1966. (B)

Drews, E.M. "Beyond curriculum; Fernwood: a free school." *Journal of Humanistic Psychology,* Fall 1968, 97-122. (B, M)

Drews, E.M. "Policy implications of a hierarchy of values." Educational Policy Research Center, 6747-6748, Stanford Research Institute, Menlo Park, California, August 1970. (B)

Drews, E.M. and Knowlton, D. "The being and becoming series for college-bound students." *Audio-visual Instruction,* January 1963. (B)

Dubach-Donath, A. *The basic principles of eurythmy.* London: Rudolf Steiner Publishing, 54 Bloomsbury Street, W.C. 1, 1937. (M)

Durckheim, K. *Hara, the vital center of man.* London: George Allen and Unwin Ltd., Ruskin House, Museum Street, W.C. 1, 1962. (B)

Educational Technology Magazine. "Simulation in education." Special issue, October 1969. (B, M)

Egan, Gerald (Ed.). *Encounter groups: basic readings.* Belmont, Calif.: Brooks/Cole Publishing, 1971. (B, M)

Elementary school mathematics. Book V. Reading, Mass.: Addison-Wesley, 1964. (M)

"Emotional stress and laboratory training." In *News and Reports,* NTL Institute, November 1969, Vol. 3, No. 4. (R)

"Encounter groups and psychiatry." Task Force Report No. 1. Washington, D.C.: American Psychiatric Association, 1970. (B)

Endore, G. *Synanon.* Garden City, N.Y.: Doubleday, 1968. (M)

Enelow, G. *Body dynamics.* New York: Information, 1960. (M)

Enelow, G. *Inner beauty, outer youth.* New York: Information, 1969. (M)

Enright, J.B. "An introduction to Gestalt therapy." Available from the author at Langley Porter Neuropsychiatric Institute, 401 Parnassus, San Francisco, Calif. (B, M)

Erikson, E. *Childhood and society.* New York: W.W. Norton, 1950. (B, R)

Erikson, E. "Identity and the life cycle." *Psychological Issues,* 1959, 1, 1, 1-171. (B)

Evans-Wentz, W. *Tibetan yoga.* New York: Oxford University Press, 1967. (M)

"Expanding the psychological awareness of teachers." (Newsletter.) Donald H. Clark, Educational Clinic, Hunter College, Bedford Park Boulevard West, Bronx, New York. (B)

Eysenck, H.J. (Ed.). "The effects of psychotherapy." *Handbook of Abnormal Psychology.* New York: Basic Books, 1961. (R)

Fagan, J. and Shepard, I.L. (Eds.). *Gestalt therapy now.* Palo Alto, Calif.: Science and Behavior Books, 1970. (B, M)

Fairweather, G.W. *Methods for experimental social innovation.* New York: John Wiley and Sons, 1968. (B)

Fantini, M. and Weinstein, G. *The disadvantaged.* New York: Harper and Row, 1968a. (B)

Fantini, M. and Weinstein, G. *Making urban schools work.* New York: Holt, Rinehart and Winston, 1968b. (B, M)

Fast, J. *Body language.* New York: Pocket Books, 1971. (B, M)

Feather, N.T. "Effects of prior success and failure on expectations of success and subsequent performance." *Journal of Personality and Social Psychology,* 1966, 3, 287-298. (R)

Featherstone, J. "Schools for children: what's happening in British classrooms." *The New Republic,* August 19, 1967, 17-21a. (B, M)

Featherstone, J. "How children learn." *The New Republic,* September 2, 1967, 17-21b. (B, M)

Featherstone, J. "Teaching children to think." *The New Republic,*

September 1967, 15-19c. (B, M)

Flanagan, J. "Functional education for the seventies." *Phi Delta Kappan,* September 1967, 27-33. (R)

Flinders, N.J. *Personal communication: how to understand and be understood.* Salt Lake City: Deseret Book, 1966. (B, M)

Foster, G.M. "Peasant society and the image of the limited good." *American Anthropologist,* 1967, 67, 293-315. (B, R)

Fox, R., Luszki, M.B. and Schmuck, R. *Problem solving in the classroom.* Chicago: Science Research Associates, 1966. (M)

French, E.G. "Motivation as a variable in work partner selection." *Journal of Abnormal and Social Psychology,* 1956, 53, 96-99. (R)

French, E.G. "Effects of the interaction of motivation and feedback on task performance." In Atkinson, J.W. (Ed.). *Motives in fantasy, action and society.* Princeton, N.J.: D. Van Nostrand, 1958. (R)

Freud, S. *The problem of lay analysis.* New York: Brentano, 1927. (B, M)

Furst, B. *The practical way to a better memory.* Greenwich, Conn.: Premier Books, Fawcett Publishers, 1960. (M)

Gardner, J. *Self-renewal: the individual and the innovative society.* New York: Harper Colophon, 1965. (B)

Garrett, H.F. "A review and interpretation of investigations of factors related to scholastic success in colleges of arts and sciences and teachers colleges." *Journal of Experimental Education,* 1949, 18, 91-158. (R)

Gebhart, G.G. and Hoyt, D.P. "Personality needs of under- and overachieving freshmen." *Journal of Applied Psychology,* 1958, 42, 125-128. (R)

Getzels, J. and Jackson, P. *Creativity and intelligence.* New York: John Wiley and Sons, 1962. (B, R)

Gilliland, S.F. "Effects of sensitivity groups on moral judgment." Unpublished dissertation, Boston University, 1970. (M, R)

Ginott, H.C. *Between parent and child.* New York: Macmillan, 1967. (M)

Glasser, W. *Schools without failure.* New York: Harper and Row, 1969. (M)

Golumbowski, B.T. and Blomberg, A. *Sensitivity training and the laboratory approach.* Itasca: Ill.: F.E. Peacock Publishers, 1970. (B, M, R)

Goodman, P. *Growing up absurd.* New York: Random House, 1960. (B)

Goodman, P. *Compulsory mis-education.* New York: Horizon Press, 1964. (B)

Gordon, I.S. (Ed.). *Reaching the child through parent education: the Florida approach.* Gainesville, Florida: University of Florida, 1969. (M)

Gordon, T. *Parent effectiveness training.* New York: Peter H. Wyden, Inc., 1970. (M)

Gordon, T. and Cartwright, D. "The effect of psychotherapy upon certain attitudes toward others." In Rogers, C.R. and Dymond, R.F. (Eds.). *Psychotherapy and personality change.* Chicago: University of Chicago Press, 1954. (R)

Gordon, W.J.J. *Synectics: the development of creative capacity.* New York: Harper and Row, 1961. (B, M)

Gorman, A.H. *Teachers and learners: the interactive process in education.* Boston: Allyn and Bacon, 1969. (M)

Goswami, S.S. *Hatha yoga.* London: L.N. Fowler and Co., 15 Bridge Street, London, E.C. 4, 1959. (M)

Gowan, J., Demos, G. and Torrance, E.P. (Eds.). *Creativity: its educational implications.* New York: John Wiley and Sons, 1967. (B, M)

Green, H.B. and Knapp, R.H. "Time judgment, aesthetic reference and need for achievement." *Journal of Abnormal and Social Psychology,* 1959, 58, 140-142. (R)

Greenlaw, P.S., Herron, L.W. and Rawdon, R.H. *Business simulation.* Englewood Cliffs, N.J.: Prentice-Hall, 1962. (M)

Gruen, G.E. "Experiences affecting the development of number conservation in children." *Child Development,* 1965, 36, 4, 963-979. (R)

Guetzkow, H. "A use of simulation in the study of inter-nation relations." *Behavioral Science,* 1959, IV, 71-83. (M)

Guetzkow, H. *et al. Simulation in international relations: developments for research and teaching.* Englewood Cliffs, N.J.: Prentice-Hall, 1963. (B,M,R)

Gunther, B. *Sense relaxation: below your mind.* New York: Collier Books, 1968. (M)

Gunther, B. *What to do until the Messiah comes.* New York: Collier Books, 1970. (M)

Gustaitis, R. *Turning on.* New York: Macmillan, 1969. (M)

Hall, E. *The silent language.* Garden City, N.Y.: Doubleday, 1959. (B)

Hamachek, D. (Ed.). *The self in growth, teaching and learning.* Englewood Cliffs, N.J.: Prentice-Hall, 1965. (B)

Hamilton, N.K. and Saylor, J.G. (Eds.). *Humanizing the secondary school.* Prepared by ASCD Council on Secondary Education, National Education Association, Washington, D.C., 1969. (M)

Handbook for staff development and human relations training: materials developed for use in Africa. Published by National Training Laboratories, Institute for Applied Behavioral Science, associated with National Education Association, Washington, D.C., 1967. (M)

Handbook of structured experiences for human relations training. Vols. I, II, and III. Iowa City, Iowa: University Associates Press, 1969. (M)

Harmin, M. and Simon, S. "Working with values in the classroom." *Scholastic Teacher*, January 6, 1967. (M)

Harmin, M. and Simon, S. "Using the humanities for value clarification." From IMPACT, New York State ASCD, Spring 1968. (M)

Harrison, R., Durham, L., Gibb, J. and Knowles, E. *Problems in the design and interpretations of research on human relations training,* (1). *A bibliography of research, 1947-1967,* (2). National Training Laboratories Institute for Applied Behavioral Science, National Education Association, Washington, D.C., 1968. (R)

Hart, H. *Autoconditioning.* Englewood Cliffs, N.J.: Prentice-Hall, 1956. (B, M)

Harvey, O.J. (Ed.). *Experience, structure, and adaptability.* New York: Springer, 1966. Note: Hunt, D. "A conceptual systems change model and its application to education," 277-302. (B)

Harvey, O., Hunt, D. and Schroeder, D. *Conceptual systems.* New York: John Wiley and Sons, 1961. (B, M)

Hawkins, D. "The informed vision: an essay on science education." *Daedalus*, Summer 1965, 94, 3. (B)

Heckhausen, H. *Anatomy of achievement motivation.* New York: Academic Press, 1967. (B, R)

Hentoff, N. *Our children are dying.* New York: Viking Press, 1966. (M)

Herrigel, E. *Zen in the art of archery.* New York: Pantheon Books, 1953. (B, M)

Heyns, R.W., Veroff, J. and Atkinson, J.W. "A scoring manual for the affiliation motive." In Atkinson, J.W. (Ed.). *Motives in fantasy, action and society.* Princeton, N.J.: D. Van Nostrand, 1958. (R)

Higgins, W., Ivey, A. and Uhlemann, M. *Media therapy: a new approach to human relations training.* Multilith paper available from A. Ivey, School of Education, University of Massachusetts, Amherst, Mass., 1968. (M)

Hills, C. and Stone, R.B. *Conduct your own awareness sessions.* New York: New American Library, 1970. (M)

Holt, J. *How children fail.* New York: Dutton, 1964. (M)

Holt, J. *How children learn.* New York: Dutton, 1967. (M)

Holt, J. *What do I do on Monday?* New York: Dutton, 1970. (M)

Holt, R.R. and Luborsky, L. *Personality patterns of psychiatrists.* New York: Basic Books, 1958. (R)

House, R.J. "T-group leadership education and leadership effectiveness: a review of the empirical literature and a critical evaluation." *Personnel Psychology,* 1967, 20, 132. (R)

Houts, P. and Serber, M. (Eds.). *After the turn on, what?* Champaign, Ill.: Research Press, 1972. (B)

Howard, J. "Inhibitions thrown to the gentle winds." *Life,* July 12, 1968, 48-65. (M)

Howard, J. *Please touch.* New York: Dell Publishing, 1970. (M)

Hoyt, D.P. "The relationship between college grades and adult achievement: a review of the literature." *American College Testing Program Research Reports,* 1965, 7, 1-58. (R)

Human relations education: A guidebook to learning activities. Prepared by the Human Relations Project of western New York, reprinted by the University of the State of New York, the State Education Department, Curriculum Development Center, Albany, New York, 1969. (B)

Hung-Min Chiang and Maslow, A.H. (Eds.). *The healthy personality: readings.* New York: D. Van Nostrand-Reinhold, 1969. (B)

Hunt, J. McV. "Parent and child centers: their basis in the behavioral and educational sciences." *American Journal of Orthopsychiatry,* 1971, Vol. 41, 1, 13-38. (B, M)

Huxley, A. "Education on the non-verbal level." *Daedalus,* Spring 1962a. (B)

Huxley, A. *Island.* New York: Harper and Row, 1962b. (B)

Huxley, L. *You are not the target.* New York: Farrar, Strauss and Giroux, 1963. (M)

Ivey, A. "Performance criteria for human relations." Appendix 1, 5-58 in *Model elementary teacher education program,* 1968. Available from the School of Education, University of Massachusetts, Amherst, Mass. (M)

Ivey, A. *Microcounseling: innovations in interviewing training.*

Springfield, Ill.: Charles C. Thomas, 1971. (M)

Ivey, A., Normington, C.J., Miller, C.D., Morril, W.H. and Haase, R.F. "Microcounseling and attending behavior: an approach to pre-practicum counselor training." *Journal of Counseling Psychology,* September 1968, 15, 5, 2, 1-12. (R)

Ivey, A. and Weinstein, G. "The counselor as specialist in psychological education." *Journal of Personnel and Guidance,* October 1970. (B)

Jacob, P.E. *Changing values in college.* New York: Harper and Row, 1957. (R)

Jacobson, E. *You must relax.* New York: McGraw-Hill, 1962. (M)

Jaffe, S.L. and Scheal, D.J. "Acute psychosis precipitated by t-group experiences." *Archives of General Psychiatry,* October 1969, Vol. 21, 443-448. (R)

Jahoda, M. *Current concepts of positive mental health.* New York: Harper and Row, 1958. (B)

James, D. (Ed.). *Outward bound.* London: Routledge Keegan Paul, 68-74 Carter Lane, London, E.C. 4, 1957. (B, M)

Jensen, A.R. "How much can we boost IQ and scholastic achievement?" *Harvard Educational Review,* Winter 1969, 39, 1, 1-123. (R)

Jones, R.M. *Contemporary educational psychology.* New York: Harper Torchbooks, 1966. (B)

Jourard, S. *The transparent self.* Princeton, N.J.: D. Van Nostrand, 1964. (B)

Jourard, S. *Disclosing man to himself.* Princeton, N.J.: D. Van Nostrand, 1968. (B)

Jourard, S. and Overlade, D. (Eds.). *Reconciliation: A theory of man transcending.* Princeton, N.J.: D. Van Nostrand, 1968. (B)

Jung, C.G. "A study in the process of individuation." In *The archetypes and the collective unconscious.* In the Collected Works, Vol. 9, Bollingen Foundation, New York, 1959a. (B)

Jung, C.G. "Conscious, unconscious and individuation." In *The archetypes and the collective unconscious.* In the Collected Works, Vol. 9, Bollingen Foundation, New York, 1959b. (B)

Kagan, J. "On the need for relativism in psychology." *American Psychologist,* February 1967, 22, 2, 131-142. (B, M)

Kagan, J. and Moss, H.A. "Stability and validity of achievement fantasy." *Journal of Abnormal and Social Psychology,* 1959, 58, 357-364. (R)

Kagan, J. and Moss, H.A. *From birth to maturity.* New York:

John Wiley and Sons, 1962. (R)

Kamiya, J. "Conscious control of brain waves." *Psychology Today,* 1968, 1, 57-60. (M, R)

Kandel, I.L. "Character formation: a historical perspective." *The Educational Forum,* March 1961, 307-316. (B)

Kapleau, P. *The three pillars of Zen.* New York: Harper and Row, 1966. (B)

Katz, R. *Self-assessment workshop, instructor's manual.* Human Development Foundation, Cambridge, Mass. (Final report of Peace Corps Contract No. 80-1531, 1970.) (M)

Katz, R. and Kolb, D. "Outward Bound and education for personal growth." Mimeographed paper available from David Kolb, Sloan School of Management, M.I.T., Cambridge, Mass., 1968. (M)

Kelley, E. *Education for what is real.* New York: Harper, 1947. (B)

Kelly, E.L. and Fiske, D. *The prediction of success in clinical psychology.* Ann Arbor, Michigan: University of Michigan Press, 1951. (R)

Kelly, G. *The psychology of personal constructs.* Vols. I and II. New York: Norton, 1955. (B, M)

Kibbe, M., Croft, C. and Nanus, B. *Management games: a new technique for executive development.* New York: Rineholt, 1961. (M)

Kirschenbaum, H. and Simon, S. "Teaching English with a focus on values." *English Journal,* October 1969, Vol. 58, No. 7, 1071-1076. (M)

Kirschenbaum, H., Simon, S. and Napier, R.W. *Wad-ja-get? The grading game in American education.* New York: Hart Publishers, 1971. (B, M, R)

Klein, A. *Role playing in leadership training and group solving.* New York: Association Press, 1956. (M)

Klinger, E. "Fantasy and need achievement as a motivational construct." *Psychological Bulletin,* 1966, 4, 291-308. (B, R)

Knapp, R.H. "Attitudes toward time and aesthetic choice." *Journal of Social Psychology,* 1962, 56, 79-87. (R)

Knapp, R.H. and Green, H.B. "The judgment of music-filled intervals and n-achievement." *Journal of Social Psychology,* 1960, 54, 263-267. (R)

Kohl, H. *36 children.* New York: New American Library, 1967. (M)

Kohl, H. *The open classroom.* New York: Vintage Press, 1969. (M)

Kohlberg, L. "The development of children's orientation towards a moral order: I: sequence in the development of moral thought." *Vita Humana,* 1963, 6, 11-33. (B, R)

Kohlberg, L. "The development of moral character and ideology." In Hoffman, M. (Ed.). *Review of child psychology.* Beverly Hills, Calif.: Russell Sage, 1964. (B, R)

Kohlberg, L. "A cognitive developmental analysis of children's sex role concepts and attitudes." In Maccobey, E. (Ed.). *The development of sex differences.* Stanford, Calif.: Stanford University Press, 1966a. (B, R)

Kohlberg, L. "Moral education in the schools: a developmental view." *The School Review,* Spring 1966b. (B, M)

Kohlberg, L. "Moral development." In *International encyclopedia of the social sciences.* New York: Crowell, Collier and Macmillan, 1968. (B, R)

Kohlberg, L. "Stage and sequence: the cognitive developmental approach to socialization." In Goslin, D. (Ed.). *Handbook of socialization theory and research.* Chicago: Rand McNally, 1969. (B, R)

Kohlberg, L. "Education for justice: a modern statement of the Platonic view." In Sizer, T. (Ed.). *Moral Education.* Cambridge, Mass.: Harvard University Press, 1970a. (B)

Kohlberg, L. "From is to ought: how to commit the naturalistic fallacy and get away with it in the study of moral development." In Mischell, T. (Ed.). *Genetic epistemology.* New York: Academic Press, 1970b. (B)

Kohlberg, L. "Stages of moral development as a basis for moral education." In Beck, C. and Sullivan, E. (Eds.). *Moral Education.* Canada: University of Toronto Press, 1970c. (B)

Kohlberg, L. "The concepts of developmental psychology as the central guide to education; examples from cognitive, moral, and psychological education." Unpublished paper available from the author, Harvard Graduate School of Education, Larson Hall, Appian Way, Cambridge, Mass., 1971. (B)

Kohlberg, L. and Kramer, R. "Continuities and discontinuities in children and adult moral development." *Human Development,* 1969, 12, 93-120. (R)

Kohlberg, L., LaCross, J. and Ricks, D. "The predictability of adult mental health from childhood behavior." In Wolman (Ed.). *Handbook of child psychopathology.* New York: McGraw-Hill, 1970. (R)

Kohlberg, L. and Turiel, E. (Eds.). *Moral development and moral education.* Cambridge, Mass.: Harvard University Press, 1971a. (B, M, R)

Kohlberg, L. and Turiel, E. "What psychology can tell the teacher about moral education." In Lesser, G. (Ed.). *Psychology and the education process.* Chicago: Scott Foresman, 1971b. (B, M)

Kolb, D.A. "An achievement motivation training program for underachieving high school boys." *Journal of Personality and Social Psychology,* 1965, 2, 6, 783-792. (M, R)

Kounin, J.S. *Discipline and group management in classrooms.* New York: Holt, Rinehart and Winston, 1970. (M, R)

Kowatrakul, S. and Stivers, H.H. *Increasing children's achievement behavior and measured intelligence through "need achievement" training.* Philadelphia: Temple University, Department of Educational Psychology, 1969. (M, R)

Kriyananda. *Yoga postures for self-awareness.* San Francisco: Hansa Publications, 1967. (M)

Laing, R.D. *The politics of experience.* New York: Ballantine, 1960. (B)

Lakin, M. *Interpersonal encounter: theory and practice in sensitivity training.* New York: McGraw-Hill, 1972. (B, M, R)

Lasker, H. "Factors affecting responses to achievement motivation training in India." Unpublished honors thesis, Harvard University, 1966. (R)

Leary, T. *Interpersonal diagnosis of personality.* New York: Ronald, 1957. (B, M, R)

Lederer, W. and Jackson, D.D. *The mirages of marriage.* New York: Norton, 1968. (B, M)

Lederman, J. *Anger and the rocking chair: Gestalt awareness with children.* New York: McGraw-Hill, 1969. (B, M)

Leeper, R.R. (Ed.). *Humanizing education: the person in the process.* ASCD-NEA, Washington, D.C., 1967. (B)

Lefcourt, H.M. "Internal vs. external control of reinforcement: a review." *Psychological Bulletin,* 1966, 65, 4, 206-220. (R)

Leonard, G.B. *Education and ecstasy.* New York: Delacorte Press, 1968. (B, M)

Lesser, G.S., Krawitz, R.N., and Packard, R. "Experimental arousal of achievement motivation in adolescent girls." *Journal of Abnormal and Social Psychology,* 1963, 66, 59-66. (R)

LeVine, R.A. *Dreams and deeds: achievement motivation in Nigeria.* Chicago: The University of Chicago Press, 1966. (B, R)

Levitt, E.E. "The results of psychotherapy with children." *Journal of Consulting Psychologists,* 1957, 21, 189-196. (R)

Lewis, H.R. and Streitfeld, H.S. *Growth games.* New York: Harcourt Brace Jovanovich, 1970. (M)

Lichtenberg, P. "Emotional maturity as manifested in ideational interaction." *Journal of Abnormal and Social Psychology,* 1955, 298-301. (R)

Lichtenberg, P. *et al.* "Mutual achievement strivings: a continuum for mental health." *Journal of Abnormal and Social Psychology,* 1961, 61, 3, 619-628. (R)

Lieberman, M., Yalom, I. and Miles, M.B. "The impact of encounter groups on participants." *Journal of Applied Behavioral Sciences,* 1972. (R)

Lincoln, C.E. *The Black Muslim in America.* Boston, Mass.: Beacon Press, 1961. (M)

Litwin, G. and Aronoff, J. "Achievement motivation training and executive advancement." Unpublished paper, Harvard University, School of Business Administration, Humphrey House 22, Cambridge, Mass., 1966. (R)

Litwin, G.H. and Ciarlo, J.A. *Achievement motivation and risk-taking in a business setting.* Technical report. New York: General Electric, Behavioral Research Service, 1961. (M)

Litwin, G.H. and Stringer, R.A. *Motivation and organizational climate.* Boston, Mass.: Division of Research, Graduate School of Business Administration, Harvard University, 1968. (B, R)

Loevinger, J., Wessler, R. and Redmore, C. *Measuring ego development,* Vols. I and II. San Francisco, Calif.: Jossey-Bass, 1970. (B, M, R)

Lombardo, A. "A mental health curriculum for lower grades." *Mental Health,* October 1968, 52, 4, 570-576. (M)

Lorrayne, H. *How to develop a super power memory.* New York: Frederick Fell, 1957. (M)

Lowen, A. *Love and orgasm.* New York: Macmillan, 1965. (B)

Lowen, A. *The betrayal of the body.* New York: Macmillan, 1967. (B, M)

Luborsky, L., Chandler, M., Auerback, A. H., Cohen, J. and Bachrach, H. "Factors influencing the outcome of psychotherapy: a review of quantitative research." *Psychological Bulletin,* March 1971, Vol. 75, No. 3, 145-185. (R)

Lyons, H. *Learning to feel—feeling to learn.* Columbus, Ohio: Charles E. Merrill Publishing, 1971. (M)

Mager, R.F. *Preparing instructional objectives.* Palo Alto, Calif.: Fearon Publishers, 1962. (M)

Mahone, C.H. "Fear of failure and unrealistic vocational aspirations." In Atkinson and Feather (Eds.). *A theory of achievement motivation.* New York: John Wiley and Sons, 1966. (R)

Makarenko, A.S. *Road to life* (translated by Stephen Garry). London, England: S. Nott, 1936. (B, M)

Malamud, D.I. "A workshop in self-understanding designed to prepare patients for psychotherapy." *American Journal of Psychotherapy,* 1958, 12, 771-786. (M)

Malamud, D.I. "Educating adults in self-understanding." *Mental Hygiene,* 1960, 44, 115-124. (M)

Malamud, D.I. "Self-confrontation in simulated family groups." 1968-1969 Psychosynthesis Seminars, December 20, 1968. Available from Psychosynthesis Research Foundation, Room 314, 527 Lexington Ave., New York, New York. (M)

Malamud, D.I. and Machover, S. *Toward self-understanding: group techniques in self-confrontation.* Springfield, Ill.: Charles C. Thomas, 1965. (B, M)

Maltz, M. *Psycho-cybernetics.* Englewood Cliffs, N.J.: Prentice-Hall, 1960. (M)

Man-ch'ing, C. and Smith, R.W. *T'ai-chi.* Rutland, Vermont: Charles E. Tuttle, 1966. (M)

Mann, J. *Changing human behavior.* New York: Scribners, 1965. (B, M, R)

Mann, J. *Encounter.* New York: Grossman Publishers, 1970. (M)

Martin, P. *Experiment in depth.* London: Routledge Keegan Paul, 68-74 Carter Lane, London, E.C. 4, 1955. (M)

Maslow, A. (Ed.). *New knowledge in human values.* New York: Harper and Row, 1959. (B)

Maslow, A. *Religions, values and peak experiences.* Cincinnati: Ohio State University Press, 1964. (B)

Maslow, A. *Eupsychian management.* Homewood, Ill.: Richard O. Irwin and the Dorsey Press, 1965. (B)

Maslow, A. *The psychology of science: a reconnaissance.* New York: Harper and Row, 1966. (B)

Maslow, A. "Synanon and eupsychia." *Journal of Humanistic Psychology,* Spring 1967. (B)

Maslow, A. "Farther reaches of human nature." *Journal of Transhumanistic Psychology,* 1968a, 1. (B)

Maslow, A. "Goals of humanistic education." Paper from Esalen

Institute, Big Sur, California, 1968b. (B)

Maslow, A. "Music education and peak experience." *Music Educators' Journal,* 1968c, 54, 72-75, 163-171. (B)

Maslow, A. "Some educational implications of the humanistic psychologies." *Harvard Educational Review,* Fall 1968d, 38, 4, 685-695. (B)

Maslow, A. "Some fundamental questions that face the normative social psychologist." *Journal of Humanistic Psychology,* Fall 1968e, 143-155. (B)

Maslow, A. "A theory of meta motivation: the biological rooting of the value life." *Journal of Humanistic Psychology,* December 1968f. (B)

Maslow, A. *Toward a psychology of being.* Princeton, N.J.: D. Van Nostrand, 1968g. (B)

Maslow, A. and Chiang, H. (Eds.). *The healthy personality: readings.* Princeton, N.J.: D. Van Nostrand, Spring 1969. (B)

Massialas, B. and Zevin, J. *Creative encounters in the classroom: teaching and learning through discovery.* New York: John Wiley and Sons, 1967. (M)

Maupin, E.W. "Meditation." In Otto and Mann (Eds.). *Ways of growth.* New York: Grossman Publishers, 1968. (M)

McClelland, D.C. (Ed.). *Studies in motivation.* New York: Appleton-Century-Crofts, 1955. (B, R)

McClelland, D.C. "Risk-taking in children with high and low needs for achievement." In Atkinson, J.W. (Ed.). *Motives in fantasy, action and society.* Princeton, N.J.: D. Van Nostrand, 1958. (R)

McClelland, D.C. *The achieving society.* New York: D. Van Nostrand, 1961. (B, R)

McClelland, D.C. "Business drive and national achievement." *Harvard Business Review,* July-August, 1962. (B)

McClelland, D.C. "Changing values for progress." In Burns, H.W. (Ed.). *Education and the development of nations.* Syracuse, N.Y.: Syracuse University Press, 1963. (B)

McClelland, D.C. "Achievement motivation can be developed." *Harvard Business Review,* November 1965a, 43, 6-8+. (B, M, R)

McClelland, D.C. "Toward a theory of motive acquisition." *American Psychologist,* May 1965b, 20, 5, 321-333. (B, M, R)

McClelland, D.C. "N-Achievement and entrepreneurship: a longitudinal study." *Personality and Social Psychology,* 1965c, 1,

389-392. (R)

McClelland, D.C. "Longitudinal trends in the relation of thought to action." *Journal of Consulting Psychology,* 1966, 3, 6, 470-483. (R)

McClelland, D.C. "Measuring behavioral objectives in the 1970s." In *Technology and Innovation in Education,* prepared by the Aerospace Education Foundation. New York: Frederick A. Praeger, 1968. (B)

McClelland, D.C. and Alschuler, A.S. *The achievement motivation development project.* Final report to USOE project No. 7-1231, Bureau of Research, April 1971. (M, R)

McClelland, D.C., Atkinson, J.W., Clark, R.A. and Lowell, E.L. *The achievement motive.* New York: Appleton-Century-Crofts, 1955. (B, R)

McClelland, D.C., Baldwin, A.L., Bronfenbrenner, U. and Strodtbeck, F.L. *Talent and society.* Princeton, N.J.: D. Van Nostrand, 1958. (B)

McClelland, D.C. with Friedman, G.A. "A cross-cultural study of the relationship between child training practices and achievement motivation appearing in folk tales." In Swanson, G.E., Newcomb, T.M. and Hartley, E.L. (Eds.). *Readings in social psychology.* New York: Holt, Rinehart and Winston, 1952. (B, R)

McClelland, D.C. and Winter, D.G. *Motivating economic achievement.* New York: Free Press, 1969. (B, M, R)

McCord, W. and McCord, J. *The psychopath.* Princeton, N.J.: D. Van Nostrand, 1964. (B, R)

McGhee, P.E. and Crandall, V.C. "Beliefs in internal-external control of reinforcement and academic performance." *Child Development,* 1968, 39, 91-102. (R)

Mehta, P. and Kanade, H.M. "Motivation development for educational growth." *Indiana Journal of Psychology,* 1969, 46, 120. (R)

Middleman, R.R. *The nonverbal method in working with groups.* New York: Association Press, 1968. (M)

Miles, M.B. *Learning to work in groups.* New York: Bureau of Publications, Teachers College, Columbia University, 1959. (B, M)

Miles, M.B. "On temporary systems." In *Innovation in education.* New York: Teachers College Press, 1961. (B, R)

Miles, M.B. "Planned change and organizational health: figure and ground." In Carlson, R.O., Gallagher, A., Jr., Miles, M.B.,

Pellegrin, R.J. and Rogers, E.M. *Change process in the public schools.* Eugene, Oregon: The Center for the Advanced Study of Educational Administration, 1965. (B)

Miles, M.B. "Some properties of schools as social systems." In Goodwin, W. (Ed.). *Change in school systems.* Washington, D.C.: National Training Laboratories Institute for Applied Behavioral Science, National Education Association, 1967. (B)

Miller, S. *Hot springs: the true adventures of the first New York Jewish literary intellectual in the human potential movement.* New York: Viking, 1971. (B, M)

Mischel, W. "Delay of gratification, need for achievement and acquiescence in another culture." Unpublished paper, Harvard University, Cambridge, Mass., 1960. (R)

Moffet, J. *A student-centered language arts curriculum,* Vol. 1 (grades K-6) and Vol. 2 (grades 7-13). Boston: Houghton Mifflin, 1968a. (B, M)

Moffet, J. *Teaching the universe of discourse.* Boston: Houghton Mifflin, 1968b. (B, M)

Mooney, R. and Eaher, R. (Eds.). *Explorations in creativity.* New York: Harper and Row, 1967. (B)

Moore, S. *The Stanislavski method.* New York: Viking Press, 1960. (B, M)

Moreno, J.L. *Who shall survive?* New York: Beacon House, 1953. (B, M)

Moreno, J.L. and Moreno, Z.T. *Psychodrama.* Vols. I and II. New York: Beacon House, 1953. (B, M)

Morgan, James N. "The achievement motive and economic behavior." In Atkinson, J.W. and Feather, N. (Eds.). *A theory of achievement motivation.* New York: John Wiley and Sons, 1966. (R)

Morris, D. *The naked ape.* New York: McGraw-Hill, 1967. (B)

Morris, V. *Existentialism in education.* New York: Harper and Row, 1966. (B)

Mosher, R. and Sprinthall, N. "Psychological education in secondary schools to promote individual and human development." *American Psychologist,* October 1970, Vol. 25, No. 10. (B, M)

Mosher, R. and Sprinthall, N. "Psychological education: a means to promote personal development during adolescence." *The Counseling Psychologist,* 1971, Vol. 2, No. 4. (B, M)

Moss, H.A. and Kagan, J. "Stability of achievement and recogni-

tion seeking behaviors from early childhood through adulthood." *Journal of Abnormal and Social Psychology*, 1961,
62, 504-513. (R)

Moustakas, C. *Personal growth.* Cambridge, Mass.: Howard Doyle,
1968. (B)

Murphy, G. *Breeding intelligence through teaching.* New York:
Harper and Brothers, 1961. (B)

Murphy, M. "Esalen, where it's at." *Psychology Today*, December
1967. (B)

Murray, Henry A. *Explorations in personality.* New York: Oxford
University Press, 1938. (B, R)

Myrers, R.E. and Torrance, E.P. *Ideabooks.* Boston: Ginn,
1965-1966. Also, Cunningham, B.F. and Torrance, E.P.
Imagi/Craft series in creative development. Boston: Ginn,
1965-1966. (M)

Navanjo, C. and Ornstein, R.E. *On the psychology of meditation.*
New York: Viking Press, 1971. (B, M)

Neill, A.S. *Summerhill.* New York: Hart, 1960. (B, M)

Newberg, N. "Education for student concerns: courses in com-
munications and urban affairs." In Alschuler, A. (Ed.).
Psychological/humanistic education. Education Opportunity
Forum, 1969, Vol. 1, No. 4. (M)

Newberg, N.C. and Borton, P. *Education for student concerns.*
Available from the authors, Philadelphia Board of Education,
21st and the Parkway, 1968. (M)

Newman, F. and Oliver, D. "Education and community." *Harvard
Educational Review*, Winter 1967, 37, 1, 61-106. (B)

News and Reports. "Emotional stress and laboratory training."
National Training Laboratories Institute for Applied Behavioral Science, National Education Association, November
1969, Vol. 3, No. 4. (R)

Nyberg, D. *Tough and tender learning.* Palo Alto, Calif.: National
Press Books, 1970. (B)

Nylen, D., Mitchell, R. and Stout, A. *Handbook for staff
development and human relations training.* Published by
National Training Laboratories, Institute for Applied Behavioral Science, National Education Association, Washington,
D.C. 10036. (B)

Olton, R.M. "A self-instructional program for the development of
productive thinking in fifth and sixth grade children." In
Williams, F.E. (Ed.). *First seminar on productive thinking in
education.* St. Paul, Minn.: Creativity and National Schools

Projects, Macalaster College, 1966. (M)

Osborn, A.F. *Applied imagination.* New York: Scribners, 1963. (M)

Otto, H.A. (Ed.). *Explorations in human potential.* Springfield, Ill.: Charles C. Thomas, 1966. (M)

Otto, H.A. *A guide to developing your potential.* New York: Scribners, 1967. (M)

Otto, H.A. (Ed.). *Human potentialities: the challenge and the promise.* St. Louis: Warren H. Green, 1968. (M)

Otto, H.A. *More joy in your marriage.* New York: Hawthorne Books, 1969a. (M)

Otto, H.A. "A new look at the human potentialities movement." *Saturday Review,* December 20, 1969b. (M)

Otto, H.A. *Group methods designed to actualize human potential: a handbook.* Beverly Hills, Calif.: Holistic Press, 1970a. (M)

Otto, H.A. "Has monogamy failed?" *Saturday Review,* April 25, 1970b. (M)

Otto, H.A. and Mann, J. (Eds.). *Ways of growth.* New York: Grossman Publishers, 1968. (M)

Parker, J.C. and Rubin, L.J. *Process as content: curriculum design and the application of knowledge.* Chicago: Rand McNally, 1966. (B)

Parnes, S. *Creative behavior guidebook.* New York: Scribners, 1967. (M)

Parnes, S. "Creative potential and educational experience." In *Fields within fields within fields,* 1969, 2, 1. (M)

Parnes, S. and Brunelle, E.A. "The literature of creativity, Part 1 and Part 2." *Journal of Creative Behavior,* 1967, Vol. 1, No. 1, 52-109; No. 2, 191-240. (R)

Parsons, T. "The school class as a social system: some of its functions in American society." *Harvard Education Review,* Fall 1959, Vol. 29, No. 4. (B, R)

Payne, B. "Extra-verbal techniques and Korzybskian formulations." *ETC,* March 1968, 15, 1, 7-15. (B)

Peck, R.F. and Havighurst, R.J. *The psychology of character development.* New York: John Wiley and Sons, 1960.

Perls, F.S. "Gestalt therapy and human potential." Esalen paper No. 1. Big Sur, California: Esalen Institute, 1965. (B)

Perls, F.S. "Workshop on individual therapy." Paper delivered at the American Psychological Association Convention, New York City, September 1966. (B, M)

Perls, F.S. *Gestalt therapy verbatim.* Lafayette, Calif.: Real People

Press, 1969. (B, M)

Perls, F.S. *In and out of the garbage pail.* Lafayette, Calif.: Real People Press, 1970. (B, M)

Perls, F.S., Hefferline, R.F. and Goodman, P. *Gestalt therapy.* New York: Dell (paperback), 1965. (B, M)

Pesso, A. *Movement and psychotherapy.* New York: New York University Press, 1969. (B, M)

Peters and Schaaf. *Algebra: a modern approach. I.* Princeton, N.J.: D. Van Nostrand, 1963. (M)

Piaget, J. *The moral judgment of the child.* New York: Collier Books, 1962. (B, R)

Piker, S. "The image of the limited good: comment on an exercise in description and interpretation." *American Anthropologist,* 1966, 68, 1202-1211. (B)

Polanyi, M. *The tacit dimension.* Garden City, N.Y.: Doubleday, 1966. (B)

Prince, G.M. "The operational mechanism of synectics." *Journal of Creative Behavior,* Winter 1968a, 2, 2, 1-13. (B, M)

Prince, G.M. *The practice of creativity.* Cambridge, Mass.: Synectics, 26 Church Street, 1968b. (M)

Prince, G.M. "Creative leadership." *Harvard Business Review,* January-February 1969. (M)

Proskauer, M. "Breathing therapy." In Otto, H. and Mann, J. *Ways of growth.* New York: Grossman Publishers, 1968. (M)

Purkey, W.V. *Self-concept and school achievement.* Englewood Cliffs, N.J.: Prentice-Hall, 1970. (B, M)

Pursglove, P.D. (Ed.). *Recognition in Gestalt therapy.* New York: Funk and Wagnalls, 1968. (B, M)

Randolph, N. and Howe, W.A. *Self-enhancing education: a program to motivate learners.* Palo Alto, Calif.: Stanford Press, 1967. (B, M)

Raser, J.R. *Simulation and society: an exploration of scientific gaming.* Boston: Allyn and Bacon, 1969. (B, M, R)

Rathbone, C. "A bibliography on open education." Newton, Mass.: Educational Development Center, 55 Chapel Street, 1968. (B, M)

Rathbone, C. "A lesson from Oughborough." *This Magazine,* Winter 1969, 3, 1. (B)

Raths, L. and Burrell, A. *Understanding the problem child.* West Orange, N.J.: Economics Press, 1963. (B, M)

Raths, L., Harmin, M. and Simon, S. *Values and teaching.* Columbus, Ohio: Charles E. Merrill Publishing, 1966. (B, M)

Reich, W. *The discovery of the orgone. Vol. I, The function of the orgasm.* (1st ed.) New York: Orgone Institute Press, 1942. (B)

Rich, J.M. *Education and human values.* Reading, Mass.: Addison-Wesley, 1968. (B)

Ricks, D. and Epley, D. "Foresight and hindsight in the TAT." Paper read at the Eastern Psychological Association, New York, April 1960. (B)

Rimmer, X. *Harrad experiment.* New York: Bantam, 1966. (B, M)

Roberts, J.M., Arth, M.J. and Bush, R.R. "Games in culture." *American Anthropologist,* 1959, 61, 597-605. (B, R)

Roberts, J.M., Hoffman, H. and Sutton-Smith, B. "Pattern and competence: a consideration of tick-tack-toe." *El Palacio,* Autumn 1965, 17-30. (B, R)

Roberts, J.M. and Sutton-Smith, B. "Child training and game involvement." *Ethnology,* 1962, 1, 2, 166-185. (B, R)

Roberts, J.M., Sutton-Smith, B. and Kendon, A. "Strategy in games and folk tales." *Journal of Social Psychology,* 1963, 61, 185-199. (B, R)

Robinson, J.A. "Simulation and games." Unpublished paper. Columbus, Ohio: Department of Political Science, Ohio State University, 1965. (M)

Robinson, J.A. *et al.* "Teaching with inter-nation simulation and case studies." *The American Political Science Review,* LX, 53-66. (M)

Rogers, C. *On becoming a person.* Boston: Houghton Mifflin, 1961. (B)

Rogers, C. "The group comes of age." *Psychology Today,* December 1969, 3, 7, 27-31, 58-61. (B, M)

Rogers, C. *Carl Rogers on encounter groups.* New York: Harper and Row, 1970. (B, M)

Rogers, C. *et al. Person to person: the problem of being human: a new trend in psychology.* Lafayette, Calif.: Real People Press, 1967. (B)

Rokeach, M. "Long range experimental modifications of values, attitudes and behavior." *American Psychologist,* May 1971, Vol. 26, No. 5, 453-459. (B, R)

Rolf, I. "Structural integration." New York: Author, 11 Riverdale Drive, 1962. (B, R)

Rosen, B.C. and D'Andrade, R.G. "The psychosocial origins of achievement motivation." *Sociometry,* 1959, 22, 185-218. (B, R)

Roth, D.M. *The famous Roth memory course.* Cleveland: Ralston Publishing, 1952. (M)

Rotter, J.B. "Generalized expectations for internal control of reinforcement." *Psychological Monographs,* 1966, 80, 609, 1. (B, R)

Rotter, J.B., Seeman, M. and Liverant, S. "Internal versus external control of reinforcement, a major variable in behavior theory." In Washburne, N.F. (Ed.). *Decisions, values and groups.* Vol. 2. London: Pergamon Press, 1962. (B, R)

Rowland, K. *Looking and seeing.* Toronto: Ginn, 1966. (B, M)

Ruesch, J. and Kees, W. *Non-verbal communication.* Berkeley, Calif.: University of California Press, 1956. (B)

Ryals, K.R. An experimental study of achievement motivation training as a function of the moral maturity of trainees. Doctoral dissertation, Washington University, St. Louis, Mo., 1969. (M)

Sadhu, M. *Concentration.* New York: Harper and Row, 1959. (M)

Satir, V. *Conjoint family therapy.* Palo Alto, Calif.: Science and Behavior Books, 1967. (B, M)

Schein, E.H. and Bennis, W.G. *Personal and organizational change through group methods.* New York: John Wiley and Sons, 1965. (B, M)

Schiffman, M. Self-therapy: techniques for personal growth. Available from author, 340 Santa Monica Avenue, Menlo Park, Calif., 1967. (M)

Schmuck, R.A., Luszki, M.B. and Epperson, D.C. "Interpersonal relations and mental health in the classroom." In Clark, D.H. and Lesser, G.S. (Eds.). *Emotional disturbance and school learning.* Chicago: Science Research Associates, 1965. (B)

Schmuck, R.A. and Miles, M.B. (Eds.). *Organizational development in schools.* Palo Alto, Calif.: National Press Books, 1971. (B, M, R)

Schmuck, R.A. and Schmuck, P. *Group processes in the classroom.* Dubuque, Iowa: William C. Brown, 1971. (B, M, R)

Schultz, J.H. and Luthe, W. *Autogenic training.* New York: Grune and Stratton, 1959. (M)

Schutz, W. *Joy.* New York: Grove Press, 1967. (M)

Schutz, W. *Here comes everybody—mind and encounter culture.* New York: Harper and Row, 1971. (B, R)

Scott, W. "Research definitions of mental health and mental illness." *Psychological Bulletin,* 1958a, 55, 29-45. (R)

Scott, W. "Social psychological correlates of mental illness and mental health." *Psychological Bulletin,* 1958b, 55. (R)

Seashore, C. "What is sensitivity training?" *National Training Laboratories Institute News and Reports,* April 1968, 2, 2. (B)

Seidman, J.M. (Ed.). *Educating for mental health: a book of readings.* New York: Crowell, 1963. (B, R)

Severin, F. *Humanistic viewpoints in psychology.* New York: McGraw-Hill, 1965. (B)

Shea, D. and Jackson, K. "Motivation training for teachers." Multilith available from the authors, Department of Sociology, Washington University, St. Louis, Missouri, 1970. (M)

Shepard, M. and Loe, M. *Marathon 16.* New York: Pocket Books, 1971. (M)

Shostrom, E.L. "A test for the measurement of self-actualization." *Educational and Psychological Measurement,* 1965, Vol. 24, 207-218. (R)

Shostrom, E.L. *Manual for self-actualization workshop.* Santa Ana, Calif.: Institute of Therapeutic Psychology, 1967a, 23-24. (M)

Shostrom, E.L. *Man, the manipulator.* Nashville, Tenn.: Abingdon Press, 1967b. (B, M)

Shostrom, E.L. "Group therapy: let the buyer beware." *Psychology Today,* May 1969.

Shrank, J. *Media in value education: a critical guide.* Chicago: Communications, 1970. (M)

Sigel, I.E., Roeper, A. and Hooper, F.H. "A training procedure for acquisition of Piaget's conservation of quantity: a pilot study and its replication." *British Journal of Educational Psychology,* 1966, 36, 301-311. (B, R)

Silberman, C.E. *Crisis in the classroom.* New York: Random House, 1970. (B, M, R)

Simkin, J.S. "Introduction to Gestalt therapy." Mimeo paper available from the author, 337 South Beverly Drive, Suite 206, Beverly Hills, Calif. 90212. (B)

Sizer, T. "Report of the president's committee on clinical training programs at Harvard University." Cambridge, Mass.: Harvard Graduate School of Education, 1968. (B)

Skinner, B.F. *Walden Two.* New York: Macmillan Paperbacks, 1962. (B, M)

Skolnick, A. "Motivational imagery and behavior over 20 years." *Journal of Consulting Psychology,* 1966, 30, 463-478. (R)

Skorpen, E. "Behavioral anthropology and the philosophy of

man." *Main Currents of Modern Thought.* November-December 1970a, Vol. 27, No. 2. (B)

Skorpen, E. "Existential ontogeny recapitulates existentialist psylogeny." Available from the author, Department of Philosophy, University of Maine, 1970b. (B)

Slater, P.E. *Microcosm.* New York: John Wiley and Sons, 1966. (B, M)

Smedslund, J. "The acquisition of conservation of substance and weight in children." *Scandinavian Journal of Psychology,* 1961, Vol. 2. (M, R)

Smith, M.B. "Research strategies toward a conception of positive mental health." *American Psychologist,* 1959, 14, 673-681. (B)

Smith, M.B. "Mental health reconsidered: a special case of the problem of values in psychology." *American Psychologist,* 1961, 16, 299-306. (B)

Smith, M.B. "Explorations in competence: a study of Peace Corps teachers in Ghana." *American Psychologist,* 1966, 21, 555-567. (R)

Sohl, J. *The lemon eaters.* New York: Dell, 1968. (M)

Sommer, R. *Personal space.* Englewood Cliffs, N.J.: Prentice-Hall, 1969. (B, M, R)

Sprawls, R.C. "Business simulation." In Borko, H. (Ed.). *Computer applications in the behavioral sciences.* New York: Prentice-Hall, 1962. (B)

Stanford, G. and Stanford, B.D. *Learning discussion skills through games.* New York: Citation Press, 1969. (M)

Stern, G.G., Stein, M.L. and Bloom, B.S. *Methods in personality assessment.* Glencoe, Ill.: Free Press, 1956. (B, R)

Stevans, B. *Don't push the river.* Lafayette, Calif.: Real People Press, 1970. (B, M)

Stevens, J. *Awareness.* Lafayette, Calif.: Real People Press, 1971. (B, R)

Stock, D. "A survey of research on t-groups." In Bradford, *et al. T-group theory and laboratory method.* New York: John Wiley and Sons, 1964. (R)

Sullivan, C., Grant, M.Q. and Grant, J.D. "The development of interpersonal maturity: application to delinquency." In *Psychiatry.* New York: Norton, 1957. (B, R)

Sutich, A. and Vich, M. (Eds.). *Readings in humanistic psychology.* New York: Free Press-Macmillan, 1969. (B, M)

Sutton-Smith, B. and Roberts, J.M. "Rubrics of competitive

behavior." *Journal of Genetic Psychology,* 1963, 105, 13-37. (B, R)

Sutton-Smith, B., Roberts, J.M. and Kozekla, R.M. "Game involvement in adults." *Journal of Social Psychology,* 1963, 60, 15-30. (B, R)

Synectics, Inc., Cambridge, Mass. *Making it strange.* (Four books and teacher's manual.) New York: Harper and Row, 1968. (M)

Tansey, P.J. and Unwin, D. *Simulation and gaming in education.* London: Methuen Educational Ltd., 1969. (B, M)

Tart, C. (Ed.). *Altered states of consciousness.* New York: John Wiley and Sons, 1969. (B, M, R)

Ten exercises for trainers. Washington, D.C.: National Training Laboratories Institute for Applied Behavioral Science, National Education Association, 1969. (M)

Ten interaction exercises for the classroom. Washington, D.C.: National Training Laboratories Institute for Applied Behavioral Science, National Education Association, 1969. (M)

Thorelli, H.B. and Graves, R.L. *International operations simulation.* New York: Free Press, 1964. (B, M)

Tiedeman, D.V. "Guidance and psychology in the 1980 secondary education of adolescents and adults." In Eurich, A. (Ed.). *High School—1980.* New York: Academy for Educational Development, 1970. (B)

Torrance, E.P. *Encouraging creativity in the classroom.* Dubuque, Iowa: William C. Brown, 1970. (B, M)

Torrance, E.P. and Gupta, R. "Development and evaluation of recorded programmed experiences in creative thinking in the fourth grade." A research project under Title VII of the National Defense Act of 1958 with the New Educational Media Branch, U.S. Office of Education, Department of Health, Education, and Welfare, 1964. (R)

True, S.R. "A study of the relation of general semantics and creativity." *Dissertation Abstracts,* 1964, 24, 4, 2390. (R)

Uhlinger, C.A. and Stephens, M.W. "Relation of achievement motivation to academic achievement in students of superior ability." *Journal of Educational Psychology,* 1960, 51, 259-266. (R)

Upton, A. and Samson, R. *Creative analysis.* New York: Dutton, 1964. (B)

Uraneck, W.O. "Creative thinking workbook." Available from the author, 56 Turning Mill Road, Lexington, Mass. 02173,

1963. (M)

Uraneck, W.O. "Young thinker." Available from the author, 56 Turning Mill Road, Lexington, Mass. 02173. (M)

U.S. Office of Strategic Services Assessment Staff. *Assessment of men.* New York: Rinehart, 1948. (M)

Van den Daele, L. "A developmental study of the ego ideal." *Genetic Psychology Monographs,* 1968, 78, 191-256. (B, R)

Waetjin, W. and Leeper, R. (Eds.). *Learning and mental health in the school.* Washington, D.C.: Association for Supervision and Curriculum Development, National Education Association, 1966. (B, M)

Walberg, Herbert J. "Teacher personality and classroom climate." *Psychology in the Schools,* 1968a, 5, 2, 63-67. (R)

Walberg, Herbert J. "Structural and affective aspects of classroom climate." *Psychology in the Schools,* July 1968b, 5, 3, 247-253. (R)

Walberg, Herbert J. "Physical and psychological distance in the classroom." *School Review,* 1969a. (R)

Walberg, Herbert J. "Class size and the social environment of learning." *Human Relations,* 1969b. (R)

Walberg, Herbert J. and Anderson, Gary J. "Classroom climate and individual learning." *Journal of Educational Psychology,* January 1969a. (R)

Walberg, Herbert J. and Anderson, Gary J. "The achievement creativity dimension and classroom climate." *Journal of Creative Behavior,* June 1969b. (R)

Walker, J.A. "Developing efficacy, sense of efficacy, and self-esteem." Thesis, Department of Educational Psychology, Eastern Michigan University, Ypsilanti, Michigan, 1970. (B, M, R)

Wallach, L., Wall, A.J. and Anderson, L. "Number conservatism: the roles of reversibility, addition, subtraction, and misleading perceptual cues." *Child Development,* 1967, 38, 425-442. (M, R)

Walstedt, J. "Teaching empathy." *Mental Health,* October 1968, 52, 4, 600-611. (B)

Watson, G. (Ed.). *Change in school systems.* Available through National Training Laboratories, Washington, D.C., 1967a. (B, R)

Watson, G. (Ed.). *Concepts for social change.* Available through National Training Laboratories, Washington, D.C., 1967b. (B, R)

Watzlawick, P., Beavin, J.H. and Jackson, D.D. *Pragmatics of human communication*. New York: W.W. Norton, 1967. (B, M)

Weber, M. *The Protestant ethic and the spirit of capitalism*. First edition, 1904; T. Parson (translator). New York: Scribners, 1930. (B)

Weinstein, G. and Fantini, M. *Towards humanistic education*. New York: Praeger, 1970. (M)

Werner, H. *Comparative psychology of mental development*. New York: Science Editions, 1961. (B, R)

Weschler, I.R. and Reisel, J. *Inside a sensitivity training group*. Los Angeles: Institute of Industrial Relations, UCLA, 1958. (M)

Whitaker, C. "The psychotherapy of married couples." Lecture delivered for the Cleveland Institute of Gestalt Therapy, Cleveland, Ohio, January 8, 1965. (M)

Whiting, C.D. *Creative thinking*. New York: Reinhold Publishing, 1958. (B, M)

Wight, A. and Castor, G. *Training and assessment manual for a Peace Corps instrumented experiential laboratory*. Estes Park, Colorado: Center for Research and Development, 1969 (Peace Corps contract 25-1708). (M)

Winter, S.K., Griffith, J.C. and Kolb, D.A. "Capacity for self-direction." *Journal of Consulting and Clinical Psychology*, 1968, 32, 1, 35-41. (R)

Winterbottom, M.R. "The relation of childhood training in independence to achievement motivation." University of Michigan, Abstract in University Microfilms, Publication No. 5113, 297, 302, 305, 313. (R)

Wohlwill, J.F. and Lowe, R.L. "Experimental analysis of the development of the conservation of number." *Child Development*, 1962, 33, 1, 153-167. (M, R)

Wolpe, J. "Experimental neurosis as learned behavior." *British Journal of Psychology*, 1952, 43, 243-268. (B, R)

Wolpe, J. *Psychotherapy by reciprocal inhibition*. California: Stanford University Press, 1958. (M, R)

Wolpe, J. "The experimental foundations of some new psychotherapeutic methods." In Bachrach, A. (Ed.). *Experimental foundations of clinical psychology*. New York: Basic Books, 1962. (R)

Wolpe, J. and Lazarus, A. *Behavior therapy techniques*. Long Island City, New York: Pergamon Press, 1967. (B, M)

Yablonsky, L. *The tunnel back: Synanon*. New York: Macmillan,

1965. (M)

Yalom, I.D. and Lieberman, M.A. "A study of encounter group casualties." *Archives of General Psychiatry*, July 1971, Vol. 25, 16-30. (R)

Yeomans, E. "Education for initiative and responsibility." Available from the National Association of Independent Schools, 4 Liberty Square, Boston, Mass., 1967. (M)

Zilboorg, G. *A history of medical psychology.* New York: W.W. Norton and Sons, 1941. (B)

Zuckerman, R. and Horn, R. *The guide to simulation games for education and training.* Cambridge, Mass.: Information Resources, 1970. (M)

JOURNALS, FILMS, RECORDS, TAPES, GADGETS, AND GAMES

"The actualization group." Film of a group interaction, conducted at Everett Shostrom's Institute of Therapeutic Psychology. For further information write American Association for Humanistic Psychology, 584 Page Street, San Francisco, Calif. (B)

Annual journal of human relations training. Institute of Human Relations Training, Indianapolis, Indiana. (B, M, R)

Audible psychogalvanometer. Aid for teacher and psychologist. Psychophysics Labs, 31 Townsend Terrace, Framingham, Mass. (M)

Big Sur recordings (tapes), P.O. Box 4119, San Rafael, Calif. (B, M)

"Body talk" (game). Psychology Today Games, DelMar, California. (M)

Borton, T., *et al.* "Prelude" (1966). "A lot of undoing to do" (1968), and "Hard to hang on to" (1969). Films about the Philadelphia Cooperative Schools. Available from the Audio-Visual Department, Philadelphia Public School Building, Room 327, 21st and Parkway, Philadelphia, Penn. (M)

Borton, T. and Newberg, N. "All's fair in love and war." Baldwin, N.Y.: Educational Activity Records, 1968. (M)

"Encountertapes for personal growth groups." Western Behavioral Sciences Institute, 34 Old Ivy Road NE, Atlanta, Georgia, 1968. (M)

"From city streets to mountain ranch." Film by Frances M.J.

Epps and Clara M. Riley. For futher information write American Association for Humanistic Psychology, 584 Page Street, San Francisco, Calif. (B)

"Group therapy" (game). Park Plastics, Linden, N.J. (M)

"Hangup" (game). Synectics, Cambridge, Mass. (M)

"High school" (film). Rental from OSTI, 264 Third Street, Cambrige, Mass. (B)

Humanizing education. Education Ventures, 209 Court Street, Middletown, Conn. (M)

"The inner world of aphasia." Film conveys humanistic concern for person who cannot communicate. For further information write American Association for Humanistic Psychology, 584 Page Street, San Francisco, Calif. (B)

"Insight" (game). Games Research, 48 Wareham Street, Boston, Mass. (M)

"In the now." (Training films for Gestalt therapy by James Simkin.) Psychological Films, 205 West 20th Street, Santa Ana, Calif. (B)

"Introduction to psychodrama." Film directed by J.L. Moreno, Beacon House, Beacon, N.Y. (B)

Journal of applied behavioral science. National Training Laboratories, National Education Association, 1201 Sixteenth Street NW, Washington, D.C. (B, M, R)

Journal of conflict resolution. Center for Research on Conflict Resolution, University of Michigan, Ann Arbor, Mich. (B, M, R)

Journal of creative behavior. Creative Education Foundation, 1614 Rand Building, Buffalo, N.Y. (B, M, R)

"Journey into self" (1968). Film on group dynamics featuring Dr. Carl Rogers and Dr. Richard Farson. Available from Western Behavioral Sciences Institute, Film Library, 1150 Silverado, La Jolla, Calif. (M)

Lewin, K. "Experimental studies in the social climates of groups" (1940). Film available through the Krasker Memorial Film Library, Boston University, 765 Commonwealth Avenue, Boston, Mass. (M, R)

Litwin, G. "Organization climate" (1966). Film available through the Audio-Visual Department, Harvard Business School, Soldiers Field Road, Boston, Mass. (M)

"Maslow and self-actualization." Film by Everett Shostrom. For further information write American Association of Humanistic Psychology, 584 Page Street, San Francisco, Calif. (B)

May, R. "Human encounter" (film). Psychological Films, New York. (B, M)

"Mental health." Info-Pak Series IDI, 166 East Superior Street, Chicago, Ill. Over 70 cassette tapes by Carl Rogers, George Bach, Carl Whitaker, and Arnold Lazarus on virtually all aspects of the human potential movement. (B, M, R)

"The need to achieve." NET Focus on Behavior Series, No. 8. Available from Indiana University Film Library, Bloomington, Indiana. (B, R)

Newberg, N., *et al.* "Build yourself a city" (1968), "It's between the lines" (1968), "Making sense" (1968). All films available through the Office of Affective Development, Room 329, Philadelphia Public School Building, 21st and Parkway, Pennsylvania. (M)

"A nude sensitivity training group." Film by Paul Bindrim, 200 Campata Drive, Los Angeles, California. (M)

Perls, F. Films made from videotapes of Dr. Perls working as a therapist, showing his Gestalt therapy approach. For further information write Mediasync, P.O. Box 486, DelMar, California. "Grief and pseudo grief" (33 min.); "The birth of a composer" (24 min.); "Demon" (14 min.); "The impasse" (22 min.); "Relentless greed and obesity" (16 min.); "The death of Martha" (40 min.); "The case of Mary Kay" (15 min.); "The treatment of stuttering" (12 min.); "A session with college students" (50 min.); "Fritz" (14 min.). (B)

"The quiet one" (1948). Film about the Wiltwick School. Distributed by Contemporary Films, c/o McGraw-Hill, Text-Film Department, Hightstown, N.J. (M)

Rogers, C. "On facilitating a group" (film). American Personnel and Guidance Association. (M)

Schrank, J. "Effective communications" (4 tapes). Argus Communications, Chicago, 1969. (M)

"Sensitivity" (game). Sensitivity Groups, Boston, Mass. (M)

Skinner, B.F. Esalen tapes on affective education which also include interviews with Maslow, Skinner, Rogers, etc. Available through Esalen Institute, Big Sur, Calif. (B)

Tapes available from American Academy of Psychotherapists tape library, 6420 City Lane Avenue, Philadelphia, Penn. "Gestalt therapy seminar," "Gestalt expressive therapy," "Individual Gestalt therapy." Available from Big Sur Recordings, P.O. Box 6633, Carmel, Calif. "Dream theory," "Fritz Perls," "Fritz' circus," "Dream sessions," "More dream sessions,"

"Gestalt therapy lectures."

"Target five, with Virginia Satir." Film by Everett Shostrom, showing Virginia Satir's approach toward helping people to communicate more openly and directly with each other. For further information write American Association of Humanistic Psychology, 584 Page Street, San Francisco, Calif. (B)

"The value game" (game). Herder and Herder, 232 Madison Avenue, N.Y. (M)

Vietnam curriculum. Department RS-1, *New York Review,* 250 West 57 Street, N.Y. (M)

"What does it need to grow?" Film by Peter Lenrow, showing diversity of individual styles among preschool children. For further information write American Association of Humanistic Psychology, 584 Page Street, San Francisco, Calif. (B)

"Where is prejudice?" (1967). Film available through the NET Film Library, Audio-Visual Department, University of Indiana, Bloomington, Indiana. (M)

INDEX

INDEX

309